Cambridge Studies in Social Anthropology

General Editor: *Jack Goody*

58

STRATEGIES AND NORMS IN A CHANGING MATRILINEAL SOCIETY

T0381845

Strategies and Norms in a Changing Matrilineal Society

Descent, succession and inheritance among the Toka of Zambia

LADISLAV HOLY
University of St Andrews

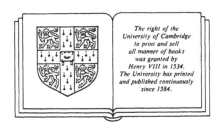

The right of the
University of Cambridge
to print and sell
all manner of books
was granted by
Henry VIII in 1534.
The University has printed
and published continuously
since 1584.

CAMBRIDGE UNIVERSITY PRESS

Cambridge
London   New York   New Rochelle
Melbourne   Sydney

CAMBRIDGE UNIVERSITY PRESS
Cambridge, New York, Melbourne, Madrid, Cape Town, Singapore, São Paulo

Cambridge University Press
The Edinburgh Building, Cambridge CB2 2RU, UK

Published in the United States of America by Cambridge University Press, New York

www.cambridge.org
Information on this title: www.cambridge.org/9780521303002

First published 1986
This digitally printed first paperback version 2006

A catalogue record for this publication is available from the British Library

Library of Congress Cataloguing in Publication data
Holy, Ladislav
    Strategies and norms in a changing matrilineal society:
    descent, succession and inheritance among the Toka of Zambia.
    Bibliography: p.
    Includes index.
    1. Toka (African people) – Social life and customs.
2. Kinship – Zambia.   3. Inheritance and succession (Toka
law) I. Title.
DT963.42.H65 1986   306'.089963   85–13222

ISBN-13 978-0-521-30300-2 hardback
ISBN-10 0-521-30300-1 hardback

ISBN-13 978-0-521-02432-7 paperback
ISBN-10 0-521-02432-3 paperback

Contents

Maps and diagrams

Tables

Acknowledgements

The fieldwork on which this book is based was carried out from March 1968 to December 1972 while I was the Director of the Livingstone Museum. It differed from standard anthropological fieldwork in that I carried it out while I was working and living in Livingstone. Mujalanyana village, in which I had a hut and where I did most of my fieldwork, is only 80 kilometres from Livingstone and, in the dry season, it could have been reached by Landrover comfortably in an hour and a half. Its inhabitants were frequent visitors to Livingstone and kept me perpetually informed about the events in their own and neighbouring villages; in consequence I was able to be in the field at the shortest possible notice. My frequent stays in Mujalanyana and in other Toka villages varied from a mere two days to several months during my annual local leaves and numerous sabbatical leaves. I wish to thank Mr Bitwell Kuwani, the Chairman of the National Museums Board of Zambia, for his understanding and for tolerating my frequent prolonged absence from my administrative duties.

From among the staff of the Livingstone Museum, my thanks are due to Dr Joseph Vogel, Keeper of Prehistory, for his intellectual support, and to Mr Patrick Siyachinga, Research Assistant in the Ethnography Department and a Toka himself, who accompanied me on my field trips and who effectively took care of all logistic and transport problems.

I wish to express my gratitude to all the Toka mentioned in this book for allowing me to participate in their lives, and especially to Amos Ilumbela and Winders Mukengami, my two successive research assistants and language instructors. During my research, the missionaries of the Church of Christ established their headquarters in Mujalanyana village; I am indebted to them, and especially to Mr and Mrs Philip Elkins, for their hospitality and companionship.

Various drafts of the manuscript were read by Dr Milan Stuchlik, Dr Kay Milton, Dr David Riches and Professor Ian Cunnison. I am grateful to them for their valuable criticism and to Dr Milton also for her laborious task of rendering the manuscript into readable English.

Special thanks are due to my wife Alice for sharing with me the joys and frustrations of the fieldwork and for her help with the manuscript.

Introduction

It is received wisdom that matrilineal systems are more liable to change than patrilineal ones when they are affected by modern economic development through absorption into the capitalist market system (Gough 1961; Nakane 1967: 143). The argument usually put forward suggests that a change from production for subsistence to production for exchange is accompanied by the advent of competition for scarce resources, which militates against the wide distribution characteristic of matriliny (Douglas 1969); this inevitably leads to the emergence of the individual family 'as the key kinship group with respect to residence, economic cooperation, legal responsibility and socialization' (Gough 1961: 631). When wealth comes to be produced and controlled by the male head of an individual family, and when his own children contribute considerably to its production, it also tends to be passed on to them instead of to those outside the productive group, as would be the case under matrilineal inheritance. Although this account has not been immune to criticism (cf. Fuller 1976: 143ff.), it has, on the whole, been accepted as an adequate explanation of the demise of matriliny in the modern world.

Assumption underlying the explanation of the decline of matriliny

Matriliny is, of course, more than the matrilineal system of inheritance. According to Poewe, it is 'a total system and consists of the combination of matrilineal ideology and those social actions and relations which are meaningfully informed by it' (Poewe 1981: 55). The matrilineal ideology itself is 'a folk-cultural theory of politics and economics' (ibid.: 54) and 'consists analytically of three ideational phenomena:

(1) kinship and descent principles,
(2) kin categories, and
(3) associated norms and values' (ibid.: 53–4).

Transmission of property through inheritance is the practice most obviously informed by, or embodying, matrilineal ideology in that it equates those who have a right to one another's property with those who share

1

common substance. In view of this fact, it is readily understandable why, when the justice of matrilineal inheritance starts to be questioned by those whose economic interests are threatened by its provisions, it becomes the 'symbolic keystone' of matriliny, as it did in Luapula (ibid.: 121). But the defining feature of matriliny is not a single social practice meaningfully informed by matrilineal ideology, but that ideology itself, i.e. the expressed kinship and descent principles, the kin categories which are recognised, and their accompanying norms and values. Analytically speaking, then, the defining feature of matriliny is the assignment of individuals to culturally recognised categories whose membership is defined by descent traced through females (Aberle 1961: 656; Douglas 1969: 124). It must follow that any explanation of the decline or demise of matriliny as such is adequate only if it accounts satisfactorily for the weakening or disappearance of the notion of matrilineal descent itself.

The explanation outlined above has been generally accepted to provide such an account; that is, it has been taken as accounting not only for the change in the transmission of property through inheritance but also for the general decline or demise of matriliny as a total system. In other words, it has been read as an explanation of the disappearance of matrilineal ideology or, more specifically, of the tracing of descent exclusively through females. We may ask what makes such a reading possible.

The answer to this question would seem to lie in the acceptance of a range of assumptions or presuppositions about the nature of social reality, facilitated by the fact that most of them have never been explicitly formulated but only tacitly entertained, and by the fact that in analysis they have frequently been treated not only as assumptions, which have a merely heuristic value, but as generalisations of empirical fact. One such specific assumption is that the regulation of economic relations is universally the most important function of a descent group. The outlined explanation can be construed as adequate only when this is accepted as a valid generalisation of empirical fact. If, however, it is relegated from its status as an empirical generalisation to its proper status as an assumption, the validity of the explanation needs to be questioned, for there is no logical reason to assume that a change in the system of inheritance has invariably to be accompanied by a change in the conceptualisation of descent. Why can men not inherit property from their fathers while considering themselves members of a category of people who are descended in the matrilineal line from a common ancestress? After all, among the Tonga, Nayar and Minangkabau, the practice of the transmission of individually earned property to one's own children has not affected the tracing of descent in the matrilineal line (Colson 1980; Fuller 1976; Kato 1982).

A more general assumption underlying the acceptance of the received explanation of the decline of matriliny is the notion of the socio-cultural

2

Introduction

reality as a system of functionally or logically interrelated parts. On analysis, the interrelation of the parts of the system (of which the most important ones in this context are the matrilineal ideology or the notion of descent and the practice of the transmission of property through inheritance) is treated as non-problematic precisely because the nature of their interrelationship is already presupposed in the assumption of their functional or logical fit. On this view, the change in one constituent part of the system leads inevitably and logically to changes in, or adjustments of, other parts. This analytical treatment is, furthermore, made possible by conceptualising matriliny not only as a total system, but as a system ridden with structural contradictions which it perpetually tries to resolve and overcome: such as the contradiction between the individual family and the matrilineal descent group, or that between marriage and sibling cohesion (Lévi-Strauss 1949: 149–50; Schneider 1961: 16–23; Nakane 1967: 143), the contradiction in the allocation of authority resulting in the 'matrilineal puzzle' (Richards 1950), which rests on the division of a man's loyalties between his children and the members of his descent group,[1] or, more generally, that between productive individualism and distributive communalism (Poewe 1981). These contradictions make matriliny vulnerable in the face of modern economic development and the capitalist market system. Matriliny's inherent inability, upon entry into the capitalist market system, to resolve these contradictions in favour of the matrilineal descent group and its distributive communalism, is ultimately seen as the cause of its demise in the modern world.

Just as the logical articulation of matriliny as a system is seen as non-problematic, so, too, is the process of its change or decline. The only problem to be dealt with is the identification of the impetus for change and the reasons for it. Once this is done, the rest logically follows. The elucidation of the process of change has been effectively ruled out by the notion of a system and its inherent contradictions. Since, for example, the structural contradiction between the individual family and the descent group has been posited as a characteristic feature of matriliny, the reasons for the weakening of the notion of matrilineal descent are already logically contained in the reasons for the strengthening of the individual family. The reasons for the increased importance of the individual family and for the strengthening of the ties between husband and wife and father and children, then become explanations for the decline in the importance of the matrilineal descent group and the weakening of ties among its members. As the ties between the members of the individual family strengthen and gain in importance, the notion of matrilineal descent, through which the unity of the descent group is ideologically expressed, is automatically affected in a negative way. There is no need to explain the process through which the notion of descent is affected upon the strengthening of the individual family.

Although every anthropologist would subscribe to the view that change

3

is a process, the need to treat it as such at the level of analytical practice is effectively removed. Change is assumed to be adequately accounted for when its original impetus has been located and the reasons for its occurrence explained.

Alternative assumptions

As indicated above, the failure to treat change as a process in analytical and explanatory practice derives ultimately from adopting assumptions about the nature of the relationship between the parts of the system, instead of making this relationship itself the object of analysis. If we want to grasp change as a process, we have to abandon the belief that we know how the parts of the system hang together, and treat their relationship as problematic. Instead of presupposing the exact nature of the relationship between the relevant constituent components or realms of the socio-cultural reality, we have only to assume that there are relevant components or realms and that a relationship between them is open to investigation.

The basic assumption underlying the analysis presented here is that the socio-cultural reality consists of two qualitatively different realms or domains of phenomena: those that constitute the knowledge or notions of the members of the society and those that constitute the actions which they perform or the social processes in which they are engaged. The distinction between these two domains is underpinned by the differences in their epistemological and existential status.

The existential status of the interactions in which people engage is given by the fact that actions are performed in order to make a visible impact on the physical and social world, that is, to change or maintain the existing state of affairs. By their nature, actions are unique and unrepeatable since each action has its specific location in time and space; once performed, actions cease to exist. But they also form a continuous flow of existence in space and time such that the state of affairs precipitated by an action continues after the action has been completed.

For social life to exist, people's actions must be meaningful to others. This presupposes that the criteria for ascribing meanings to actions and the ways of interpreting them must be known and shared by them. The fact that people share criteria, or, more generally, knowledge of how to behave and how to interpret actions, entails the existence of the actions at another level: as models, plans, 'blueprints' or schemata for actions in the minds of the people. The existence of these models is perduring: people hold them regardless of whether or not the corresponding action is at the moment being performed; they are related not to any particular action located in space and time, but to classes of actions.

Performed actions and models for actions (or, more generally, notions about actions) have different epistemological statuses. While actions are, to

4

Introduction

some extent, available to others through observation (for fuller discussion of the concept of observation, see Holy and Stuchlik 1981: 2–3; 1983: 33–7), models for actions are in no acceptable sense of the word observable. Neither the anthropologist nor the actors can 'witness' them in the sense that they can 'witness' actions; they have to be told of their existence or to infer it. Actions and models for actions also have different existential statuses: through their actions people make a direct impact on the world, through holding a model of action people do not directly maintain or change the existing state of affairs. By themselves, models for actions do not 'do' anything; they form part of an individual's knowledge and are part of social life only to the extent that they are shared. On both existential and epistemic grounds they form a realm or domain of reality different from that formed by actions.

However, simple models of actions form only a small part of the notional domain of reality. People perform their actions in concrete physical and social environments, situations and circumstances. They have to know all these conditions to be able to perform their actions effectively and in a way acceptable to and understandable to others. Their notions about all these conditions are again mental constructs, just as models of actions are, but they differ from the latter in that they are not simple descriptions of actions, but more complex models of relations between actions, representations of parts of the physical and social world, notions about the way things are or should be, etc. In their totality these models, representations and notions constitute what, in the broadest possible sense, could be described as people's knowledge of their natural and social world.

This knowledge is never made available to other actors or to the observer simply as a multitude of separate bits of information. It is always presented in an organised form, as more or less coherent structures of differing generality. It is not intended here to discuss the organising principles of presented knowledge in any detail; they should follow from the research rather than be defined *a priori*. It is, however, necessary to point out that organised sets of notions, be they called structures, systems or models, are differently related to the natural and social world, and on the basis of that difference it is possible to make a useful distinction between two types of model.

In the last instance, whatever people know about their world and however they think about it is relevant for their actions. Nevertheless, there is a basic difference between knowledge concerning the existing state of affairs, what they are, why they are so, how the social world is constituted, etc., and knowledge of what to do and how to do it. Probably the best formulation of this difference is that drawn by Caws:

Among the mental structures belonging to the members of a given social group, then, will be some that model various features of the physical and social world in which the group lives ... These structures will have been formed by experience and education

5

and will determine the individual's conception of his world as well as his behaviour in it ... I therefore introduce a first distinction between 'operational models' and 'representational models'; the representational model corresponds to the way the individual thinks things are, the operational model to the way he practically responds or acts (Caws 1974: 3).

Irrespective of some conceptual problems of Caws's scheme discussed elsewhere (Holy and Stuchlik 1981: 19–20; Jenkins 1981: 97–101; Holy and Stuchlik 1983; 100–2), it appears to me that the knowing subject must be capable of at least two conceptual operations, or, put differently, that his knowledge must fulfil two ideally separate functions, of which one is that of reflection on the nature of things and the other a practical, task-oriented application. It seems heuristically useful to refer to them as two separate models and to retain Caws's terminology for their designation. People's perception and representation of their natural and physical world as a more or less stable structure and a more or less lasting distribution of people, tasks, resources, products, physical objects, rights and duties, etc., can be called their representational model. Such a model does not contain notions about what to do and how to go about doing it; it is informative rather than instructive and it stipulates only the limiting conditions within which people have to decide on the most appropriate courses of action. The rules or norms which stipulate what these courses are, differ from the representational notions in that they are not predominantly informative but instructive; as such they form part of what can appropriately be called operational models.

The relationship between these two analytically distinguishable models is not a conceptual question but an empirical one which can be answered only through concrete research. Particular attention is paid to it in Chapters 1 and 9.

The distinction between the conceptual or cognitive world of the actors, and the realm of events and transactions in which they engage, is not a novel one. It parallels to a certain extent the linguists' distinction between language and speech. In one form or another, some version of it has repeatedly been used by many scholars. In the field of anthropological and sociological studies, it has usually been expressed as a distinction between an ideational system or 'culture' and a system of interactions or 'social structure' (Kroeber and Parsons 1958; Kay 1965; Goodenough 1964, 1970; Geertz 1966; Keesing 1971, 1975). Nevertheless, even when it has been made, the analytical and explanatory consequences of the distinction have not always been fully explored. Very often, the distinction has led to an unrealistic overstressing of one domain over the other: one of the domains carries the full research and explanatory load, while the other is simply attached to it. The accepted explanation of the demise of matriliny invariably locates the cause of this change in the domain of events and transactions in which the actors engage; the changes in their notions follow non-problematically from changes which have occurred in the domain of their interactions. On the other hand, various analytical approaches that conceptualise culture as a system of symbols and meanings, which is then treated as an autonomous entity endowed with its own logic, ascribe to it a determining effect on the social and economic processes and on events and transactions in which its members engage; in this case the behavioural reality is assumed non-problematically to follow from the notions themselves.

In this study, I follow an analytical and explanatory procedure which stresses neither actions nor notions, but focuses instead on the relationship between the two domains constituted by them. This relationship is not prejudged to be one of entailment or automatic congruence but is taken to be problematic and hence the main object of analysis. Having taken this approach, I am not concerned with the organising principles of actors' knowledge as such, but rather with its organisation in relation to actions.

Anthropological approaches which have explicitly rejected the assumption that the conceptual or cognitive realm and that of events and transactions are isomorphic, and which treat the relationship between them as problematic, have considerably enhanced our understanding of the processes through which the actors' cultural notions enter into the events and transactions in which they engage. Several excellent studies have amply demonstrated that cultural notions do not pattern behaviour by themselves, but do so by being brought into the situation as one of the possible relevant factors on which the actors base decisions about the course of their actions (Pospisil 1958; Scheffler 1965; Keesing 1967; Stuchlik 1977b). If we abandon the assumption that people's notions have a compelling force on their actions, and instead consider the relationship between notions and actions as problematic, we obviously need to stipulate some mediating motivational mechanism through which they can be brought to bear upon actions, either summoning them or restraining them. In other words, we need to employ in our analyses some bridging concept which would relate them to actions. I consider the goal of an action to be such a concept.

The goal of an action indicates some future state of affairs to whose attainment the action is oriented. It obviously presupposes the existence of an agent, who needs to be a particular individual. Treating the relationship between notions and actions as problematic thus not only makes it necessary to account for actions by the goals they are intended to attain, it also entails conceiving of people as agents behaving purposively so as to attain goals. Although it is only specific agents that have goals, an individual can have as his goal not only his own particular future state but a future state for his group. In the discussion of the succession to headmanship in Chapter 1, I argue that the choice to invoke one of two alternative norms depends basically on the way in which the future state of the village is defined.

The assumption that people have goals and behave purposively so as to attain them has in itself specific consequences for the conceptualisation of the relationship between notions and actions. We have to realise that to invoke or disregard a notion (e.g. a specific norm), within the course of an interaction, is an action in itself and must be seen as having a specific purpose. It is not the notion which has been invoked or disregarded in the action, but the purpose of the action which gives it its meaning. I pay specific attention to this problem in Chapter 2 and again in Chapter 10.

Explaining people's behaviour in terms of its goal orientation or purposiveness calls for the construction of a different explanatory model from the normative model of social structure. An important aspect of the latter is that it treats social actors as occupants of statuses and sees the collection of rights and duties comprising each actor's status, or the norm of behaviour pertaining to it, as determining the interpersonal relations and alignments or, in short, the structure of the society. The structure so conceived is then an abstraction which does not necessarily reflect the actual social relations and alignments, but merely the norms which are ideally supposed to shape them and give them their form. Following Leach, I regard social structure not as a reflection of the jural and moral rules which form part of the actors' conceptual realm, or of their culture, but as the outcome of their choices (Leach 1960: 124).

On this view, 'structure' is not something that lies behind the recurrent pattern of activities; it emerges from them and is created and changed by them. When social structure is conceptualised in this way and when the question of its generation is answered in terms of the reasons, intentions and purposes of the people who create it through their actions, then concrete activities enter into research procedures not only at the descriptive level, but also at the analytical and explanatory level. They are not only something that has to be drawn upon to explain how the structure is generated; their actual, as opposed to their ideal or normative, pattern has also to become the object of explanation.

Chapter 2 is, among other things, specifically concerned with showing that the observable ploughing teams and their perpetual change cannot be explained by the normative model of their composition, which could easily be formulated on the basis of the Toka's elucidation of the relevant norms. Similarly, the actual composition of particular meetings at which the successor to the deceased is chosen cannot be contained in a normative model of such meetings, which it would again be possible to formulate and which the Toka indeed do formulate; again, the actual division of any particular estate cannot be fully accounted for by invoking the normative model of inheritance. It is for this reason that Chapters 7 and 8, which deal with succession and inheritance, provide a detailed description of actual 'cases', although the methodological point made in Chapter 2 is not reiterated in them. It is not only these chapters which may be seen as burdened with such excessive 'ethnographic detail', and those who subscribe to the view that anthropology should aim at formulating normative models of social structure will probably find the description of actual residence alignments and the accounts of actual actions of specific individuals unnecessary and superfluous. It is only hoped that this view will not be shared by those who believe that the anthropologist's task is to explain how the structure of the society is created, sustained and gradually changed in the process of its ongoing re-creation, and that the way in which the normative model relates to the observable social processes and alignments is an important problem for investigation. Such investigation is grounded in the assumption that, although the actors' choices are not directly determined by their cultural notions, they are made within the context of these notions; in this sense cultural notions impinge on social processes by defining a set of constraints within which these processes occur. This point is again further elaborated in Chapter 2.

If actions are continually re-creating the world about which knowledge is held, this knowledge itself has to be viewed as being continually re-created. This means that we have to view particular bits of knowledge or specific cultural notions as being continually organised, reorganised and changed, both to take into account the existing state of affairs and to make possible their future state. Without trying to assign any explanatory priority either to people's notions or to their actions, we may say that, on the one hand, their behaviour derives from their knowledge and therefore can be understood only by being related to it, or, more exactly, behaviour can be accounted for as rational or purposive only in the context of the world known to the actors; and, on the other hand, people's notions derive from their cognitive (theoretical) and practical activities in the world known to them. On this view, the relationship between the cultural realm of held notions and the realm of social transactional order is characteristically dialectical. We may assume that in circumstances of accelerated change the two realms may markedly diverge. Although this has been theoretically recognised (Keesing 1971: 126), the recognition has not had a sufficient impact on existing analytical practice. I have mentioned above that, until now, anthropological studies which made use of the analytical distinction between notions and actions have been mainly concerned to investigate the process whereby people's notions or their knowledge affect or shape their actions. Only a few studies have so far paid specific analytical attention to the process whereby the social transactions in which the actors engage affect the cultural notions which they hold (Leach 1961; Stuchlik 1977a; Holy 1979). After considering, in Chapter 2, the process whereby the actor's notions enter into their transactions, in Chapters 3 and 5 I change my analytical focus and concentrate on the process whereby their interactions affect the notions which they hold.

Dissatisfaction has been expressed above with explanations claiming the

demise of descent in the matrilineal line to be implicated in the demise of
the practice of matrilineal inheritance, or non-problematically to follow from
it. Instead of seeing the change from matrilineal inheritance to inheritance
by sons as the cause of the demise of matrilineal descent, it is suggested that
the change in the system of inheritance and the change in the mode of tracing
descent are better viewed as two parallel processes. The former is analysed
in Chapter 3, the latter in Chapter 5. Although they are triggered off by the
same factors (described in Chapter 2), they do not causally affect one another.
Unlike the change in the inheritance system, the change in the mode of tracing
descent is not so much a direct result of the restructuring of the relations
of production (described in Chapter 2), as a response to the changed structure
of local groups (described in Chapter 4). No doubt the two processes, which
are treated analytically as separate, reinforce and mutually affect one another
and, in doing so, they facilitate the overall adjustment of existing notions
about categories of people, the criteria by which their members are recruited
and the normative rights, entitlements and duties which ensue from their
membership. This adjustment is discussed in the latter part of the book.

It is in terms of the adjustment of the various cultural notions to one
another and to the actual social transactions in which the actors are
continuously engaged that the process of change which has occurred in Toka
society over the past few decades can best be described. In analytical terms,
this historical process can be envisaged as the process of the declining
importance of Toka matriliny. Anthropologists who see descent as the main
principle of social organisation necessarily conceptualise the demise of
matriliny as a major revolutionary change in the society's organisation. In
contrast to this view, for the Toka themselves, the change in their system
of inheritance and succession and in their mode of descent-reckoning was
natural, smooth, gradual and almost imperceptible; it certainly was not
traumatic and revolutionary. The reason for this is that the changed
practices, while necessarily accompanied by specific changes in the Toka
operational model, did not alter significantly the Toka's representational
model of their society. The description and analysis of change, which is the
main topic of the book, is at the same time inevitably a description and
analysis of the underlying continuity.

The Toka

Linguistically, the Toka form part of the Tonga-speaking peoples who
inhabit much of the Southern Province of Zambia. The Tonga speakers do
not form a unity either politically or culturally. They inhabit four districts
of the Southern Province and consequently they are nowadays administered
by four different rural councils. The people who, for administrative purposes,
are referred to as the Plateau Tonga live in the Mazabuka and Choma

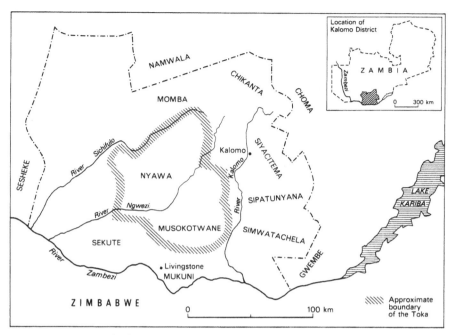

Map 1. Kalomo District

Districts, and those referred to as the Valley Tonga inhabit the Gwembe District. The Toka live on the Trust Land in Kalomo District and are administered by the Kalomo Rural Council, which has its seat in Zimba and which has taken over the duties and responsibilities which, before the independence of Zambia, were discharged by the District Commissioner and the Tonga–Leya Native Authority. The cultural differences between the Plateau and the Valley Tonga have been brought out in the writings of Elisabeth Colson, who carried out research among both these peoples (see especially Colson 1958, 1960, 1962). As this monograph should indicate, the Toka differ in many significant respects from both of them.

There are nowadays nine chiefs in the Kalomo District (Map 1) who are recognised as such by the administration: Momba, Chikanta, Siyacitema, Simwatachela, Sipatunyana, Nyawa, Musokotwane, Mukuni and Sekute. The inhabitants of Chikanta's chiefdom, which occupies the northern part of the district and borders on Machila's and Macha's chiefdoms in the Choma District, consider themselves to be Tonga like their neighbours across the district boundary. The same is probably true of the inhabitants of Siyacitema's chiefdom which lies in the north-eastern part of the district, and of the inhabitants of Simwatachela's chiefdom in the easternmost part of the district

11

adjoining Choma and Gwembe Districts. The inhabitants of Sipatunyana's, Nyawa's and Musokotwane's chiefdoms consider themselves to be Toka and, in support of their claim, they point out the differences between themselves and the Plateau Tonga to whom they refer either as the 'Tonga on the plateau' or the 'Tonga around Choma'. The inhabitants of Momba's chiefdom in the north-western part of Kalomo District are partly Lozi-speaking Nkoya and partly Toka. Chief Momba is classed in the government list of chiefs as 'Nkoya and Toka (Tonga)' (Brelsford 1965: 64). Chiefs Mukuni and Sekute refer to the people under their jurisdiction as the Leya. According to Chief Mukuni's version of Leya history recorded in the archives of the Livingstone Museum (see also Brelsford 1965: 72–3), his people are a branch of the Lenje who migrated southwards from Central Zambia and settled on the northern bank of the Zambezi above and below the Victoria Falls. Whatever their historical origin, the people in Mukuni's and Sekute's chiefdoms nowadays speak Tonga, although with a noticeably stronger admixture of Lozi words and expressions than in other areas of Kalomo District.

The division between the Leya and the Toka is, however, a very tenuous one. The people in and around Mukuni's and Sekute's capital refer to themselves as the Leya and so do the people in the southern parts of these two chiefdoms. The further northwards one progresses, the more the people conceive of themselves as Toka. Although the whole of Mukuni's chiefdom has been classified as 'Baleya Native Reserve', the people in its northern part, in the area which used to be under Chief Katapazi before his chiefship was abolished in the 1950s and amalgamated with Mukuni's chiefship, consider themselves to be Toka. There is a lot of intermarriage between the people from the Katapazi area and those from Musokotwane's chiefdom and a number of people living in these two areas are mutually interrelated. Several village communities in Musokotwane's chiefdom have migrated there from the Katapazi area. All their members consider themselves to be Toka. A similar situation to that in the Katapazi area obtains in the northern part of Sekute's chiefdom. The boundary between Sekute's and Musokotwane's chiefdoms is partly formed by the Ngwezi river. The headman of Linda, a village which is located on the southern bank of this river and thus under Sekute's jurisdiction, was at one time one of Sekute's two assessors. In spite of the fact that the inhabitants of Linda have to have their cases heard at the court at Sekute, they consider themselves to be Toka and they are closely interrelated with the inhabitants of Mujala, one of the most important and oldest villages in Musokotwane's chiefdom.

Brelsford's suggestion that the name Toka is the Lozi or Sikololo mis-pronunciation of Tonga (Brelsford 1965: 64) is probably correct. Holub, who travelled in 1886 through the Toka and Tonga areas, relied heavily on his

Lozi guides and interpreters and in consequence the names of people and places and their spelling in his travelogue are heavily Lozi-ised. He consistently refers to the Tonga-speaking peoples as the 'Matoka' (Holub 1975).

Holub also indicated, at least partly, the eastern boundaries of the political influence of the Lozi state under King Lewanika at the end of the nineteenth century. It appears from his account that chiefs, Sekute, Mukuni, Musokotwane, Nyawa, Momba, Siyacitema, Sipatunyana and a few others whose chiefships were later abolished by the British administration, recognised the sovereignty of King Lewanika. At the time of Holub's travels, the village of Chief Siyacitema was about 80 km north-west of Choma around the headwaters of the Kasangu river (Holub 1975: 286); nowadays it is located about 27 km north-east of Kalomo in an area which, according to Holub's account, was at that time already outside the direct political influence of the Lozi state. The area of the present Chief Chikanta also lies outside the limits of past Lozi influence. It is doubtful whether their direct political influence extended eastwards across the lower course of the Kalomo river; the area of the present Chief Simwatachela, which lies there, has also probably never been subject to Lozi dominance. The boundaries of Lozi influence thus clearly coincide with the Toka–Tonga divide and it seems that, as far as the distinction between the Tonga proper and the Toka is concerned, the latter are those who at one time were under Lozi dominance.

The Lozi were instrumental in appointing chiefs among the Toka from among the important headmen, in a way similar to that in which the British administration later appointed chiefs among the Plateau and Valley Tonga. The oral histories of Toka chiefships clearly indicate the role that the Lozi played in the appointment of the first chiefs. They were all considered to be Lewanika's representatives in their respective areas, and they were responsible to him for the collection and delivery of tribute paid in slaves, cattle, honey, skins, mats and grain. The Toka chiefs were recognised as such by the early British administration although some of them were later deprived of their titles in various successive efforts to make the administrative system more effective. The chiefs together with their assessors formed the Tonga–Leya Native Authority with the right to pass ordinances and rules. Each chief had his own court with jurisdiction to hear cases referred to it by village headmen, and with a limited jurisdiction to try minor criminal offences. He was responsible to the District Commissioner for the maintenance of law and order in his area and for the implementation of the current laws, ordinances and rules. The boundaries of chiefdoms were precisely delineated, but only partly took into account the actual area which had traditionally been under the chief's jurisdiction. As a result, the existing boundaries ignore the ethnic or cultural distinctions among the people themselves: the boundaries of the population conceiving of themselves as Toka nowadays cut across the boundaries of Sekute's, Mukuni's, Momba's and probably Sipatunyana's chiefdoms.

After Zambia's independence, with the abolition of head tax and of the chief's presidency over his court, accompanied by the bringing of native courts under the jurisdiction of the Ministry of Justice, the chief's status was greatly diminished. For the Toka themselves, however, as indeed for all other Zambian peoples, the chiefs are still figures of respected authority. The Zambian government recognises them as important agents of local government and relies heavily on their traditional authority in implementing its own policies.

Subject to the chief are the headmen who represent the lowest level in the hierarchy of authority. The headman is a representative of his village *vis-à-vis* the chief, the native court, the rural council or the various officers of the local government.

Toka villages are rather small. According to the population census of 1963, there were 44 villages in Chief Nyawa's area and 136 villages in Chief Musokotwane's area. Their population varied from 7 people to 455 in Chief Musokotwane's own village, which was the biggest in both chiefdoms. The next village in size had 245 inhabitants, 32 had between 100 and 200 inhabitants and the remaining 146 had fewer than 100. The mean number of inhabitants in a village was 66.1, the median being 88.

The villages are not scattered evenly over the whole tribal area. In some parts of it, their concentration is quite dense, while in others there exist vast areas of unoccupied bush. Availability of water and of good agricultural soil are the main factors determining their location. The villages tend to be situated along the river and stream banks or on the slopes of shallow grassy valleys, which get flooded during the rainy season. From both streams and valleys water is readily obtainable during the rains, and it is easy to get water from shallow wells dug during the dry season either in the sandy riverbeds or in the lowest points of the valleys.

The village under a headman is the smallest officially recognised administrative unit, but it does not necessarily form a compact settlement. More often than not it is divided into separate hamlets, each consisting of several households.

The core of every household is a rectangular dwelling-house with a thatched roof and with walls built of vertical poles plastered with mud. It usually consists of only one room. At the time of my fieldwork very few houses had tin roofs or were built from dry bricks or contained two or three rooms. From the second decade of the twentieth century on, the rectangular house, which is now the most common form of dwelling, started gradually to replace the round hut with a conical thatched roof and walls built from poles and mud. Nowadays, usually only divorcees and widows or widowers living alone inhabit small round huts that resemble the old traditional type of Toka dwelling. Some of these huts have only grass walls or their walls consist simply of poles to which several mats, normally used to sleep on, are attached.

Some households consist of only one dwelling-house, some have two or three. An additional house is needed as a sleeping-place for children who are considered too old to share a house with their parents at night. Quite often an old house which has been replaced by a new one is used as a sleeping-place for children or as a store. Most households have a kitchen attached to the dwelling. Invariably, this has a thatched conical roof supported by poles. Sometimes it has no wall at all, in other cases it has a grass wall or a wall formed by mats attached to the supporting poles. A properly built kitchen has a mud wall built up for about two thirds of the space between the roof and the ground or it has a pole and mud wall extending up to the roof, in which case it does not differ in appearance from the traditional round dwelling-hut.

Every household has its own table-platform on which corn, flour, fish and other foodstuffs are dried as well as dishes after they have been washed. These platforms are usually close to the dwelling-house, as are pole frames, interwoven with rope. These are used for drying maize cobs after they have been brought from the fields and before they are stored in the granaries or the corn put in sacks. Other structures usually owned by a household are the grass hen-coops on platforms, and sometimes small hen-houses built of sticks and grass on the ground. Each household has several granaries – round straw huts with conical grass roofs, built on pole platforms, usually standing behind the house on the outskirts of the settlement.

The structures of one household quite often stand next to the structures of another, so that it is difficult to say which house belongs to which household and where one household ends and another starts.

A Toka household is always made up of an elementary family or a fragment of such a family. Rarely, other people may live with the family as attached members of the household. As the household is defined by one fire and as co-wives never cook together, a polygynous family never constitutes one household; each wife has her own household in which she lives together with her children.

The household is the basic unit of production. The Toka are sedentary agriculturalists; except in areas infested with tsetse fly, cattle are their main domestic animals. Chickens are kept in all villages, pigs, goats and ducks in some. However, it is fishing, and to a lesser extent hunting and trapping, which provide the people with their main source of meat. While hunting by shotgun, mostly at night, and trapping (mostly for birds) is carried out by few men, fishing is a widespread activity in which a wide range of techniques is used. It is practised in the rainy season and in the early months of the dry season when there is water in the streams and in the shallow valleys along which the villages are situated.

Of over a dozen species of subsistence crops cultivated, only bulrush millet, sorghum and maize rank as staples. Millet used to be the main crop before maize started to be extensively grown wherever possible in the mid-1920s and 1930s. Maize is the only cash crop and, together with sorghum, it is now the main subsistence crop. When deciding which cereal and how much of it to plant, various factors are taken into consideration: the time of ripening, the yield, the crop's susceptibility to disease and attack by birds, the ease with which the grain can be crushed into flour in a mortar, the grain's nutritive value, taste, and its value for making beer or as a cash crop. Various crops require a specific type of soil to grow successfully, and an important limiting factor in deciding what to plant is obviously the availability of suitable soil. Any soil in which maize thrives would be wasted if planted with anything else; as a rule then, the best soil around every village is used for growing maize. Manure can easily be transported to the fields round the village from the cattle pens situated nearby, and the soil on which maize is grown is fertilised at least every two or three years and very often yearly. Other cereals, as well as groundnuts, are grown in fields which are situated farther away from the village and which are never manured. The usual practice is to cultivate the field for two or three years (or, depending on the quality of the soil, possibly even longer) and then to let it lie fallow for three to six years. The fields of different households are not scattered haphazardly in the bush around the village, but are concentrated in one or more distinct clusters in an area where the bush has been cleared.

Sorghum, maize and millet are used to make a thick porridge which is the staple food. It is eaten twice a day with a cooked sauce or relish which is used as a dip for handfuls of porridge. Groundnuts are the most important ingredient for relishes, but they are made from a wide range of cultivated and wild vegetables, and from domestic and wild animal products and fish.

The subsistence production is supplemented by the migration of younger men and very often young married couples as labourers to urban centres. It is not unusual for as much as half the adult male population of a village to be away at any given time as labour migrants.

In this book, I do not aim at generalisations valid for the whole Toka population. I worked only in Nyawa and Musokotwane chiefdoms (Map 2) and I am unable to say how far the conclusions of my analysis would be true for other Toka chiefdoms I have never visited.

Musokotwane chiefdom has a population of over nine thousand people living, as I mentioned before, in 136 villages. Nyawa chiefdom has about three thousand inhabitants living in 44 villages. Even as far as these two chiefdoms are concerned, I have detailed knowledge of only some areas within them. I did most of my fieldwork in the village of Mujalanyana, in which

16

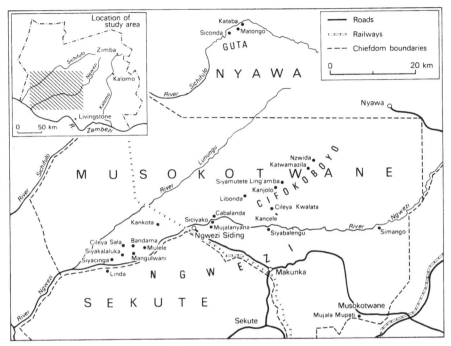

Map 2. Guta, Cifokoboyo and Ngwezi

I had my own hut. It is a fairly big village with a population of about 160, situated on the bank of the Ngwezi river about 5 km east of Ngwezi Siding, a halt on the narrow-gauge Livingstone–Mulobezi railway operated by the Zambezi Sawmills. Ngwezi Siding is one of the centres of the area referred to as Ngwezi, which consists of some forty villages in the western part of Musokotwane's chiefdom. It is a small settlement with a store run by the Zambezi Trading Company, and with a population consisting of railway workers and their families, mostly Lozi, housed in prefabricated huts built by the timber company. There are also a few Toka, who operate small grocery stores and about half a dozen illicit bars. Every Saturday afternoon, the bars, selling locally brewed maize, sorghum and millet beer, cater for dozens of railway workers and hundreds of Toka men and women from neighbouring villages. Ngwezi Siding is located on the bank of the Ngwezi river some 75 km north-west of Livingstone. There are some thirty villages stretching along both banks of the Ngwezi river to the west and east of it. Apart from the railway, Ngwezi Siding is connected to Livingstone by a road which, although impassable for any kind of vehicle in the rains, is good enough even for an ordinary car during the dry season. Another centre of

17

the Ngwezi area is Makunka, a settlement situated in a shallow grassy valley about 10 km south of the Ngwezi river and some 50 km north-west of Livingstone. It houses a Catholic mission with its own clinic and several stores and bars. It is easily accessible from Livingstone either by rail or by road. There are some ten villages clustered around it.

Using Mujalanyana as my base, I visited most of the villages in Ngwezi. I was a frequent visitor to villages neighbouring on Mujalanyana; in others I spent only a few hours. In many of them, however, I stayed for a few days, mostly attending final mourning ceremonies together with the people from Mujalanyana, or conducting a census. In some of them (e.g. Siyabalengu, Mangulwani and Cileya Sala) I stayed for a few weeks collecting data comparable to those I had from Mujalanyana.

Cifokoboyo is another area of Musokotwane's chiefdom in which I worked systematically. It consists of eleven villages along the Nanyati stream, a tributary of the Ngwezi, in the northern part of the chiefdom. Cifokoboyo was in the 1930s still infested with tsetse, particularly in its north-eastern part. As late as 1967, one village in the area moved south-eastwards from its site near Lunungu stream because of the fear of tsetse flies. The biggest and most centrally located village in Cifokoboyo is Siyamutete Ling'amba. It was founded by immigrants from Nyawa's chiefdom, who left it in the early 1940s because of tsetse flies pestering their cattle. They settled first in Kanjolo, a village about 1.5 km south-west of the present Siyamutete Ling'amba. In 1955, Siyamutete and his followers left Kanjolo and founded the present village. It is some 27 km north-west of Ngwezi Siding and about 32 km south-east of Chief Nyawa's village and it is connected by paths and bush roads to both these places. I stayed there twice, each time for about three weeks and, using it as my base, I visited most of the other villages in Cifokoboyo.

Apart from brief visits to numerous villages in Nyawa's chiefdom, my work there was limited to an area called Guta, in which I spent about three months. It is located on the southern bank of the Sichifulo river some 100 km north-north-west of Livingstone, and it consists of three small isolated villages, Matongo, Siconda and Kataba, which are 35 km north-west of the nearest settlement and school in the cluster of villages around Nyawa's large village. Guta is 44 km from Nyawa itself. Nyawa is connected by a good all-weather road with the main Lusaka–Livingstone road and the railway, and thus easily accessible from Livingstone, Kalomo and other urban centres of the Southern Province; but Guta is, for the most part, connected with Nyawa simply by a footpath which is passable for fourwheel drive vehicles in the dry season only. It is situated deep in the tsetse-infected area which lies around the Kafue National Park: the nearest tsetse fly control post is about 20 km south-east of Guta on the path connecting it with Nyawa and the other nearest villages.

Introduction

Just as I do not aim in this book at generalisations applicable to the whole Toka population, I also do not aim at an exhaustive description and analysis of the social structure and culture as it exists in Ngwezi, Guta and Cifokoboyo. I limit myself solely to a discussion of the way in which the people conceptualise the categories to which they belong by virtue of their descent, and the way in which their membership of these categories affects their behaviour in specific situations of interaction, particularly those connected with ritual, succession and inheritance. It became obvious during my fieldwork that there are significant differences between the social structure and culture in Guta and Cifokoboyo on the one hand, and Ngwezi on the other. In this book, I am taking this regional variation as indicative of the process of change which has been taking place in Toka society over the past four or five decades: I treat the present situation in Guta and Cifokoboyo as indicative of the social structure and culture of the Ngwezi Toka as it was before the recent process of change had taken place. To treat regional cultural variations as indications of various stages of cultural development is always problematic, and the difficulties involved in such an approach are well known. In this particular case, they are alleviated by the fact that the Toka themselves were very well aware of these differences and interpreted them unambiguously in developmental terms. People from Ngwezi who travelled with me to Cifokoboyo, and particularly to Guta, perpetually pointed out to me customs which were not observed any more in their home areas, but which had been in existence there some decades before. An independent justification for taking the present structure and culture in Guta and Cifokoboyo for the initial historical zero point from which to view the change that has occurred in Ngwezi, were the still very vivid recollections of many Toka men and women of the life and customs which had existed in the latter area some forty or fifty years before, and which were perfect descriptions of the life and customs I myself observed in Guta and Cifokoboyo.

In the first chapter, I describe the traditional Toka culture and social structure as it exists in Guta and Cifokoboyo. All subsequent chapters are devoted to the description and analysis of the changing culture and social structure in Ngwezi.

1

Descent categories and local ties in traditional Toka society

In Guta and Cifokoboyo, the two areas which have not yet been fully affected by the modern development taking place elsewhere among the Toka, all people to whom an individual can trace a genealogical connection are his or her *babululu* (kinsmen, sing. *mubululu*). Within this category he or she distinguishes *babululu ba bataata* (paternal kinsmen) and *babululu ba mama* (maternal kinsmen). There is no corresponding collective designation for affines. A distinct category of kinsmen are the *basimukowa*, the matrilineal kin. They are members of a social category called *mukowa* or *luzubo*.

Descent categories

Every Toka is a full member of his or her mother's, and a 'child' of his or her father's *mukowa*. These two *mikowa* (pl. of *mukowa*) are distinguished in verbal reference to membership. A Toka whose mother's *mukowa* is that of Bankombwe (sing. Munkombwe) and whose father's is that of the Bwoono (sing. Moono), refers to his or her membership of the former by saying *ndili Munkombwe* (I am Munkombwe), or *ku mukowa ndili Munkombwe* (I am Munkombwe to my lineage). When referring to his membership of his father's *mukowa*, he says *ndili mwaana wa Bwoono* (I am a child of the Bwoono) or *ku kuzialwa ndili Moono* (I am Moono to my birth). Others acknowledge his membership of the Bwoono *mukowa* by referring to him as Siyamoono. Through his mother and father he is attached to his mother's father's and to his father's father's *mikowa*. He refers to their members as his *basikulu* (grandfathers) and *banene* (grandmothers) and describes himself as their *muzikulu* (grandchild). The members of his FFM's, MFM's as well as members of his four great-grandfathers' *mikowa* are strangers to him and his behaviour towards them and theirs towards him is not affected by common *mukowa* membership.

The Toka apply the terms *mukowa* or *luzubo* to two different categories of people which they clearly distinguish conceptually and which can be distinguished analytically. One of these is a category which, for lack of a better term, I call a clan. I recorded the existence of at least 15 different clans.

Members of some of them are scattered all over Toka territory; members of others live only in some parts of it. The clans have no recognised heads, they do not claim any common property and common clan membership is not a principle of recruitment into any group.

The other category of people referred to as *mukowa* or *luzubo* is conceptualised as a subdivision of the clan. It has a genealogical depth of five or six generations counted from the youngest adults and it comprises matrilineal descendants of one recognised ancestress. I shall retain the Toka term *basimukowa* in referring to the members of this category and the term *mukowa* when referring to the category as such.

When talking about the differences between the clan and the *mukowa*, the Toka usually point out that, unlike the *basimukowa*, the clan members cannot attend the funerals of fellow members nor partake actively in the division of the deceased's estate because they are too numerous and too widely scattered. Apart from considering common clan membership to be a bar to marriage, they ascribe very little importance to clan membership and it seems that it is meaningful only when people travel in foreign areas. The Toka claim that all the tribes they know have the same clans as they themselves do, so that even among tribal foreigners they can always find people who are their clansmen and from whom they can therefore expect protection and offers of hospitality.

Unlike a clan, every *mukowa* has a recognised head (*mupati wa mukowa*), usually the oldest living male member or the one with the highest political status. After his death, the successor to his 'name' also succeeds to his position as *mukowa* head. The *mukowa* head performs the libations to ancestors on behalf of his *basimukowa* during the rain-making ritual, and on the more serious occasions when the ancestors need to be placated. In cases of less serious misfortune, the libation is performed by some kinsman of the victim without the *mukowa* head being specifically summoned to do so.

The Toka state that the head of the *mukowa*, together with its members, attends the funeral of any of their number. When he cannot do so, he always attends the final mourning ceremony (*mayobo*), which takes place later and at which the deceased's successor is chosen and ceremonially installed, and his estate divided among his *basimukowa*. They also state that the head is informed about the marriages of his *mukowa* members and his opinion about prospective marriages is sought. It seems, however, that in practice the head attends the funerals and final mourning ceremonies only of important members of his *mukowa*, for example the village headmen, and of those members who lived either in his own village or in one nearby. In this respect, his behaviour does not differ from that of the ordinary members. Likewise, it seems, he is informed only about the marriages of those members of his *mukowa* who live in his own village or in a village close to it.

21

Descent categories and local ties

According to informants' statements, in the past *mikowa* were groups collectively responsible for avenging the killing of one of their members. The matter was, however, usually settled by the injured *mukowa* accepting compensation. This was paid in cattle and the injured *mukowa* also received a child from that of the killer to compensate for the loss of their member. A boy was given to replace a dead man, a girl to replace a woman. The children were always young ones, so that they would grow up in their new homes as members of the compensated *mukowa* and would not remember from where they had originally come. Nowadays *mikowa* are certainly not groups carrying out vengeance or accepting compensation for members who have been killed.

Every *mukowa* has its own name. Either it is called after its present or previous head or its founder, or it is referred to by the name of the clan of which it is a subdivision. So, for example, the *mukowa* headed by Kambole is known as *mukowa wa* Kambole, *mukowa wa* Mutwanjili (Mutwanjili being its head before Kambole), *mukowa wa* Kasimbo (Kasimbo being its founding ancestress) or as Bazamba (Bazamba being the clan of which it is a subdivision).

Basimukowa represent the most important category of kin among one's *babululu*. Generally, the latter term designates more distant kinship than the former one, which means in practice that only those kin who are not *basimukowa* will be referred to collectively as *babululu*. For Toka, *basimukowa* is a collective designation of those of their kin whose relationship to them is conceptualised in terms of common descent. The Tonga term *basyanausi*, denoting the members of the father's *mukowa* (Colson 1958: 53), is unknown among the Toka, who refer to the members of this category simply as the paternal *basimukowa* (*basimukowa wa bataata*).

The Toka's notions of their descent categories are sustained by a specific spatial distribution of people. Unlike the clans, the *mikowa* are localised in the sense that the majority of their members live in a more or less closely defined territory and that their rights in that territory are recognised. Social relations into which people enter in their social identities defined on the basis of descent, are defined at the same time as being relations among the residents of the territory in which the *basimukowa* have recognised rights. Territorial ties thus parallel descent ties in a range of situations which the Toka clearly see as *mukowa* affairs, and the spatial distribution of *mukowa* members considerably affects a wide range of situations in which they act in their social identity relationships (Goodenough 1965), defined on the basis of their membership. I shall discuss some of these situations later. As it would be meaningless to embark on this discussion without understanding how spatial proximity and distance between the *basimukowa* affect the relations between them, I shall first describe the physical and social aspects of Toka villages.

Village topography

A typical Toka village, whether in Guta, Cifokoboyo or Ngwezi, consists of dwelling-houses built in two parallel rows some twenty or thirty metres apart. This arrangement is, however, not always clear. In villages which have existed on the same site for many years and gradually grown bigger, additional houses have often been built between the original rows as other suitable building sites were no longer available. If some of the houses in the two rows have been abandoned and left to fall down, the original spatial arrangement of households can be completely disrupted and the village may have the shape of a cluster of houses with no clear spatial structure. On the other hand, villages which have existed for only a few years have not yet had time to grow big enough to have houses built along both sides of the village street. Their households are arranged either in one line, with only a few houses forming the nucleus of the other one, or in a cluster from which the two lines of houses will develop only later, after new households have been added to the village.

The maize gardens are located close to the village, clearly separating it from the surrounding bush. Only in villages in which goats and/or pigs are kept in big numbers, are they situated further away from the village to prevent them being damaged; this arrangement is, however, not common. Fruit trees like pawpaws and mangoes are planted in almost every village; in some of them plantains are also grown. Mangoes are so commonly planted that an abandoned village site can almost always be recognised by its mango trees.

A small village constitutes one single settlement. In all big villages powerful social tensions exist which ultimately lead to the fission which divides them into smaller units. The fission has a two-fold character: the seceding group either builds far from the parent village and ultimately establishes itself as a new, independent village under its own headman, or it builds close to the parent village recognising its headman as its own even after the secession. In the latter case the original village merely splits into two, or sometimes three, hamlets. They are separated from one another by maize gardens or even by areas of uncultivated bush and they can be as far apart as five kilometres, although such a distance is exceptional. Some of the hamlets are formed by only two houses; the biggest one I encountered in Guta and Cifokoboyo consisted of twenty-one households. Physically, the hamlets resemble in every respect an independent village. Without knowing the social structure of a settlement and its relationships to the neighbouring ones, it is impossible to say whether it is an independent village or merely a hamlet. Metaphorically, it is possible to say that, just as a household is defined by one fire, a village is defined by being under the authority of one headman. In the following, when using the term 'village' I shall be referring to residential units so defined; by 'hamlets' I shall mean settlements constituting parts of a single village.

Toka villages change their sites quite frequently. Some of their moves take place in a narrow orbit within a few kilometres of the original site, other moves shift a village over a large distance. From the statements of informants it seems that the reasons why a village changes its site can be considerably varied. Villages moved for various reasons: because water became scarce, because cattle and people were troubled by tsetse flies, because the original site used to become muddy during the rainy season, because the soil conditions were not favourable and the fields had to be too far from the village or were across the river and difficult to reach when the river became flooded, because the village was located in such a position that there was not enough land close to the settlement, etc. Although these economic and ecological factors often caused a village to move, it seems that the main reasons for a village changing its site were of a ritual nature. In the past, a village always moved if several deaths occurred there within a short time-span.

The village headman

A village comprising several hamlets emerges as a unit (primarily in the political sphere) by recognising the authority of a single headman. He is responsible for the maintenance of law and order in the village and for hearing the disputes among its inhabitants when asked to do so by a party to the dispute. Unless the dispute is considered to be a trivial one which can be settled by the headman himself in an informal hearing, he informs the headmen of neighbouring villages about the case and requests them to attend the hearing. Not all the headmen are of equal status. The headman of the village whose residents first settled in a certain area is the senior one there. His higher status derives from the fact that the headmen of other villages, or their predecessors, had to ask him, or his predecessors, for permission to build their villages in that area before they could settle there. The senior headman presides over the hearing of cases in all villages in his area. After a hearing the headmen from the neighbouring villages each give their judgement; the final judgement is then passed by the senior headman. The headman in whose village the case was heard does not give judgement.

If the headmen are not able to reconcile the parties to the dispute, or if any party is not satisfied with their judgement, the senior headman will refer the case to the local court. In fact the court will refuse to try a case unless it has already been heard unsuccessfully by the village headmen.

Individual hamlets do not have distinct territories and the fields of the inhabitants of one hamlet are often intermingled with the fields of the inhabitants of another hamlet or hamlets. Only a village as such has its own territory whose borders, against the territories of neighbouring villages, are more or less clearly delineated. The headman exercises certain rights of control over land within this territory. Anybody wanting to open a new field can do so anywhere on so far uncultivated soil, and no special permission to do so has to be sought from the headman. It is assumed that this has been tacitly given, as the headman does not interfere. In fact he could interfere only if the piece of land on which somebody intends to start a field has already been claimed. Anybody leaving the village with no intention of returning can allocate his fields to anybody in the village. If he does not do this, the right to dispose of them is again that of the headman, who can allocate them to anybody who approaches him. The hamlet heads have no similar rights and it is always the village headman who is responsible for the allocation of land to the inhabitants of his village, irrespective of whether they are members of his own or of any other hamlet.

An abandoned village site remains forever the property of the village which once stood there. The right of ownership to such a site is vested in the village headman, whose approval has to be obtained by anybody who wants to build or to start a field there.

Status within the village

The inhabitants of a village fall into three categories:

(1) *Bweni ba munzi* (sing. *mweni wa munzi*) – owners of the village
(2) *Bakumbizi ba munzi* (sing. *mukumbizi wa munzi*) – strangers of the village
(3) *Bakwatizi* (sing. *mukwatizi*) – uxorilocal residents in the village

When the Toka explain the concept of village ownership they point out that the owners of the village are those whose mothers were born there, i.e. those who are tied to the village by a matrifilial link. The concept of village ownership is also often explained by saying that people are owners of the village of which their mother is an owner. On a practical level, however, when somebody's status in a village is being disputed (e.g. when the question of succession to village headmanship is being discussed), and it is pointed out that his or her mother was herself born in the village, the dispute is settled: the person in question is an owner of the village. It means that the Toka have an ownership status in their mother's natolocality, irrespective of whether it is her patrilocality or her matrilocality. In no case I know of has it been queried whether the village in question is their mother's matrilocality, i.e. whether their mother was herself an owner of that village. This practice is fully in line with the realities of the structure of local *mikowa* which, due to the frequent fission of villages, rarely have a depth greater than three generations, as I shall show later. An adult person's mother's mother is thus typically the ancestress of the local *mukowa* and the question of whether she was herself born in the village in which her *mukowa* is localised or brought into it by her husband is irrelevant. Consequently, as far as the status of her daughters' children is concerned, it is irrelevant whether her daughters were born in their matrilocality (i.e. in their mother's matrilocality) or patrilocality (i.e. in their mother's virilocality). The rule which says that people are owners of the village that is their mother's natolocality does not imply that the village of which they are owners has to be at the same site or even has to be known by the same name as that in which their mother was actually born. Due to the perpetual fission of villages and their frequent shifts from one site to another, quite the opposite is typically the case. For example Musoe (E13) now lives in Siyamutete Ling'amba (Diagram 2) and is one of its owners. She was born in Kanjolo, while her mother Munkombwe (D10) was born in Nyawa. Although Siyamutete Ling'amba was only founded in 1955, for the purpose of defining who is and who is not an owner it has, as it were, existed for generations, albeit only as part of another village. For this purpose it traces its continuous existence through the times when it was part of the village of Kanjolo to the time when it was part of Nyawa's village.

Under the conditions of prevailing virilocal residence, the Toka are typically born in villages of which they are not owners; it is their attachment to their mothers, as against their fathers, which brings them eventually back to their own village, usually after their father has died or their mother has been divorced. The life history of Musoe (E13) is illustrative of this pattern. She herself was born in Kanjolo, but after her marriage moved to Nzwida, her husband's village. All her children were born there. After their father died they followed her to Siyamutete Ling'amba, of which they are owners.

Being an owner of the village does not necessarily mean being a member of its headman's *mukowa*. For example, Mukasilumbe's *mukowa* of the Mucimba clan is the headman's *mukowa* in Kataba's village (Diagram 3) and Kataba (H5) and Siyamonga (I4), who are its only members, are owners of the village. But other inhabitants of Kataba are owners as well. Siconda's wife, Moonga (G5), married into Guta and her daughters, Muncindu (H6) and Mukacoobwe (H7), were born there. Muncindu (H6) is dead, but her sister, Mukacoobwe (H7), lives with her children, Mukanyambe (I7) and Sikapula (I8), in Kataba's village. Although Mukacoobwe (H7) herself is not one of its owners, Mukanyambe (I7) and Sikapula (I8) are. So are Muncindu's children, Muntemba (I5) and Malumani (I6). Muntemba (I5), Malumani (I6), Mukanyambe (I7) and Sikapula (I8) are all members of Moonga's *mukowa* of the Muntanga clan. Similarly, Kamela's wife, Mukwazi (G1), married into Guta and her two children, Musiko (H1) and Nason Muyoba (H2), were born there. Nason Muyoba (H2) is not an owner of Kataba, but Musiko's children, Anderson Limwanya (I1) and Nasimoono (I2), are. So is Nasimoono's son, David Liyambai (J1). Anderson Limwanya (I1), Nasimoono (I2) and David Liyambai (J1) are all members of Mukwazi's *mukowa* of the Mudenda clan. The fact that members of other *mikowa* than that of the headman are village owners can often have important repercussions for the succession to village headmanship, as I shall show later.

All those whose residence in the village is neither matrilocal nor uxorilocal, are referred to as *bakumbizi*, strangers. This category includes not only those who are not linked by kinship ties to the village, but quite a number of the headman's close kinsmen as well, his own children included. Thus in Kataba (Diagram 3), for example, Nason Muyoba (H2), Kataba's (H5) mother's brother's son, and Alec (J2), Kataba's sister's son's son, are strangers. So is Malumani's (I6) father-in-law and the latter's brother, and so would be Kataba's (H5) and Gadi's (H4) own children.

The last category of village inhabitants are *bakwatizi*, uxorilocal residents. Due to the instability of marriage, they are quite often nothing more than transients in a given village. Upon divorce, it is the *mukwatizi* and not his wife who has to leave the village and settle somewhere else. The house which he built for himself and his wife will be left for her. The Toka say that a *mukwatizi* actually did not build it for himself as other men do, but for his wife.

All this accounts for the *mukwatizi* having the lowest status of all three categories of village residents. His status is even worse if he has his father-in-law living in the same village. He is forced to carry out in full his duties and obligations towards him, of which the other men are relieved simply because they do not reside with their fathers-in-law and see them only once in a while. A *mukwatizi* whose father-in-law lives in the same village as he himself, has to help him with building his house and his cattle enclosure, with looking after his cattle, with cultivating his fields, transporting corn from the fields or water from the well, providing firewood, etc. This is something which the other men do not have to do. He is not only constantly subject to their ridicule but quite often he is considered as nothing better than a slave working for his father-in-law.

Low as their status may be, the *bakwatizi* play an important role in the political life of the village. From among them – preferably from among the headman's own sons-in-law – is recruited the headman's representative (*ng'ambela*). He acts for the headman if the latter cannot show up or does not consider the matter important enough for his personal presence. Thus the *ng'ambela* may be sent to the local court to convey the headman's message or he may attend funerals or mourning ceremonies at which the village headman has to be formally represented, but which are not considered important enough to require his personal attendance. The *ng'ambela* is apparently chosen from among the *bakwatizi* for two reasons. First, apart from his own children, no members of the village are bound to him by kinship ties, and his bias towards those who might otherwise be his kinsmen is thus automatically eliminated; living in a village where hardly anybody is closer to him than anybody else, he can easily remain impartial. Second, his low status among the village residents eliminates the possibility that he will pursue his own policy when acting for his headman: especially when he is the headman's son-in-law, there is a reasonable guarantee that he will always abide by the headman's own instructions.

When the Toka explain their marriage arrangements in general terms, they always mention that a couple establish residence in the bridegroom's village; post-marital virilocal residence is invariably depicted as an ideal. But uxorilocal residence is quite frequent: out of fifty-five married couples in Guta and Cifokoboyo, thirty-seven (67.3%) reside virilocally, fifteen (27.3%) reside uxorilocally and three (5.4%) reside neolocally. There are basically three reasons leading to uxorilocal residence. As I will show in detail later, the hamlet head relies on his own children and possibly even on the kinsmen of his children's spouses when building up his hamlet. He tries to keep in it not only his married sons but also his married daughters. Their husbands are thus exposed to a much stronger pressure to reside uxorilocally than the other men are. This pressure is particularly effective if they have not fully completed their bridewealth payments. While only 25% of men with married children who are not hamlet heads have one married daughter living patrilocally with them, 50% of hamlet heads with married children have on average two married daughters living patrilocally.

Another reason leading to uxorilocal residence is the tendency of the matricentric family or a remnant of such a family – the group of uterine siblings – to maintain its local unity (see pp. 35ff. for further discussion). If a married woman wants to live with her mother and her siblings, her husband has basically two options: he can either divorce her, if he does not want to live in the village she has chosen, or follow her to the village where her mother and/or her uterine siblings live. If he decides on the latter step, uxorilocal residence will result. As with the previously discussed cases, the husband's bargaining position *vis-à-vis* his wife and her kin is much weaker if he has not paid full bridewealth. Thus again, uxorilocal residence can be a result of the combination of both factors.

It is bridewealth which makes any marriage a formal one and the fact that the husband has not paid it in full can stand alone as a sufficient reason for uxorilocal residence, for unless the bridewealth is transferred, he is not allowed to take his wife to his own village. He is, however, allowed to live with her in the village of her parents and, if the situation continues for long, to establish his own household and cultivate his own fields there. He nevertheless has to cope with various strains, on top of the social disadvantages faced by every man living uxorilocally. For instance, the children of the marriage belong solely to their mother and her kin, and their father has to leave them behind should he choose to 'divorce' his wife. As the Toka put it: 'He has to go alone as he came.' To be bound in this way to a single locality (or to be able to leave it only at the expense of a divorce and loss of one's children) can become extremely difficult in many situations (e.g. when in dispute with fellow villagers, when accused of sorcery, etc.).

Individual mobility

When deciding on their place of residence, the Toka aim at securing for themselves lasting access to land, and at establishing the highest possible degree of security in relation to other people. Their aim is to live in a village in which their status is such that they are guaranteed a say in the important village affairs and, in the case of a dispute with a neighbour or strained relations with their fellow villagers, they will not be forced to leave the village. They aim at living in a village in which they can exercise their moral authority, in which they are able to secure for themselves the cooperation of others when they need it, and in which they are unlikely to be bewitched or to be accused of being witches. They aim either at living in a village of which they are owners or in which their close relationship, either to its headman or some hamlet head, guarantees them a reasonable amount of the desirable economic and social security.

A striking feature of the social structure of Guta and Cifokoboyo is that individuals tend to circulate rapidly through villages in the course of their lifetimes. Behind this degree of individual mobility lies each individual's perpetual pursuit of his immediate and long-term interests and goals: people leave villages in which their interests have been for one reason or another frustrated or have remained unfulfilled, and move to those in which they will, under their momentarily given circumstances, achieve a higher degree of both economic and social security. Typically, those will be the villages in which they will enhance their status. Obviously, each specific reason for each specific move differs from the specific reasons which lie behind other moves; there is no need in the present analysis to go into them in detail. It suffices to say that the multiplicity of individual decisions on inter-village moves leads to the emergence of virilocal residence, the coherence of the matricentric family and the ties of uterine kinship as the most important principles of village affiliation (see Chapter 4 for a more detailed discussion of individual mobility and the social composition of villages in Guta and Cifokoboyo).

The social composition of villages in Guta and Cifokoboyo reflects the interplay of these three most important principles. Virilocal marriage disrupts the matricentric family by separating daughters from mothers and sisters from brothers. At the same time, it enables men, particularly the hamlet heads, to retain their children in their own hamlets after the latter have matured and married. Nevertheless, the dominant attachment of children is not to their fathers but to their mothers, and the main bond of kinship is between a mother and her children, who form a matricentric family.

This family may be attached for longer or shorter periods to a woman's husband. In this way a man can retain the residential affiliation of his children while his marriage to their mother endures. On divorce or after the death of their father, the children invariably follow their mother. If children and mothers are temporarily separated during their lifetime as a result of virilocal marriage, they come together again after the mother's divorce or widowhood. This is one of the important factors behind individual mobility and the instability of an individual's residence. In fact, the system can only operate when there is high mobility.

The main principles of village affiliation can also be expressed in terms of the strategies followed by hamlet heads when building up their hamlets. A hamlet head tries first of all to attract his own uterine kinsmen. Although he invariably tries to attract his patrilateral kinsmen as well, he does not usually succeed as their loyalty lies, in the first place, with their own uterine kin. In consequence, the uterine kinsmen of the hamlet head outnumber his patrilateral kinsmen by at least fifteen to one. The hamlet head further relies on his own children and possibly on the kinsmen of his wife or even his children's spouses, when building up his hamlet. His degree of success in attracting them depends directly on his success in retaining his own wife and on the success of his children in retaining their spouses. As divorce is frequent, to be able to maintain successfully a sizeable hamlet in prolonged existence, its head first of all has to attract to it his own uterine kinsmen. Many hamlets have collapsed only because their heads have been unable to gather any other support than that of their children and the latter's affines.

The following two cases of the founding of Libonda and Siyamutete Ling'amba villages in Cifokoboyo indicate clearly the people from whom hamlet founders attract the necessary following.

Libonda (Diagram 1) was founded by its present headman, Namadula (B6), in 1953. Until then, Namadula (B6) had lived with his parents in Kancele, his father's matrilocality. After his father died, he and his widowed mother, Cilikwazi (A2), left Kancele but did not move to Namadula's mother's village. Instead, Namadula (B6) started his own village not far from Kancele. He was able to attract to it his uterine brother, Sibeso (B5), who until then had been living in his wife's village, and his uterine sister, Zita (B4), together with her husband, Thomas (B3). The nucleus of Namadula's village was thus formed by members of the matricentric family headed by Namadula's mother, Cilikwazi (A2). Three other households in Namadula's village consisted of his uterine kin: that of his mother's matrilateral parallel cousin, Maliya (A3), and her husband, Simango (A4), and those of Maliya's two sons, Nais (B9) and Siyampunga (B10). These three households moved to Namadula's new village from Simango. Namadula (B6) also attracted two of his wife's brothers, Siyakweziya (B7) and Silimi (B8), who moved to Libonda from the village of Siyantalusiya. Another household in the new

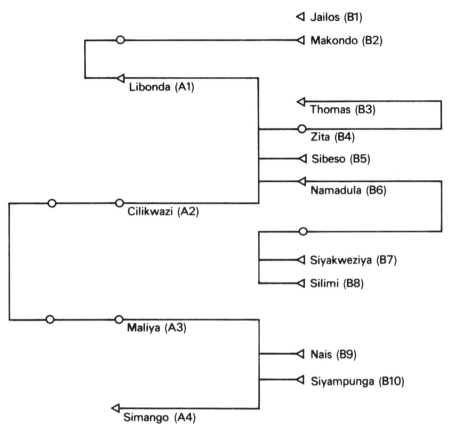

Diagram 1. Social composition of Libonda village in 1953

village was that of Makondo (B2), Namadula's (B6) patrilateral kinsman, who moved to the new site with him from Kancele. The last man attracted by Namadula was Jailos (B1), a stranger with no kinship ties to anybody in Libonda. By being able to persuade his various kinsmen to settle down with him, Namadula (B6) mustered a following of nine tax-paying male household heads and, with himself included, had thus a village of ten tax-payers. He fulfilled the requirements stipulated by the Native Authority for the minimum size of Toka villages and his headmanship was recognised by the chief and confirmed by the Native Authority.[1]

Siyamutete Ling'amba (Diagram 2) was founded in 1955 when Janki Siyamutete (D9) and his followers left the village of Kanjolo and settled on a site about 1.5 km away. Among the followers of Janki Siyamutete (D9) were, first of all, his mother, Mukanamunyuku (C1), his uterine sisters,

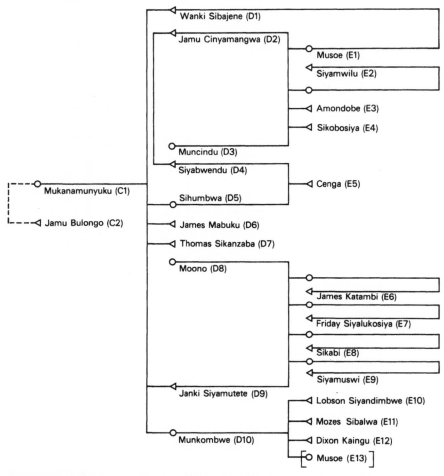

Diagram 2. Social composition of Siyamutete Ling'amba village in 1955

Sihumbwa (D5) and Munkombwe (D10), and his uterine brothers, Wanki Sibajene (D1), James Mabuku (D6) and Thomas Sikanzaba (D7). As in Libonda, the core of Siyamutete's new village was formed by members of the matricentric family headed by Mukanamunyuku (C1). Just as she herself was followed by her married children, so were her two daughters, Sihumbwa (D5) and Munkombwe (D10). Munkombwe (D10) came with her three married sons: Lobson Siyandimbwe (E10), Mozes Sibalwa (E11) and Dixon Kaingu (E12). All these people were uterine kinsmen of the village founder. Another of his uterine relatives whom he attracted to the new village was Jamu Bulongo (C2). Apart from his uterine kinsmen, Janki Siyamutete (D9)

32

succeeded in attracting the husbands of his four daughters, James Katambi (E6), Friday Siyalukosiya (E7), Sikabi (E8) and Siyamuswi (E9). The remaining three men who moved to Siyamutete's new village from Nyawa, Amondobe (E3), Sikobosiya (E4) and Siyamwilu (E2), are all related to Siyamutete (D9) through affinal links. It was not Siyamutete (D9) himself so much as his sister, Sihumbwa (D5), and his brother, Wanki Sibajene (D1), who were instrumental in attracting these three. Jamu Cinyamangwa (D2) was a uterine brother of Sihumbwa's husband and the father of Wanki Sibajene's wife. Sihumbwa (D5) and her husband, Siyabwendu (D4), followed her mother, Mukanamunyuku (C1), and her uterine brother, Siyamutete (D9), into the new village founded by the latter. Jamu Cinyamangwa (D2), his wife, Muncindu (D3), his sons and his daughter's husband left Nyawa and joined Cinyamangwa's brother, Siyabwendu (D4), in the new village in which Cinyamangwa's and Muncindu's daughter, Musoe (E1), was already living. When Siyamutete Ling'amba started in 1955, it was composed, with the sole exception of Jamu Bulongo (C2), of members of five matricentric families: that headed by Mukanamunyuku (C1), those headed by her two daughters, Sihumbwa (D5) and Munkombwe (D10), that headed by Jamu Cinyamangwa's wife, Muncindu (D3), and that headed by Janki Siyamutete's wife, Moono (D8).

The fact that adult males in Guta and Cifokoboyo take into account first of all the links of uterine kinship when deciding on their residence, results in the male *basimukowa* being kept in spatial proximity. Out of fifty-four adult men residing in Guta and Cifokoboyo, twenty-three (42.6%) were members of the hamlet head's *mukowa* and thirty-one (57.4%) were members of other *mikowa*. It is basically the high incidence of uxorilocal marriages and, to a lesser extent, the tendency of a hamlet head's children to reside in their father's village, which prevents a village in Guta and Cifokoboyo from being composed solely of the male members of one *mukowa*.

Fission of villages

The high mobility of villages is influenced by fission, which divides larger villages into smaller units; it occurs quite frequently and is an important factor in Toka social structure.

Out of eleven villages in Guta and Cifokoboyo whose histories I recorded, six (i.e. 54.5 %) originated by seceding from another village. In the remaining five cases it was not possible to establish the way in which the village originated; only the name of its founder was known and the informants were not able to say where he came from and what the circumstances were under which the village had started.

The principles of village fission can be illustrated by the history of Matongo, one of the three villages in Guta which originally formed a single

Descent categories and local ties

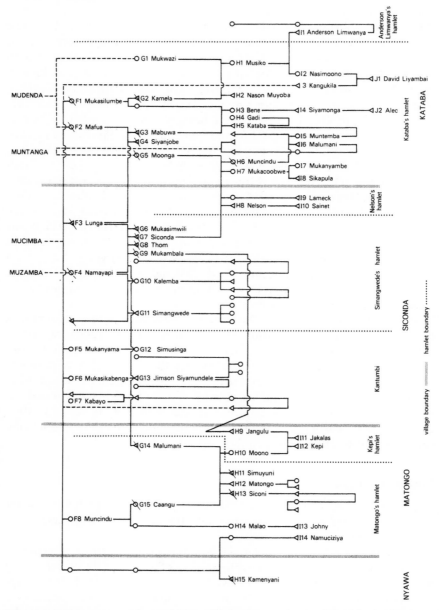

Diagram 3. Master genealogy of Guta. (Only the people mentioned in the book are indicated in the diagram.)

34

village founded by Chief Lunga (F3) some time in the second half of the last century (Diagram 3; the history of the other two villages is described in Appendix 1). When Lunga (F3) died in 1930 (?), his sister's daughter's son, Kamenyani (H15), succeeded him as chief and village headman and in 1935 he moved his court to its present site in Nyawa. He was followed there by descendants of his maternal grandmother (Lunga's sister), who formed a distinct *mukowa* within the Mucimba clan. The members of other *mikowa* of this clan, i.e. the descendants of Lunga's other four sisters, Mukasilumbe (F1), Mukanyama (F5), Mukasikabenga (F6) and Muncindu (F8), stayed behind in Guta. The senior man of Muncindu's *mukowa* was Matongo (H12). Like Kamenyani (H15), he is a son of Lunga's sister's daughter and hence he too was qualified to succeed to Lunga's headmanship. However, not he but Kamenyani (H15) succeeded and Matongo (H12) exercised his right to become a village headman by forming his own village. Apart from his mother, Caangu (G15), his father, Malumani (G14), and his own children and his two wives, he attracted to it his sister, Moono (H10), and her sons (I11 and I12), the son of his deceased uterine brother, Siconi (H13), and his brother-in-law, and his mother's sister's daughter, Malao (H14) and Malao's son (I13). His last recruit was Namuciziya (I14), a member of Kamenyani's *mukowa*, whom he attracted mainly because Namuciziya was married to a daughter of one of Matongo's uterine brothers. With the exception of Namuciziya (I14), Malao (H14) and her son (I13), Matongo's village consists entirely of the members of the matricentric family headed by his own mother, Caangu (G15), their descendants and one of the latter's affines. Caangu (G15) is now dead and the unity of her matricentric family is fading. There is now a separate hamlet within Matongo's village which is headed by Matongo's sister's son, Kepi (I12). It consists of three households: Kepi's own, that of his mother, Moono (H10), and his father, Jangulu (H9), and that of his brother, Jakalas (I11). The emergence of a matricentric family – such as that of Moono (H10) – as a local unit established in a separate hamlet or village, is a process which lies at the very root of *mukowa* segmentation and village fission (or emergence of hamlets within a village), which is its spatial expression. When a daughter's children mature and establish their own families, a new matricentric family comes into existence headed by the daughter of the founder of the original family. The daughter's matricentric family may very often now start to assert its own unity as against that of the original matricentric family. Particularly when the founder of the original family is dead and the structural point on which the unity of that family hinged is removed, the unity of the new matricentric family leads inevitably to a pulling-apart of the members of the original matricentric family, i.e. the group of uterine siblings. A *mukowa* may be viewed as composed of overlapping matricentric families, each of which is structurally a minimal *mukowa* segment. While in a sense a *mukowa* is nothing but a matricentric family grown large, the unity of any immediate matricentric family within it perpetually disrupts the unity of the *mukowa* and the emergence of a local matricentric family leads to the segmentation of the *mukowa* of which it is a part. Although the women are the focal points of *mukowa* unity and segmentation and of village unity and fission, it is primarily, although not exclusively, the men who manipulate these points. An ambitious man who wants to be a village headman or to have his own hamlet – hopefully as a first step on the way to his own village – is more likely to attract his own uterine siblings and their descendants if his mother is still alive and if he can persuade her to settle down with him in his own hamlet. It is the bond to their mother which will attract them to his hamlet. Whether he will be able to persuade his mother to settle down with him in a new hamlet and attract her other children to it, will largely depend on whether her own mother is still alive or not. In the former case she might prefer to reside with her and her own uterine siblings. The mother's brother–sister's son relationship and other relationships between members of *mikowa* three generations deep (e.g. MZS–MZS) are thus as much principles of village affiliation as they are of village fission. Whether they will be one or the other depends on the development stage of the matricentric families of both men involved. Relationships linking together members of *mikowa* of a four- or five-generational depth (e.g. MMB–ZDS, MMMZDS–MMZDDS) rarely recruit people to a hamlet. Only four household heads residing in Matongo's hamlet are members of a *mukowa* more than three generations deep: Matongo (H12), Malao (H14), Johny (I13) and Namuciziya (I14). This is an indication that a village inhabited by members of a *mukowa* more than three generations deep is unlikely to persist and withstand fission, or, expressed in other words, that a woman's matricentric family of procreation is unlikely not to exert its spatially expressed independence of her matricentric family of orientation, particularly if her own mother (i.e. the head of her matricentric family of orientation) is dead.

The history of Matongo's village demonstrates that the fission of villages is a territorial expression of *mukowa* segmentation; a *mukowa* segment expresses its unity against other segments by establishing itself in its own settlement. Whether this settlement is an independent village or merely a hamlet has no significance within the process of *mukowa* segmentation and fission, since it is solely determined by the administrative requirement for a village of consist of at least ten adult male householders. The head of every *mukowa* segment establishing itself in its own settlement ideally aims at founding an independent village. Very few achieve this aim, however, as the local unity of the matricentric family in many cases disrupts the local unity of the *mukowa* by pulling apart the group of uterine siblings on whose co-residence it is based. It is mainly due to the strong tendency of the matricentric family to reconstitute itself as a local unit, at the expense of the local unity of a sibling group, that the localised *mikowa* have only exceptionally more than three generations' genealogical depth (counted from the youngest generation of household heads). The local unity of the *mukowa* segment within its own village or hamlet has significance only at the political level; at the ritual level there exists a wider unity among segments of the same *mukowa* within a specific area.

Mukowa and ritual

The *basimukowa* living together in the same village are members of a local *mukowa* that is usually three and never more than four generations deep when counted from the youngest adult generation. The term *basimukowa* refers, however, not only to the members of such a localised group of matrilineal kin; it denotes a wider category of people: all those who are matrilineal descendants of a common ancestress who can be as many as five or six generations removed. The awareness of belonging to this wider category is manifest in the rain-making rituals and the final mourning ceremonies, in which the *basimukowa* who live within an area covering several villages take part. Each *mukowa* is associated with one such particular area, that where its ancestors are buried. Thus Guta (Diagrams 3 and 4) is the area of the Bacimba; it is the burial place of their most important ancestor, Chief Lunga (F3). Although they recognised his successor, Kamenyani (H15), as the head of their *mukowa*, most Bacimba did not follow him to Nyawa when he moved his court there in the mid-1930s. They preferred to stay in their proper ancestral home of Guta, in spite of the fact that this area is infested with tsetse. After Kamenyani (H15) died, Matongo (H12) succeeded him as the *mukowa* head and he is recognised as such not only by the Bacimba of Guta but also by the Bacimba who live in other areas (e.g. Nyawa, Cifokoboyo).

Guta is also the ancestral home of the Bazamba, whose founding ancestress was Namayapi (F4), Chief Lunga's wife. She is buried in Guta, as are her two sons, Siconda (G7) and Malumani (G14). Siconda (G7) was recognised as the head of the Bazamba and after his death Simangwede (G11), the present headman of Siconda's village, succeeded to this position.

Although there are not many Badenda living in Guta, two of their ancestors are buried there: Mabuwa (G3) and Siyanjobe (G4), the sons of Lunga's junior wife, Mafua (F2).

The rain-making ritual, *lwiindi lwemvula* (or *mupai mwemvula*, libation for rain), was traditionally performed, as it still is in Guta, every October before the beginning of the rainy season. In most Toka areas it is now only performed if the rains are late or, particularly, if there is a prolonged break in the middle of the rains and the drought threatens to kill growing crops. As its name implies, the ritual consists in libations to ancestors who are begged to provide rain.[2]

Members of all the *mikowa* whose ancestors are buried in Guta, i.e. Bacimba, Bazamba and Badenda, take part in the same ritual. This is because these *mikowa* are closely interrelated as both Siconda (G7) and Malumani (G14), ancestors of the Bazamba, and Mabuwa (G3) and Siyanjobe (G4), ancestors of the Badenda, are at the same time children of Bacimba, Lunga (F3) having been their father. The Bacimba are the autochthonous *mukowa* in Guta as Guta is Lunga's matrilocality while it is Bazamba's and Badenda's patrilocality: both Bazamba's ancestress Namayapi (F4) and Badenda's ancestress Mafua (F2) were Lunga's wives and were brought to Guta by him. In the same sense in which only those whose mothers were born in a village are its owners, only the Bacimba are owners of Guta. Their seniority there is recognised in the concepualisation of the ritual as that of Bacimba in which the Bazamba and the Badenda actively participate at relevant points. Matongo (H12), as the head of the Bacimba, is the organiser and leader of the ritual which starts with each village headman – Matongo (H12), Kataba (H5) and Simangwede (G11) – pouring a libation of beer at a shrine which has been built in front of his house by the men from the village. The libation is accompanied by an incantation to God for rain so that the crops might grow well; a desire for meat and a wish to live in peace and to keep all evil away are mentioned as well.

The libation at the shrines is followed by libations at the graves of the ancestors, which are accompanied by similar incantations. The participants in the ritual accompany each libation by clapping their hands rhythmically and the libation is followed by the singing of special songs, drumming, the sprinkling of water into the air and impromptu dances mimicking the work in the fields. Libations are always poured on the graves of important ancestors but the graves of less important forebears are often bypassed. Libations performed during the rain-making ritual in Guta in October 1971 are indicated in Diagram 4.

All inhabitants of Guta participate in the ritual but only those who are matrilineally descended from the ancestors or who are the 'children' or 'grandchildren' of their *mukowa*, pour libations on their graves. It is thus mostly the Bacimba and Bazamba – Matongo (H12), Kataba (H5), Moono (H10), Kepi (I12), Simangwede (G11) and Kalemba (G10) – who take an active part in the ritual, by making offerings to the ancestors of their two *mikowa*. Nason Muyoba (H2), the head of the Badenda, only makes offerings to the Badenda ancestors, Mabuwa (G3) and Siyanjobe (G4), and pours libations on the graves of the Bacimba – e.g. Siconi (H13) – of whom he is a 'child'. Although the members of the Bantanga attend the rain-making ritual in Guta like anybody else, they do not participate in it by making libations. Lameck (I9) and Malumani (I6), who are Bantanga, poured libations on Siconda's (G7) grave. They did this, however, not as Bantanga or on behalf of members of this *mukowa*, but as 'grandchildren' of the

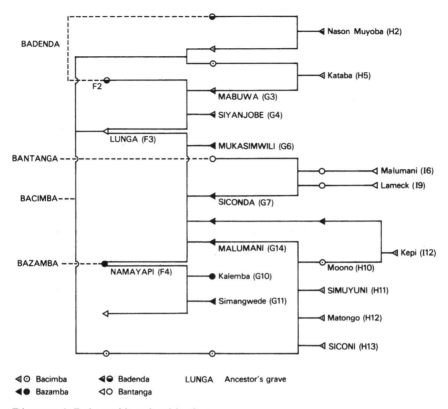

⊲○ Bacimba   ⊲● Badenda   LUNGA   Ancestor's grave
⊲● Bazamba   ⊲○ Bantanga

Diagram 4. Rain-making ritual in Guta

Graves in order of visit	People performing libation at the grave
1. Siconda–G7	H12, G11, I6, I9
2. Namayapi–F4	H12, G11, H10, I12, G10
3. Lunga–F3	H12, H5, G11, H10
4. Malumani–G14	H12, G11,[a] I12
5. Mukasimwili–G6	H12, G11, I12
6. Mabuwa–G3	H5, H2
7. Siconi–H13	H12, H5, G11, H2, I12

[a] Simangwede (G11) is the successor to Siconda (G7), the son of the Bacimba

Bazamba (Siconda was their mother's father). There are no Bantanga ancestors buried in Guta and this is not a place where Bantanga could make offerings to their ancestors. Unlike the Bacimba, Bazamba and Badenda, the Bantanga living in Guta are only a segment of a *mukowa* whose ancestral home is elsewhere and whose head lives elsewhere.

Similarly, the Bacimba living in Siyamutete Ling'amba in Cifokoboyo (Diagram 2) cannot perform a rain-making ritual on their own. Their ancestors are not buried there, except for Janki Siyamutete (D9), the founder of the village. When Cenga (E5), the headman of Siyamutete Ling'amba, wants to perform a rain-making ritual in his village, he has to summon Matongo (H12), the head of the Bacimba. The women in Siyamutete Ling'amba brew beer and Cenga (E5), with other representatives from his village, takes it to Matongo in Guta. Matongo (H12) pours it on the grave of Lunga (F3) and other Bacimba ancestors in Guta. He then goes himself to Siyamutete Ling'amba, where he and Cenga (E5) pour a libation at the grave of Janki Siyamutete (D9).

In the same way in which a *mukowa* segment expresses its unity against other segments by establishing itself in its own settlement, a *mukowa* expresses its unity against other *mikowa* of the same clan by performing its own rain-making ritual. A *mukowa* segment becomes recognised as such after it has established itself in its own hamlet or village; a *mukowa* becomes recognised as such after its senior member has performed its own rain-making ritual. Village fission is the territorial expression of *mukowa* segmentation at both levels. But while it is sufficient, in order that a *mukowa* segment be recognised as such, for its senior member merely to found his own village or even a hamlet, a *mukowa* segment has to be associated for several generations with a particular locality to be recognised as an independent *mukowa* within its clan. The founder of a new village can never become the head of a new *mukowa*: his ancestors are not buried there and in the ritual sphere he is dependent on the existing *mukowa* head, who usually lives in the locality from which the new segment originated. It is only one of the successors of the village founder who will become a recognised head of the new *mukowa* with a right to perform his own rain-making ritual. If a brother succeeds the founder of the new village as a headman he is unlikely to become recognised as the head of a new *mukowa*. His dead brother is not sufficiently far removed for his successor to make offerings to him. A sister's son who succeeds as a headman has a better chance of becoming the head of a new *mukowa*; but this is not always the case. Cenga (E5), the contemporary headman of Siyamutete Ling'amba (Diagram 2), is the sister's son of the founder of the village, Janki Siyamutete (D9). But Janki's mother (C1) and four of his siblings (D1, D6, D7, D10) are still alive and residing in the village. Janki Siyamutete (D9) is thus not sufficiently far removed to be recognised as a common ancestor of all the Bacimba in Siyamutete Ling'amba. For many of them he is no more important than their own mother's brothers who are still alive. After Janki's mother, Mukanamunyuku (C1), has died and been buried in Siyamutete Ling'amba, she might become recognised by all the Bacimba there as the founding ancestress of their *mukowa*. Offerings for rain will then be made to her as well as to her son, Janki (D9), and her other children and the Bacimba in Siyamutete Ling'amba will become a *mukowa*, independent of other Bacimba, and with their own rituals. Cenga (E5), as a village headman, will then become the head of this new *mukowa*, which will be bound to the Bacimba in Guta only by ties of common clanship. When Kamenyani (H15) in Guta succeeded Lunga (F3), the situation was different. Lunga's own mother was long dead and Lunga (F3) had only one living brother (Kabayo's (F7) husband) at that time. Kamenyani (H15) could become the head of the Bacimba *mukowa* as his predecessor was genealogically far enough removed to be recognised as a common ancestor of all the Bacimba in Guta.

Like a rain-making ritual, the final mourning ceremony, called *mayobo* or *mapaila*, is a situation which brings together a wider range of *basimukowa* than those who live together in the same settlement. It is organised in the same way in Guta, Cifokoboyo and Ngwezi; to avoid repetition I shall discuss its organisation in Chapter 7.

Succession and inheritance

Among the Toka the transmission of relatively exclusive rights in social position and material goods usually occurs only on the death of the holder. The successor of the deceased is chosen during the final mourning ceremony at a meeting held secretly during the night. Its participants are first of all some of the deceased's *basimukowa*, both men and women, who are either members of an older generation than was the deceased, or, if they belong to his generation, are older than he was himself. The successor is chosen from among the younger *basimukowa* of the deceased and these usually do not attend the meeting. The meeting may also be attended by some of the deceased's affines and by men without any connections with the deceased, usually headmen of neighbouring villages or their representatives. They attend at the invitation of the *basimukowa*. The criteria for choosing the successor include more than genealogical relation to the deceased; the character and personal qualities of the candidate are always taken into consideration. The Toka are aware that the *basimukowa* might easily be biased and might try to push through their favourite as the successor, without taking into consideration whether he is the best qualified in all respects. The role of the headmen, who are not biased in favour of any of the deceased's kinsmen and who know the conduct of those who come under consideration, is to express an independent opinion about them. If the deceased left a widow, her kinsmen, or more often kinswomen, are sometimes present at the meeting to look after her interests.

The final mourning ceremony is attended by the *basimukowa* living in the deceased's village as well as by his *basimukowa* from other villages. The latter are the guests of the local *basimukowa* and as such they are treated with respect and deference. The most senior man among them is usually asked to convene the meeting. Although he does not necessarily have the main say in choosing the successor, he is always the one who eventually declares his name in accordance with the sense of the meeting.

Succession follows the matrilineal line and ideally and most frequently the sister's son succeeds. More rarely it is the uterine brother or a more distant member of the deceased's *mukowa* (e.g. MZDS) who succeeds to his name. The successor inherits the *muzimu* (spirits, shade) and the kinship duties and responsibilities of the deceased. If the deceased himself had an inherited *muzimu*, two successors are usually chosen: the first inherits the deceased's own *muzimu*, the other the *muzimu* which the deceased himself had inherited.

The last part in the final mourning ceremony is the division of the deceased's estate among his inheritors. The things constituting the estate are allocated to individual kinsmen and affines of the deceased by one of his *basimukowa*, usually the man who presided over the meeting for choosing the successor. He picks up one thing after another and allocates them to the assembled kinsmen, affines and even non-relatives (either headmen or other important men who are attending the final mourning ceremony or who themselves live in the deceased's village). The division of inheritance usually proceeds smoothly as long as those who feel entitled to a share of the deceased's estate receive one. About a quarter of the estate is allocated to the member of the deceased's father's *mukowa*. The rest is divided among the deceased's own *basimukowa*, with only a token going to the affines and non-kinsmen. Such a division is normal rather than normative, for only those of the deceased's kinsmen who attend the final mourning ceremony receive a share. Rather than deriving from the norm stipulating that a certain proportion of the estate should be allocated to the members of the deceased's father's *mukowa*, the fact that its members receive only a small proportion of the estate is a consequence of the fact that more members of the deceased's own *mukowa* than those of his father's *mukowa* attend the ceremony. The former usually outnumber the latter by about three to one. This again is a consequence of the spatial distribution of the members of both *mikowa*. Whereas most of the deceased's own *basimukowa* live either in his own or in neighbouring villages, the members of his father's *mukowa* are more widely dispersed. Those who live far from the deceased's village are unlikely to turn up at the final mourning ceremony and consequently they are disqualified from inheriting from him. When a close kinsman of the deceased is away as a labour migrant, his mother or siblings protect his rights and often claim inheritance for him. He will always be given a beast from the deceased's herd if he is entitled to one but his other shares are bound to be smaller than they would be if he actually attended.

The successor is always the main heir but the estate is distributed as widely as possible among the men and women present at the final mourning ceremony. If the deceased was a man, the successor always inherits his gun (if he had one), spear, axe, fly-whisk, walking-stick and cap. These are the things closely connected with the deceased's personality, and their transfer to the successor symbolises the transfer of his social role to him; they are always the first part of the estate to be distributed. Cows are only rarely the object of inheritance in Guta. Only few people there own cattle, which are always looked after by their kinsmen living in areas which are free of tsetse. Cattle are, however, common in Cifokoboyo nowadays and if the deceased had any cows, one of them is inherited by the successor; it is *ing'ombe yo mweemvule*, the cow of the shadow. Other cows are divided among various kinsmen of the deceased and, if the herd was big, the successor is most likely to receive another animal besides the cow of the shadow. If there are not enough cattle for all, inheritors are instructed to pass on any progeny to others, usually to their younger siblings. Anyone who received a beast during the deceased's life is thought to have received a share already. If the herd was small, those who received cattle from the deceased during his lifetime may be invited to bring a beast from the progeny to share with those who would not otherwise inherit. This mainly concerns the children of the deceased, to whom he was most likely to have made gifts of money or cattle during his lifetime. If he did not inform his *basimukowa* about them, they may insist that such property be regarded as part of the estate. A man's children are never his primary heirs, though they should receive one cow from the deceased's herd, or part of his other goods if he had no cattle. If the deceased leaves a big herd, his and his father's *basimukowa* usually do not object to his children receiving more than one cow. Children also inherit from their father the right to continued assistance from the members of his *mukowa*. A wife never inherits from her husband, nor he from her; some grain from the husband's granary is, however, left to her if she has not enough grain in her own granaries to support her and her children until the next harvest. Otherwise the grain in the dead man's granary becomes part of the estate. If the widow stays in her late husband's village, she goes on using the fields which he cleared.

If a woman dies, her daughter usually becomes her successor and main heir. If she leaves cattle, the cow of the shadow will be inherited by her daughter and another beast might be given to her children; the rest is then divided between the members of her and her father's *mikowa*. Very often, however, she may leave only the contents of her granaries and a few plates, pots and baskets, which will mostly be left to her children.

Whoever receives an inheritance holds this property as his own. Those who have not received a share still have a right to assistance for bridewealth, fines and damages if their kinship link to the deceased entitles them to it. Such assistance is the responsibility of the successor, who for this very reason receives the biggest share; this is thus in a sense held in trust for the deceased's *basimukowa*, from among whom he is chosen.

The Toka are aware that no man can acquire riches alone and that every man's property is built up through the joint efforts of himself, his wife and his children. They are aware that to be married is the first condition of becoming wealthy and, as marriage depends on the transfer of bridewealth, they fully realise that to provide it means to set up a man on the path to possible wealth. If a father provides the bridewealth for his son or contributes considerably to it, his *basimukowa* very often feel that they are entitled to inherit a substantial portion of his son's wealth. On the other hand, if bridewealth is provided by the mother's brother, or if he contributes considerably to it while the man's own father does not, the man's own *basimukowa* may feel that only they are entitled to inherit his wealth and may be very reluctant to share it with the members of his father's *mukowa*. Both *mikowa* may thus have conflicting claims to shares in the estate and the division of inheritance may become subject to much bargaining, particularly if the deceased was a rich man and considerable wealth is at stake. In particular, cattle, cash and objects of considerable value like sewing machines, grinding machines, pieces of European furniture and ploughs, are quite often only allocated to individual inheritors after prolonged arguments between the members of both *mikowa*.

There is yet another reason for possible disagreements about the division of the estate: if a member of one of the *mikowa* is suspected of having killed the deceased by sorcery, the members of the other *mukowa* usually object to members of the suspected sorcerer's *mukowa* receiving conspicuous shares, for they feel that it was precisely this greed for the deceased's wealth which led to his death.

Succession to village headmanship: a process within the *mukowa* and the village

The selection of the successor of a village headman follows the same pattern as the selection of the successor of any other man, although some factors enter into the decision about the headman's successor which do not have to be taken into consideration when the deceased was not a headman. During the final mourning ceremony, the headman's successor is chosen by the deceased's *basimukowa*, both men and women. The head of the *mukowa* usually attends the final mourning ceremony for a deceased headman, and he and those *basimukowa* who are themselves headmen of other villages have the main say about the successor. A number of headmen from neighbouring villages who are not members of the deceased's *mukowa* also usually attend. When Cenga (E5) succeeded Janki Siyamutete (D9) as a headman of

Siyamutete Ling'amba in 1962 (Diagram 2), Kamenyani (H15) (Chief Nyawa and head of the Mucimba *mukowa*), headmen Matongo (H12) and Kataba (H5) (of the Mucimba *mukowa*), Janki Siyamutete's mother, Mukanamunyuku (C1), his elder sister, Munkombwe (D10), and a number of headmen from Cifokoboyo (of other *mikowa* than the Mucimba) were the most important of those deciding on the successor.

Succession to village headmanship again follows the matrilineal line but genealogical position alone is not a sufficient qualification. A headman has to have certain qualities to be able to keep people in the village together: he must not be quarrelsome, he must put the interests of the people in the village before his own personal interests, he must have proved through his past behaviour during the hearing of cases that he is not biased in favour of only some members of the village, and, above all, he has to command the natural respect of all the people in the village. When choosing a headman's successor, a distinct preference is given to those who have themselves been living in the village; the Toka feel strongly that a man who has been living in a different village will hardly make a good headman for the simple reason that he does not know the people in the village or their life histories and that they will distrust him as a stranger. This preference for appointing a local man quite often disqualifies a sister's son who has been living in his father's village, unless he has been a frequent visitor to his mother's village and is well known and generally respected by its inhabitants. When choosing a successor from among those who are genealogically qualified, the *basimukowa* and the headmen take into account the opinion of the people in the village. Succession to headmanship is an important matter; it will be widely discussed in the village after the headman's death, and very often during his lifetime. The feelings of the members of the village are thus generally known. If this is not the case, the people choosing the successor explicitly ask the most important members of the village for their opinion.

Succession to headmanship is, in every case, the outcome of the feelings of both the *basimukowa* of the deceased headman and the members of his village. These can sometimes be contradictory and the individual cases of succession reflect an interplay of *mukowa* and village pressures. When collecting the histories of the villages in Guta and Cifokoboyo, I recorded sixteen cases of succession to headmanship.[3] They spread over seven decades but the pattern of succession does not show any change over time as Table 1 indicates.

In thirteen cases out of the sixteen, the successor was of the same *mukowa* as the deceased headman (in ten cases he was a sister's son, in two cases a uterine brother and in one case a mother's sister's daughter's son); in the other three cases the headmanship passed to a different *mukowa*. In two out of the last three cases this happened through the son succeeding his father.

Table 1. *Succession to headmanship in Guta and Cifokoboyo*

Relationship of the successor to the deceased	1900s	1910s	1920s	1930s	1940s	1960s
Uterine	ZS	ZS	ZS	ZS	B	ZS
	ZS		ZS	MZDS		ZS
	ZS					ZS
						B
Agnatic	S			FBS	S	

This last kind of succession is a deviation from the proclaimed ideal of succession in a matrilineal line; it is, however, in line with another ideal, i.e. that an inhabitant of the village and not an outsider should succeed. These two ideals can very often be in conflict with one another. If they are, it is the result of a deeper structural conflict between the actual composition of the village and an ideal situation in which a village is inhabited by members of one *mukowa*. When preference is given to a member of the village, and headmanship passes from father to son, this is very often the result of an effort to reconcile the reality of village composition with the village headmanship, and is the main mechanism by which the numerically strongest *mukowa* in the village becomes the dominant one there.

Although Kataba (H5) himself is a member of Mukasilumbe's *mukowa* of the Mucimba clan, most of the inhabitants of his village, including his own wife, Muntemba (I5), are members of the Muntanga clan (Appendix 1 and Diagram 3). Even the Mudenda clan – the third one represented in Kataba's village – is numerically stronger than Kataba's own clan, the Mucimba. It is generally expected that Kataba's sister's son, Siyamonga (I4), will succeed him as headman but that he will be unable to keep in his village the members of the Muntanga and Mudenda clans. They will secede and establish their own villages or will join some already established villages inhabited by members of their respective clans and Siyamonga (I4) will be left with only a few households. If Kataba (H5) had sons, they would be members of the Muntanga clan, numerically the strongest in the village. If one of them succeeded to village headmanship, their clan would become the dominant one and Kataba's son would be in a much better position than Siyamonga (I4) to maintain the unity of the village. The chances are that he would be able to keep in the village not only the members of the Muntanga clan, but also the members of the Mucimba clan, of which he is a son. How far he would be able to keep in the village the members of the latter clan would depend on the political ambitions of Siyamonga (I4). Should

Siyamonga (I4) feel that, by right, he should himself have succeeded Kataba (H5), and should he decide to compensate for his deprivation of this right by founding his own village, Kataba's son would not be able to keep the members of the Mucimba clan in his village. Should Siyamonga (I4) lack such political ambitions, the chances would be that not only he would stay, but also Kangukila (I3), who is a Mucimba, although not of Mukasilumbe's *mukowa*. Together with him would stay his wife, Nasimoono (I2), who is a member of the Mudenda clan, and with her would stay her son, David Liyambai (J1), and possibly her brother, Anderson Limwanya (I1), and her mother's brother, Nason Muyoba (H2). Even if Kataba's son did not succeed in keeping all these people in his village, it would still remain much bigger than it would with Siyamonga (I4) as headman. This hypothetical case illustrates well the reasons which lead to sons occasionally succeeding their fathers as headmen, in defiance of the ideal of matrilineal succession.

Every headman aspires to headmanship of a big village inhabited by his own *basimukowa*, but very few achieve this ideal. Paradoxically, the same principles of village affiliation, particularly virilocal residence and the unity of the matricentric family, which in one generation help him to achieve this ideal, prevent its maintenance in the next. It is mainly through the local unity of his own matricentric family of orientation (consisting of his mother and his siblings) that a strong core of members of his own *mukowa* is formed in his village. But when his family of procreation (consisting of his wife and children) constitutes itself as a local unit around his wife in his village, a strong core of members of *mukowa* other than his own develops. As his sisters progressively marry out and their children reside with them in their father's villages, it is mainly his own sons (provided his marriage endures) and the sons of his brothers (provided again that their marriages endure) who inhabit the village. They are all members of *mikowa* other than his own. What started as a village inhabited mainly by his own *basimukowa*, develops gradually over time into a village inhabited by members of other *mikowa*. Some of them can easily become numerically stronger than his own and the strongest one will try to become the dominant one in the village. This will be achieved by one of its male members (typically his son, more rarely his brother's son) succeeding him as headman. The histories of some villages are of the successive development of new dominant *mikowa* within them through this process, the headmanship perpetually passing from one *mukowa* to another. The fission of these villages exhibits the repeated pattern of a *mukowa* once dominant in a village in which it has been outgrown by some other *mukowa* establishing itself as a dominant *mukowa* in a break-away settlement. The histories of Katwamazila and Nzwida villages in Cifokoboyo illustrate well this developmental cycle, in which the processes of fission and succession are closely and logically interconnected.

Katwamazila (Diagram 5), the oldest village in Cifokoboyo, started

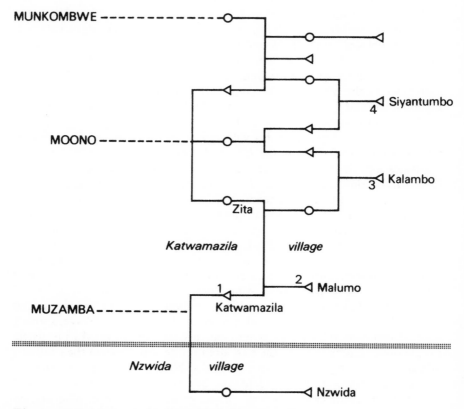

Diagram 5. Succession to headmanship in Katwamazila

probably some time in the early 1850s. Its founder, Katwamazila, was a member of the Muzamba clan and his wife, Zita, was of the Moono clan. At the time of Katwamazila's death, the latter clan was numerically the strongest in the village and it became the dominant one through Katwamazila's son, Malumo, succeeding to headmanship. Soon after this, Nzwida, Katwamazila's sister's son, left the village, together with other members of the Muzamba clan, and founded his own village, in which Katwamazila's clan was still the dominant one. Moono was still numerically the strongest clan in Katwamazila at the time of Malumo's death and the village headmanship remained within it: Malumo's sister's son, Kalambo, succeeded as headman. At the time of his death, Bwoono were outnumbered in the village by members of the Munkombwe clan, that of Zita's brother's wife. She was the founder of a big matricentric family and most of her children, together with their offspring, remained in Katwamazila. Kalambo was succeeded as headman by Siyantumbo, his father's sister's son and a member of the numerically stronger Munkombwe clan. He is the present headman of Katwamazila and he was able to keep together most of its members after Kalambo's death. This was mainly due to the fact that, although he was himself a member of the Munkombwe clan, he was a child of the Moono clan, the second biggest in Katwamazila (his father and Kalambo's father were sons of Zita's sisters).

When a son succeeds his father as a village headman, the ideal of matrilineal succession is usually preserved through the appointment of two successors instead of the usual one. One of the dead man's younger matrilineal kinsmen succeeds to his name and inherits the *muzimu* (spirit, shade) and together with it the kinship duties and responsibilities of the dead. His son succeeds to the name of the village (*izina yokuyobola munzi*),[4] which was born by the deceased.

Succession to village headmanship and the fission of a village, which usually follows the headman's death, are processes resulting from the interplay of *mukowa* and local ties. It is, however, only segments of existing *mikowa*, usually three and never more than four generations deep, which are involved in them. By one of its members succeeding to headmanship, the numerically strongest *mukowa* becomes the dominant one in the village and the association of the village with a particular *mukowa* effectively changes. The formerly dominant *mukowa* asserts its right to its own locality by seceding from the village and establishing itself in a different settlement. It is, however, not only *mikowa* of different clans which compete among themselves in this way for the control of villages. Through the same process of village fission a *mukowa* segment also expresses its unity against other segments of the same *mukowa*. At this level, the system exhibits a high degree of fluidity over time. Not only do individuals move perpetually from one village to another, but new hamlets and villages come into existence while other villages either diminish in importance or perish completely. The composition of existing villages changes all the time and often new *mikowa* emerge as dominant ones. The death of the village headman is always the crucial time at which these structural reshuffles take place.

Succession to chieftainship: a process within the *mukowa*

Within the gradual process of segmentation, a *mukowa* segment becomes recognised as an independent *mukowa* when it starts performing its own rain-making rituals. Another main activity whose participants are recruited from among the members of the whole *mukowa* and not merely a local segment, is the choosing of successors to headmen, *mukowa* heads and chiefs. The process of succession to chieftainship is similar to the succession to

Descent categories and local ties

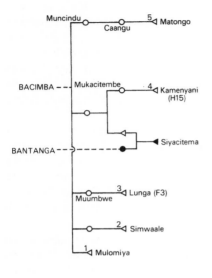

◁○ Bacimba
◀● Bantanga

4   Numbers indicate the order of succession

Diagram 6. History of the Nyawa chieftainship (Bacimba's version)

village headmanship in the sense that the chieftainship, too, is vested in a particular *mukowa*. Unlike village headmanship, which may pass from one *mukowa* to another to reflect the actual *mukowa* membership of the villagers, the chieftainship is for ever vested in the first chief's *mukowa*. Its right to the office is substantiated by the history of the chieftainship.

Thus the Nyawa chieftainship is vested in the Bacimba *mukowa*; this is substantiated by its history as perpetuated within this *mukowa* (Diagram 6):

Mulomiya of the Bacimba *mukowa* was 'owner of the land' (*mweni cisi*) a long time before the Europeans came. Other village headmen recognised his authority; the most important of them were Sikabalenga, Mufuzi, Muliyandelele, Kangumu and Sitemba. When Mulomiya died, his sister's son, Simwaale, who lived in his village, became his successor. Mulomiya had another sister's son, Siyankobe, who lived in a different village. When he heard that his mother's brother had died, he started drumming, thinking that he would be Mulomiya's successor. When the Lozi heard the drumming, they thought that there was a fight and they started fighting his people. Lunga [F3], another son of Mulomiya's sister, was taken by them as a prisoner to Barotseland. He was released and sent back to his area to be responsible for peace and for collecting tribute. He gave a girl called Cibuyu as a slave to the Lozi king, Lewanika, and headmen Sikabalenga and Mufuzi also sent him a female slave; headman Sitemba sent him a boy slave and headmen Muliyandelele and Kangumu sent elephant tusks as tribute. Lunga [F3], accompanied by these five headmen, took this tribute to

50

Lewanika and in return was recognised as a chief. When the Europeans came and asked headman Nankupaisiya who was the chief in the area, he named Lunga [F3]. Lunga was confirmed as the chief by the British administration. When he died in the 1930s, he was succeeded by Kamenyani [H15], the son of Lunga's mother's sister's daughter.

The successor of a chief is chosen during a final mourning ceremony as are the successors of all the deceased. The mourning ceremony for a chief is a big event attended by hundreds of people. Before it, the important men from among the chief's *basimukowa* usually meet to select the successor, whom they then propose to the neighbouring chiefs, headmen and the chiefs' councillors, who formally choose the successor at their meeting during the ceremony. In the morning the successor is installed in the same way as the successor to any other man. To be recognised as a chief, the proposed successor has to be approved by the higher political and administrative authorities. All the successive authorities, whether the Lozi overlords or British and Zambian administrations, have always retained this right and exercised their veto if not satisfied, for whatever reason, with the proposed successor.

When Kamenyani (H15) died in 1964, his younger classificatory brother (his MMZDS), Matongo (H12), was chosen as his successor by the Bacimba, the headmen and Kamenyani's councillors. But, as a staunch supporter of the African National Congress, the opposition party, Matongo (H12) was not acceptable to the administration governed by the ruling United National Independence Party, who thought, probably rightly, that Matongo (H12) would be reluctant to implement the decisions of the administration whose policies he publicly opposed. The administration proposed as chief, Lunga's (F3) grandson, Siyacitema, who was a member of the ruling UNIP party. He was 'approved' as a chief at a meeting of the people called by the administration. The administration's decision to have Siyacitema appointed as a chief is quite understandable in the light of the government's policy which considers chiefs, as the traditional authorities respected by their subjects, to be the most important agents in the programme of development in rural areas. Moreover, by replacing Matongo (H12) with Siyacitema, the administration only exercised its right to interfere in chiefs' appointments.

But at the time of my fieldwork, Siyacitema had still not been recognised as a legitimate chief by the Bacimba nor indeed by most people in the chiefdom. He is a member of the Muntanga *mukowa* and only a son of the Bacimba, and he is generally considered to be a usurper of the Bacimba's legitimate rights, who was not appointed by the people, as he should have been, but by the government. For most, not he, but Matongo (H12), is the chief.

Although fully backed by the administration, Siyacitema is aware that he

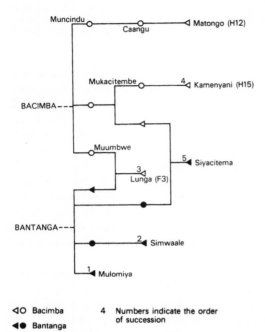

◁○ Bacimba   4   Numbers indicate the order
◀● Bantanga   of succession

Diagram 7. History of the Nyawa chieftainship (Bantanga's version)

can succeed as a chief only when accepted as such by his people, which would require the legitimacy of his chieftainship to be substantiated by history. According to Siyacitema and the Bantanga (Diagram 7), Mulomiya and his successor, Simwaale, were not members of the Bacimba *mukowa* as the Bacimba claim, but they were Bantanga. Lunga (F3), who was appointed by the Lozi as the first Chief Nyawa, was not Mulomiya's sister's son but the son of Mulomiya's brother, who was married to Muumbwe. Muumbwe was a member of the Bacimba *mukowa* and so was her son, Lunga (F3). When he was appointed as a chief by the Lozi, he usurped the Bantanga's right to the Nyawa chieftainship. By the appointment of Siyacitema, the illegitimate situation has been at last terminated and the chieftainship has returned into the Bantanga *mukowa* in which it was originally vested.

Conclusion

The two versions of the history of the Nyawa chieftainship substantiate the legitimacy of the claims of both contenders for the office in terms of matrilineal ideology, not in terms of different ideologies or images of social order. The ideology of matriliny forms an important part of the cultural notions of the people in Guta and Cifokoboyo and it is perpetually revalidated through being invoked in a multitude of concrete interactions which, in their turn, can then be seen as being informed by it.

In this chapter I have paid little attention to these concrete situations or to the actual events and transactions that occur in Guta and Cifokoboyo. I was not concerned with the analysis of the way in which particular concrete estates were actually divided among individual inheritors, nor with the way decisions were actually reached about successors of particular concrete individuals, nor by whom and why they were reached. I was primarily concerned with the notions the Toka themselves hold about their society and concentrated on describing the concepts, categories and norms which form some of these notions, so as to establish a baseline against which the changes that have occurred in Ngwezi can be measured and evaluated.

By concentrating on the description of the cultural notions which the Toka in Guta and Cifokoboyo entertain, I did not intend in any way to suggest that such a description accounts for the observed interactions. The latter are not compelled by the existing cultural notions. They are the result of the multiplicity of decisions of individual actors, into which their notions enter merely as one of the considered factors. In this respect, culture can be seen as a set of constraints within which decisions about the course of action are made and individual choices exercised (see Chapter 2 for a further elaboration of this point).

Cultural notions, however, do not impinge on the social processes merely by defining a set of constraints within which these processes occur. Another aspect of the relationship between the conceptual or cultural level of phenomena and transactional processes can usefully be considered: it is because of the shared cultural notions that the ongoing social transactions are meaningful for the actors themselves. The cultural knowledge of the people not only defines constraints they have to consider in their interactions, but at the same time it provides the framework within which the actors interpret the ongoing interactions and on the basis of which they assign meaning to them. It is because of this knowledge that the actor is able to ascertain and understand what others do and why they do it.

The normative rules which belong to the operational level of the actor's cognitive or cultural order are always situation-specific in the sense that they are invokable in clearly defined situations. The notions that things are what they are and that a society has a certain form, which belong to the representational level of the actor's cognitive or cultural order (to their model *of* social reality), do not necessarily have to be situation-specific. By referring to the enduring form of society they transcend specific interactional situations and have an existence above and beyond them. In the way in which they are formulated, they account for a multiplicity of situations and conceptually subsume them.

Empirically, it seems that normative rules remain unquestioned insofar as they do not disturb the representational level of the actors' cognitive or cultural order, i.e. as long as their enactment does not contradict the notions of what things, and relationships between things, are. The Toka in Guta and Cifokoboyo recognise a rule of uterine succession to the name of the deceased. This normative rule forms a part of their operational model (their model *for* social reality). Its invocation in appropriate situations does not require any specific legitimisation, for the behaviour that is in congruence with the normative rule is normal and expected. But it remains such only insofar as it does not disturb the Toka's representational model of their own society, their notions about the form of their society, about the categories of people and the relationships between them. Among other things, the Toka's representational model consists of their notion of the relationship between descent categories and local communities, their knowledge that certain *mikowa* and their segments are localised in certain villages of which the *basimukowa* are the owners, their knowledge that the village headmanship is vested in these *mikowa* and that they are dominant in the given villages not only because the headmanship is vested in them but also because the majority of the village inhabitants are their members. Unlike the normative rules, these notions are not concerned with what should or should not ideally be done or said under certain circumstances. They are concerned with what things or relationships between things actually are.

As I mentioned before, the behaviour which is in congruence with the normative rule is expected, understandable and meaningful to everybody, and as such does not need to be further legitimised. Behaviour that is not in accordance with the normative rule ordinarily seen by the actors as guiding it, is not quite normal, does not have to be expected by all concerned and can be incomprehensible and meaningless to at least some. Being such, it has to be explicitly legitimised; it has to be made meaningful and understandable in the given context by the explicit invocation of the shared representational model. When, in spite of the normative rule of uterine succession, a son and not a sister's son or any other member of the previous incumbent's *mukowa* succeeds to village headmanship, such a succession is explained and justified by invoking the representational model and by explicitly presenting it as an effort to entrust with headmanship the numerically strongest *mukowa* in the village, which, being the strongest, is *de facto* the dominant *mukowa* which owns the village. What is being considered by the actors in the given situation is which of the possible candidates for headmanship will be best qualified to keep the village together, or at least to retain most of its inhabitants. Values of wider applicability than the pragmatic, situation-specific normative rules (like the value attached to a big village), or principles of what might be called natural justice (like the idea that the accepted situation should suit the majority of the people concerned), are upheld in the actual situation.

When culture is seen not as simply compelling behaviour but rather as a set of constraints which the actors bring to bear on their transactions, it becomes useful to conceive of it, not only as a set of 'plans, recipes, rules, instructions (what computer engineers call "programs") ... for governing behaviour' as Geertz has done (Geertz 1975: 44; see also Geertz 1970: 57), but rather as the total stock of the actors' knowledge, which contains not only the plans, recipes, rules and instructions on which they base their decisions about their course of action in particular situations, but also their notions about the form of their society and their accompanying values. Culture is then best seen as consisting of two sets of notions of varying degrees of generality and specificity, which can be invoked by the actors for differing reasons and which, when invoked, are brought to bear on different actions. On the one hand, there are situation-specific normative rules, which form part of the actors' operational model (whose other elements are their goals, strategic plans, recipes, etc.); on the other hand, there are the situation-transcendent values and notions about the form of society, which can be invoked by the actors to legitimise their invocation of particular normative rules (in a situation where two or more norms are invoked as rules to be followed in action) and their pursuit of particular goals or their following of particular plans or recipes. In this sense, the culture of the Toka in Guta and Cifokoboyo is more than a complex of pragmatic rules about the mode of tracing descent, about the allocation of people to descent categories and about succession and inheritance. All these rules are formulated in an idiom or ideology of matriliny. People's values and notions about the relationship between descent categories and local and territorial groups are formulated in terms of the same idiom or ideology. What might, on the one hand, be seen as a deviation from this idiom or ideology at the level of pragmatic rules, or at the level of the operational model (e.g. the son's succession to village headmanship), is fully consistent with the same idiom or ideology at the level of the representational model. In this respect, the culture of the people in Guta and Cifokoboyo is homogeneous in the sense of employing one and the same idiom. As a result of the technological development that has taken place among the Toka in Ngwezi and which I describe in the next chapter, the culture of the latter area is less homogeneous and employs different, though mutually understandable, idioms. Its analysis is the subject of the following chapters.

2

Technological development and the restructuring of the relations of production

The agricultural economy which the Toka practise in the tsetse-infested area of Guta is still strongly oriented to subsistence production by each household. Agriculture depends on typical slash-and-burn techniques. Clearing a portion of woodland for the fields with an axe is done by men, although women and children might assist, particularly with the piling of the cut vegetation on the site and its subsequent burning. The digging of the field with a hoe and its sowing immediately after the onset of the rains is the work of women. Subsequent weeding is mainly carried out by women and children, though men often help. Harvesting is exclusively women's work.

A household consisting of an elementary or polygynous family is a viable unit of production. Under normal circumstances it disposes of enough labour to carry out all the agricultural work, and does not cooperate regularly with other households in the village. It seeks their help only if the successful performance of the work in the fields is threatened due to a temporary lack of labour, typically caused by illness, the woman's pregnancy or the man's temporary absence from the village as a labour migrant. The help of other households, which might then be needed in clearing the new field or possibly in weeding, can easily be mobilised through an offer of beer.

In other Toka areas which are free of tsetse fly, the use of the plough has radically altered the traditional relations of production. One such area is Ngwezi, where ox-drawn ploughs have been in use for the last fifty years or so. All my informants agreed on having seen the first plough some time during the second decade of this century. Ploughs used at that time were wooden ones with a steel share and they were pulled by six oxen specially trained for the job. During the 1920s, enterprising men who had oxen started to use them for ploughing and at the end of the decade there were men in every village who ploughed their fields regularly and who were prepared to plough the fields of their neighbours for cash. But it was only during the 1930s that the plough ceased to be a fanciful novelty and became a generally used agricultural implement; in this decade, the sowing of seed into the furrow behind the plough replaced completely the sowing under the hoe. Only the gardens and beds inside the villages are nowadays cultivated by hoes, being too small for ploughing. In the 1930s, the all-steel ploughs of the type used nowadays became available and gradually replaced the wooden ones. As they were lighter than the wooden ploughs, only four oxen were needed to pull them; this was considered to be the great advantage of the modern steel plough as six oxen were often very difficult to control. To train oxen for ploughing is a difficult, tiresome and lengthy job. It starts when they are about three years old and takes three seasons; they are at first yoked to a sledge and later to the plough itself. The training with both sledge and plough is made easier when they are yoked behind a pair of experienced oxen. But very often men who train oxen in ploughing have no experienced oxen, and the young oxen have to be trained by being yoked on their own. The Toka consider the handling of untrained oxen not only a frustrating undertaking but a dangerous one as well, and men who are prepared to train oxen for their owner are always welcomed.

A man who does not have his own oxen can acquire them by undertaking to train them for their owner. He does not receive anything for doing so but has the use of the oxen for three years for ploughing his own fields. Should the owner of an ox claim him back before the end of the three-year period, he is supposed to pay the trainer K10 for every year for which the latter is deprived of its use.[1] Nothing is paid in such a case if the two parties are close kinsmen; among them, lending oxen for training is not merely a matter of contract through which both parties maximise their gains, but a matter of assistance to those in need. If the circumstances of the man who has rendered this assistance change, so that he is no longer able to maintain it without suffering a loss, it is simply withdrawn with apologies which the other man is obliged to accept.

Although milk is an important part of the diet and its nutritive value, particularly for small children, is clearly appreciated, the role of cattle as capital and in farming clearly surpasses their contribution to the diet. In an environment in which agricultural wealth can hardly be stored without damage or loss for more than a year or two, cattle naturally become the preferred form of capital for they can be converted into cash in time of need. They are also valued for their role in farming, with oxen used as plough animals and cows as potential bearers of oxen. The role of cattle as a durable form of capital is, however, not easily compatible with their role in farming. No ritual value is attached to cattle and they are frequently sold for the cash needed for bridewealth and elopement payments, damages, and the purchase of household goods, implements, clothes, furniture, and even food. Although wage labour cash is apt to supply the major portion of bridewealth and elopement payments, and although the sale of maize provides at least some people with the cash they need throughout the year, the sale of cattle is often the only way out for those who suddenly and unexpectedly find themselves in financial difficulty. The Toka try to avoid having their herds depleted in this way and are always reluctant to sell cows unless they are apparently barren. It is thus typically the oxen who frequently end up as market animals. Most of them are sold to butcheries in Livingstone and only very few to other villagers. A newly weaned calf costs about K18. This is a sum of money which can easily be raised through the sale of grain, fowl or even beer, or which can possibly be borrowed. The Toka are, therefore, not usually pressurised into the sale of calves. An adult ox, on the other hand, averages about K140. This is a sum of money which even those whose regular cash income is through the sale of grain can hardly expect to raise in this way alone.[2] If men are faced with substantial unexpected expenditure, usually in the form of damages, bridewealth or elopement payments, or if some of their kinsmen whom they are obliged to help are faced with such an expenditure, the sale of an adult ox is very often the only way of obtaining the required cash. As a result of this perpetual drain on plough animals, they are a scarce resource. In Siyabalengu, a village of seventeen households, there were about a dozen ploughs, thirty-seven cows, two bulls, and fourteen oxen at the time of my census. The calves are not included in these numbers. Only nine oxen of the fourteen were fully trained for ploughing. All the oxen in the village were owned by five household heads. In the 1969–70 agricultural season, there were twenty-seven households in the two hamlets of Mujalanyana village and the fields of twenty-six of them were ploughed. Eight ploughs were in use during the season. There were altogether eighteen oxen in the village, belonging to seven household heads, and seventeen of them were engaged in ploughing. Twelve were trained oxen and five were in training. One young ox being trained for ploughing was borrowed from a man in a neighbouring village. In the following season, there were twenty-nine households in the two hamlets of Mujalanyana village and the fields belonging to twenty-eight of them were ploughed. Seven ploughs were in use and there were seventeen oxen in the village belonging to nine household heads. Fifteen of them were engaged in ploughing. Ten were fully trained and five were in training; again, one trainee ox was borrowed from a man in the neighbouring village. A similar situation obtains in all Toka villages where ploughs are used, and the average number of plough animals (both experienced and in training) per household, which ranges from 0.82 in Siyabalengu to 0.70 and 0.62 in Mujalanyana,[3] is fairly typical.

Not only are oxen a scarce resource, but so, too, is the labour. The ploughing and sowing behind the plough has to be performed cooperatively as it consists of four different tasks: leading the oxen, driving them, ploughing and sowing. If the oxen are experienced, some of these tasks may either be left out or possibly performed by one person only. Although ploughing is typically a man's job, it can be done by women if there is no male labour available in the household. The sowing is always done by women. Both men and women can lead and drive oxen and these two jobs are the only ones which can be done by boys and girls. If the oxen have been properly trained, the task of driving them can be left out altogether and two people only are needed; one leads the oxen and sows at the same time; the other ploughs. Such an arrangement is, however, very rare and usually a team of at least three people is necessary to handle a plough pulled by a pair of oxen; one person leads or drives the oxen, the second one ploughs and the third one sows. If the oxen are not yet properly trained four people are often necessary, one to lead the oxen, the other to drive them, the third one to plough and the fourth one to sow. As ploughing is a very tiring job, particularly when the oxen are not well trained, two ploughmen are preferred so that one can relieve the other every now and then. Very often a regular team may thus consist of at least four adults and a boy. This is more labour than an average household can provide.

Among the Toka, a household is established as a place of residence for each newly married couple. It enters into the second phase of its development when the children are born and it is composed of the members of one elementary family. When all the children marry and establish their own independent households, the original household enters the third and final phase of its development, when, as in its initial phase, it is again composed of only the man and his wife. The number of people in the household in each of its three developmental phases can be reduced through divorce, death, or labour migration; on the other hand, it increases when extra familial kin become attached to it. This is not too frequent an occurrence, however, apart from cases in which grandchildren occasionally live, for various reasons, as attached members of their grandparents' household. In consequence, Toka households are relatively small. The actual number of members varies from one to eleven with the mean number being 4.1. Considering that some members of a great many households are either too old or too young to participate in production, it is typically only the household approaching the end of its second phase of development which can provide enough labour for a ploughing team, and only occasionally one at a different stage of its development. In my sample of 182 households, in various phases of development, only 63 (34.6%) had enough labour for ploughing.

Shortage of labour in most households leads to the necessity of their cooperating with others in ploughing. The fact that most households lack oxen, including many of those who have sufficient labour, has the same effect. The ownership of a plough is usually not a limiting factor; they cost less than oxen and any man with oxen is certain to possess a plough. But if the plough gets broken and the owner fails to get spare parts in time, he is also forced to enter into cooperative arrangements with others.

Out of the seventeen households in Siyabalengu only three had both labour and oxen available for ploughing their fields. One household had oxen but

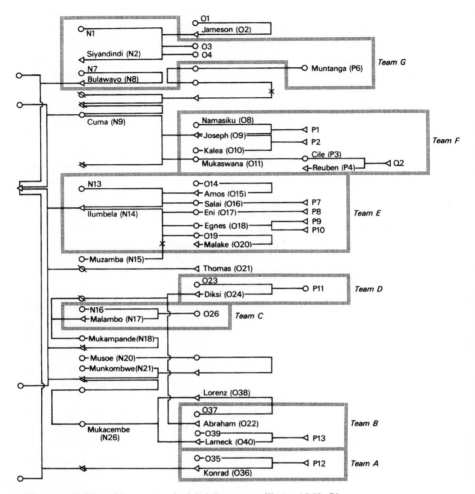

Diagram 8. Ploughing teams in Mujalanyana village, 1969–70

not sufficient labour, many households had sufficient labour but not oxen, and several lacked both resources. In 1969–70, out of twenty-seven households in Mujalanyana, only two had both oxen and labour available for ploughing their fields. In the next season, none of the twenty-nine households in this village could have ploughed its fields using only its own resources; all had to cooperate with others in ploughing or to rely on their help.

Seven ploughing teams were formed in Mujalanyana in the 1969–70 agricultural season (Diagram 8). Only three of these were each composed of one household. Of the two households which had both oxen and labour, one was that of Konrad (O36), who had two trained oxen, and another one was that of Malambo (N17), who likewise had two well-trained oxen. The third was that of Diksi (O24), who had no oxen of his own but was training two, one belonging to Joseph (O9), and another one to a man from a neighbouring village.

The remaining four teams were each composed of members of more than one household. Team B ploughed with oxen belonging to Lameck (O40) and his brother, Lorenz (O38), who each had one trained ox and one young ox in training. Team E had four oxen at its disposal: two of them were Ilumbela's (N14) adult oxen, which were experienced in ploughing, the remaining two were in their first season of training. One belonged to Ilumbela (N14), the other to his sister, who is married in a different village. Team F ploughed with two oxen belonging to Joseph (O9). The last team (G) used two oxen belonging to Bulawayo (N8).

Both the human and cattle population of the village changed to some extent in 1970 (Diagrams 8 and 9). Ilumbela's son, Amos (O15), and his wife (O14) left the village to work in town. Muntanga (P6) remarried and went to her husband's village. Davidson (O7), the son of Bulawayo's wife (N7) from her previous marriage, and his wife (O6) returned to Mujalanyana from the town where he had been working. Also Siyalwindi (N4), Bulawayo's brother, and his wife (N3) returned to the village after Siyalwindi's abortive attempt to establish his own hamlet. Two more households came into existence in the village: one was that of Siyakuwa (O29) and his wife (O28), who moved to Mujalanyana from a nearby village, and the other was that of Malita (Q1), who had been divorced and came to take up residence with her mother.

Konrad's (O36) children burnt down one house in the village when playing, and to be able to pay damages, Konrad had to sell one of his two oxen. Ilumbela's sister removed her cattle, including one young ox, from Ilumbela's (N14) care and took them to her husband's village. At the beginning of the agricultural season, Ilumbela was left with a pair of experienced oxen and one young ox which had been trained for only one year. One of Malambo's (N17) oxen injured itself and Malambo hoped that it would recover in time to be able to plough; consequently he did not make any alternative arrangements. The ox, however, did not recover and, when the agricultural season started, Malambo was desperately looking for an ox he might borrow. There were two spare young oxen in Mujalanyana, one belonging to Ilumbela (N14) and one to Bulawayo (N8). Ilumbela's ox had had only a year of training and Bulawayo's had not yet been trained at all. Malambo (N17), being an old man, did not fancy the idea of ploughing with one experienced and one untrained ox, which is always very strenuous. He did not succeed in finding an experienced ox which he could borrow and he was not able to plough his fields himself. One of Joseph's (O9) oxen died during the year

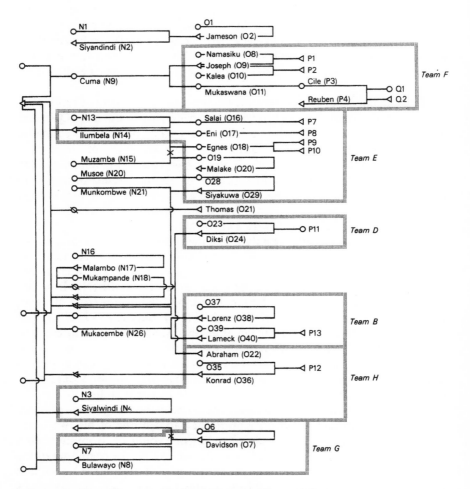

Diagram 9. Ploughing teams in Mujalanyana village, 1970–1

and he took back a young ox which he had given to Diksi (O24) to train; the ox had already been ploughing for two seasons and Joseph yoked it together with his remaining ox.

There were six ploughing teams in Mujalanyana in 1970–1 (Diagram 9); only Diksi's (O24) team (D) consisted of members of one household only. One of the oxen Diksi used was the same young ox, borrowed from a man in a neighbouring village, which he had used the previous season; the other was a young ox, belonging to his mother's sister, Mukampande (N18), which was in its first season of ploughing.

All the remaining teams were each composed of more than one household. Teams B, F and G used the same oxen as the previous season. Team H had two trained oxen at its disposal, one belonging to Konrad (O36) and one to Siyalwindi (N4). The plough animals of Team E were Ilumbela's (N14) adult oxen, and his ox which had started ploughing for the first time in the previous season was occasionally yoked alongside one of them.

Most teams change in this way from one year to the next. They do not have to be composed only of members of the same village; sometimes members of two adjoining villages form a joint team. In 1968–9, before she ploughed with Bulawayo (N8) and Siyandindi (N2), Muntanga (P6) helped to plough the fields belonging to Reuben's (P4) brother, who lives in a neighbouring village and who would then take his oxen and plough her fields in Mujalanyana. In 1971, Bulawayo (N8) died; his oxen were inherited by his son, who works as a policeman in Kalomo. In 1971–2, Davidson (O7) ploughed with them with his wife (O6), his mother (N7), and a couple from a neighbouring village as members of his team. Together they ploughed the fields belonging to all three households.

When explaining to me the composition of ploughing teams in general terms, the Toka pointed out that a man who does not have oxen helps to plough the fields of a man who does and the latter then ploughs with his oxen the fields of the former. But even a cursory look at who ploughs with whom and who does not plough at all clearly shows that there is more to it than that. In 1969–70, Konrad (O36) and Malambo (N17) had their own oxen and Diksi (O24) had oxen at his disposal, and although there were many people in the village who did not have oxen, nobody ploughed with Konrad (O36), or Malambo (N17) or Diksi (O24). If the rules for forming ploughing teams were as simple and straightforward as the Toka state them in general terms, a more even distribution of people around ploughs and oxen than is actually the case would result. A significant feature of the actual distribution is that it is highly uneven and ploughing teams range from three members of one household (A, C and D) to as many as thirteen people from six different households around one plough (E). The rule which governs the formation of the team consisting of members of different households is that one household provides the oxen while another or others provide the labour. Following this rule, households which dispose of different types of resources combine to form joint ploughing teams. The Toka readily explained to me the composition of particular teams in terms of this rule. I was told, for example, that Team G (1969–70) was composed of members of Bulawayo's (N8), Siyandindi's (N2) and Muntanga's (P6) households because Bulawayo (N8) had oxen but lacked labour. He himself was an old man for whom ploughing was already a strenuous job and the only other member of his household was his wife (N7). These two old people alone could not form a team, so Bulawayo (N8) ploughed with Muntanga (P6) and with Siyandindi

(N2) and his wife (N1). These three people provided the labour which Bulawayo (N8) needed for ploughing his fields; in return he used his oxen to plough their fields and Muntanga (P6) and Siyandindi (N2), through investing their labour, gained access to the resources they themselves lacked.

People who lack both labour and oxen are excluded from joining the ploughing teams as they have nothing to invest. Typically, they are widows or old divorced women living alone or, more rarely, widowers or old divorced men. Not all of them are incapable of doing any work, but due to their age they can generally perform only lighter tasks, like sowing the seeds or leading the oxen. These are the tasks for which it is easiest to find labour; it is the ploughing and, to a lesser extent, the driving of the oxen for which labour is difficult to find. These are the tasks whose performance is generally beyond the ability of those who stand outside the ploughing teams. This does not mean that their fields will remain unploughed and that they will have of necessity to resort to hoeing. For these people, however, the kinship ties are instrumental for having their fields ploughed and sown. They will have it done as a result of recognition by others of the rights inherent in their kinship status. For this reason, it is much more important for them than for anybody else to live among the kinsmen whose assistance they can demand as a right. If the kinship relationship is close enough to guarantee such a right, the right will be recognised. It is certainly always recognised within the relationship of familial kinship. Thus Cuma (N9) relies on having her field ploughed by her son, Joseph (O9), Mukacembe (N26) by her sons, Lameck (O40) and Lorenz (O38), and Muzamba (N15) by her daughter, Eni (O17), and her son-in-law, Malake (O20). The children do not relinquish the responsibility if for some reason they themselves are not able to fulfil their obligation. Thus, when Joseph (O9) did not manage to plough Cuma's field he asked Konrad (O36) to do so; similarly, Konrad (O36) ploughed the fields of Mukacembe (N26) when Lameck (O40) was unable to do so.

Those who are not members of ploughing teams and who do not have any close kinsmen in the village on whose assistance they can rely, have to pay for having their fields ploughed. Thus Munkombwe (N21) hired Konrad (O36), and Musoe (N20) hired Amos (O15) to plough their fields in this way. Later, when Siyakuwa (O29) moved into the village, he ploughed Musoe's field for free.

It is not only old men and women lacking both labour and oxen who do not get recruited into ploughing teams, but also, sometimes, younger married men who could perform well as ploughmen, but who have no kinship ties in the village which they could successfully manipulate to this effect. Having families, their fields are always bigger than those of bachelors and in comparison with the latter their labour contribution is considerably outweighed by the demands they make on the resources of other team members. Unless they can manipulate kinship ties, they rank below bachelors as potential recruits. In Mujalanyana, Jameson (O2) is in this position. His fields were ploughed for money by Amos (O15) and, in the following season, by Davidson (O7).

The fields of those who are not members of ploughing teams get ploughed only after the ploughing of the fields of team members has been completed, very often towards the end of the ploughing season. This does not adversely affect the old men and women living alone; virtually all the cash they need they can raise by brewing beer and they need to grow only a little more grain than they need for their subsistence. In consequence, their fields are quite small. Even if they have to start weeding much later than those whose fields have been ploughed and sown earlier, they have comparatively little weeding to do and can finish it in time to reap a reasonably good harvest. The late sowing is, however, a serious handicap for younger men with families. They need to cultivate much more land for subsistence than do widows and widowers and, unlike the latter, they usually need to sell at least some grain to obtain cash for buying goods which they themselves cannot produce. In their case, the late sowing adversely affects them and for this reason they prefer to borrow oxen for training, as Diksi (O24) does. If they do not manage either to join someone in ploughing or to borrow oxen for training, they usually leave the village. After having his field ploughed for money for two consecutive seasons, Jameson (O2) and his family left the village to seek employment on the Copperbelt with the hope of earning enough money to be able to buy his own oxen.

Another rule which governs the formation of teams from the members of different households, states that close kinsmen should plough together; cooperation in ploughing is one form of the expression of mutual obligation among kinsmen. The composition of certain teams was explained to me by invoking this rule. Thus it was pointed out that Team E (1969–70) consisted of Ilumbela's children (O15, O16, O17, O18, O19) and their spouses (O14, O20). Joseph (O9) ploughed with his sister (O11), his sister's daughter (P3) and his sister's daughter's daughter (Q1). Lameck (O40) and Lorenz (O38) ploughed together because they were brothers.

Since both the rules in whose terms the Toka explain the composition of particular ploughing teams are always offered as *post facto* statements, they are treated by them, and could be treated by the anthropologist as well, as non-manipulable and hence explanatory; a normative model would result. However, a close examination of cases shows that both sets of rules can be manipulated. The rule stating that households which dispose of different types of resources combine to form ploughing teams was, for example, obviously disregarded when Malake (O20), who has no oxen, joined the team using Ilumbela's oxen (Team E), in spite of the fact that Ilumbela (N14) did not depend in any way on Malake's labour. Although the Toka explained to me the composition of this particular team by invoking the rule prescribing the cooperation of close kinsmen in ploughing, this rule was disregarded in other cases: Abraham (O22), who has no oxen, did not plough with his brother Diksi (O24), who had oxen at his disposal; when Malambo's ox was injured, Malambo (N17) did not plough with Diksi (O24), his sister's son and his nearest kinsman in the village.

From the inspection of these cases, it is obvious that the composition of ploughing teams cannot be explained simply as being structured according to ideal jural or moral rules. The Toka's ideal normative model and empirical facts are quite distinct. When that is the case (as it generally seems to be on closer inspection), Leach suggests that 'social structures are sometimes best regarded as the statistical outcome of multiple individual choices rather than a reflection of jural rules' (1960: 124). Social structure so conceived is:

a social fact in the same sense as a suicide is a social fact. It is a by-product of the sum of many individual human actions, of which the participants are neither wholly conscious nor wholly unaware. It is normal, rather than normative; yet, since it clearly possesses some degree of stability, we are still faced with Durkheim's problem – what relates a suicide rate with the motivations of an individual suicide? (Leach 1961: 300).

The statistical model of social structure, which Leach advocates, has no explanatory value (Keesing 1967); it is at best an attempt at an accurate and exact description of actual, as opposed to normative, social relations and alignments. As the last sentence in the above quotation suggests, the explanation can only be achieved by elucidating what generates the statistical distribution, i.e. by explaining the pattern of individual choices of which the statistical distribution is the outcome, or, as Goodenough pointed out, by explaining the rules or principles whereby actual decisions are made (Goodenough 1961: 1343). The jural and moral rules which are invoked in some particular instances and disregarded in others are only a part of the total stock of rules, principles or factors taken into account in any decision. The degree to which an individual will let himself be constrained by them in his decision depends on what constraining value he attributes to other rules, principles or factors which he has to take into account. It is the goal he pursues which is, as it were, the basic yardstick by which the relative significance of the directly and remotely relevant rules, principles and factors is evaluated. Each decision would be a simple and clear-cut process if each goal stood in isolation and if its attainment had no repercussions on other goals which the individual tries to achieve. Empirically, the opposite is true and various goals, e.g. economic and social ones, are not only interdependent but quite often mutually conflicting. Consideration of the way in which other goals will be achieved, modified or nullified in the course of the attainment of any given goal is thus yet another factor which enters into the decision on a course of action. The construction of a satisfactory decision model requires not only the enumeration of all these factors but also the specification of the ways in which they interplay. Such a model is much more complex than the structural model which is simply constructed through the enumeration of jural rules.

Because of its inevitable complexity, I can outline only the most important elements of the decision process generating the formation of the observed ploughing teams. This process takes place within the existing framework of constraints, which are both natural and cultural and which can be analytically distinguished as existing on three different planes. The first one is the ecological plane where natural conditions determine when the sowing can be started and when it has to be completed so that the crops will mature and so that the subsequent weeding, which is instrumental for their maturation, can be successfully carried out. This plane cannot be manipulated and in this sense its determining force is absolute.

The other two planes can be, and are, manipulated. One is the plane of existing resources, i.e. labour and plough animals. Depending on the degree of scarcity of available resources, the force of ecological determinism can be, to a certain extent, alleviated. If enough labour is available, some of it can be employed in weeding while ploughing is still in progress; the ploughing season can thus be effectively extended. The use of enough oxen to pull more than one plough has the same effect in that more fields can be ploughed in the same time and the labour so saved employed elsewhere. In 1968–9, Ilumbela (N14) had four adult oxen and his team used two ploughs, one operated by Amos (O15) and another one by Eni (O17), with Malake (O20) relieving them. They succeeded in ploughing their fields in much less time than usual and Amos (O15) did a lot of ploughing for money for others.

The third constraining plane is the plane of social relations, of which the most important are close kinship relations, close neighbourly relations, the relations of friendship and those established through previous cooperation.

The Toka have to pursue their goals within this framework of constraints. The direct goals, in pursuance of which the ploughing teams crystallise, are both long-term and short-term ones. The long-term goal is to produce enough wealth to secure one a comfortable life in a dry brick house with a zinc roof furnished with pieces of European furniture. Apart from securing a comfortable life, which is valued in itself, there is yet another incentive for producing wealth: through its display a man makes or builds his name (*usumpula zina* or *upanga zina*) or becomes known (*uzibinkana*). He gains the reputation of a *muvubi* or a *mupukusi* (a big or rich man). One man I knew planned to buy a grinding-machine, his chief motivation being to become a *muvubi* or a *mupukusi* in this way and to be remembered for it in posterity. There are many ways in which one can become a *muvubi*. One can have a grinding-machine, one can have a dry brick house with a zinc roof, one can have plenty of cattle, which one farms out to the less fortunate, or one can have a store and possibly a truck. But for whichever course one opts, the precondition is to have money. This can be earned through hawking, or the educated minority can earn it as teachers or government employees. But for the majority of the villagers, the quickest way of making money is through the sale of cattle. When opting for this strategy, one of course needs money in the first place to build up a sizeable herd, and for the majority of men the first step on the way to becoming a *muvubi* is to sell corn and to earn additional money by ploughing for others.

Not everybody has an equal chance of becoming a *muvubi*. A bachelor without education and with no oxen has no chance at all. At the other end of the scale is a man who not only has oxen, but who also has children in their teens who are capable of taking an active part in production. His household is big enough to form its own ploughing team and it maximises its gains by ploughing alone; it would only lose by cooperating with another household or households. The team composed of the members of one household has only the fields of that household to plough. All things being equal, it completes that ploughing in half the time which a team composed of members of two households needs for ploughing their fields. Where there is no shortage of land, a household which can manage its own team is able to cultivate more land than a household which needs to cooperate with others and it is able to produce more corn for the market. All the men who are regularly selling maize in substantial quantities to the Agricultural Marketing Board, are men who have been ploughing alone. In Mujalanyana, Konrad (O36) and Malambo (N17) are the only men who sell corn more or less regularly.

After ploughing its own fields, a household with labour and oxen can employ its resources to plough for money for the rest of the ploughing season. Thus in 1969–70, Konrad (O36) ploughed for money for Munkombwe (N21) and some people in neighbouring villages; in the following season when Malambo (N17) was not able to plough, Konrad (O36) ploughed all his fields for money. Malambo (N17) himself also ploughs for money although he did not do so in 1969–70. A household which hires somebody to plough its fields provides its own labour for sowing and for driving the oxen. The wife of a man who ploughs is free to weed her own fields while her husband is still ploughing for others.

A man who disposes of both labour and oxen has a considerable economic advantage over anybody who lacks one of these resources and an even greater advantage over somebody who lacks both. Only such a man has a chance of becoming a *muvubi*. But he pursues this goal within the framework of existing social relations and the attainment of his various social goals has a bearing on the way in which he pursues this long-term goal. From the purely economic point of view his most effective strategy would be to plough as much land as can be successfully weeded by the labour available in his household, and to plough for cash in his spare time. To be able to do so, he would have to disregard his obligations towards the people who, due to their close kinship relationships with him, have a right to demand his assistance. But this is not feasible and such a strategy might even frustrate the attainment of his long-term goal. The kinsmen who have a right to demand his assistance are those among whom he lives and on whose assistance he himself relies in numerous ways. They are the people on whom he might, himself, be fully dependent should his oxen die or should he lose them in some other way, or should he lose the labour which is instrumental to the production of his wealth. The support of his kinsmen is his ultimate insurance and any strategy he pursues would not be reasonable if it did not take this into consideration. Thus Konrad (O36) ploughed free for Cuma (N9), the mother of Joseph (O9), when the latter was not able to do it. Malambo (N17) ploughs free the fields of his sister, Mukampande (N18), and when he did not plough himself in 1970–1, his sister's son, Diksi (O24), ploughed her fields free. Similarly, when Lameck (O40) was not able to plough the fields of his mother, Mukacembe (N26), Konrad (O36) again did it free. These cases indicate two things. Firstly, it is not only close kinship ties, but often distant kinship or affinal relationships which are strategically exploited. Cuma (N9) is Konrad's father's paternal half-sister and by ploughing for her Konrad (O36) put his own cousin, Joseph (O9), under an obligation to provide support should Konrad decide to solicit it in the future. Mukacembe (N26) is Konrad's distant affine. Secondly, it is not only the distance of kinship or affinity as such which is taken into consideration in deciding whether a field be ploughed free or for money, but the assessment of the strategic importance of each particular kinship link and the spatial proximity or distance of the relative in question, as well as the character, nature and intensity of previous interaction between them. Although the Toka are able to enumerate the rules of behaviour appropriate between any two kinship types, these rules are nothing more than ideals which might, but need not, be invoked in particular interactions. One year when Joseph (O9) did not manage to plough the fields of his first wife (O10), Amos ploughed them for her for money unlike Konrad (O36), who ploughed the fields of Joseph's mother, Cuma (N9), free. Here, a reference to the mutual rights and obligations between two kinship types fails to account for the differences in Konrad's and Amos's behaviour. Joseph (O9) is a patrilateral cross-cousin of both Konrad (O36) and Amos (O15). However, for Konrad (O36), whose closest kinsmen in Mujalanyana are his father's half-siblings, this is a close kinship link. Amos (O15), whose closest kinsmen in the village are his parents and siblings, treated the same link as a link of distant kinship for he does not need Joseph's support, and might not need it in the future, to the same extent as Konrad.

Living together inevitably intensifies interaction, and frequent interaction leads to the creation of multiplex ties of mutual obligation which will be recognised or can be invoked in any future interaction. The relationship between two relatives in close spatial proximity and frequently interacting with one another will therefore tend to be much more intimate than the ideal rules of behaviour between the two kin types would suggest. Simply, close spatial proximity and the resulting frequency of interaction narrows the kinship distance. Konrad (O36), Lameck (O40), Lorenz (O38) and Lameck's and Lorenz's mother, Mukacembe (N26), live in their own hamlet, set apart from all the other people considered here, who live in the main hamlet of the village. Mukacembe (N26) is as much a 'grandmother' to Konrad's children as she is a grandmother of Lameck's and Lorenz's children. When Lameck (O40) was not able to plough Mukacembe's field and Lorenz (O38) was away, Konrad (O36) did it free as he would have done were he Lameck's and Lorenz's brother. We might see this as a part of his strategy of establishing and maintaining close ties in a village in which he has no close kinsmen of his own. This strategy impinged here on his main economic strategy. Munkombwe (N21) is in fact a closer affine to Konrad (O36) than is Mukacembe (N26). When he ploughed her field for money, Konrad was following his main economic strategy; unlike in Mukacembe's case, there was nothing to be gained in terms of social relations by refusing the monetary reward to which he was normatively entitled.

A man who has children old enough to participate actively in ploughing by at least leading or driving the oxen, but who has no oxen himself, can, by borrowing some for training, follow a strategy similar to those who possess both resources. Diksi (O24) does this. Compared with those who have their own oxen and who have enough labour available in their household, he is in a disadvantageous position in that he ploughs all the time with untrained oxen. To be able to do so, he has to be very skilful in their handling. He never had difficulty in borrowing oxen for training for he had the reputation of being very good at it and nobody was afraid to entrust animals to his care. Siyandindi (N2) was in a different position. When Davidson (O7) returned to the village and Siyandindi (N2) lost Bulawayo (N8) as his ploughing partner, he tried to borrow oxen for training and to plough with them on his own. But he could not find any as he had the reputation of being rather bad at handling animals and nobody seemed to be prepared to entrust oxen into his care as long as there were better-skilled men around who wanted to borrow them for training. Even if a man has an exceptional skill at handling plough animals, he cannot expect to plough as much land with untrained oxen as he might with experienced ones. To plough with untrained oxen is always much more strenuous and slower. Diksi (O24) has always been able to plough enough land to produce some corn for the market but he has never finished ploughing his fields soon enough to be able to plough for money. Even so, to plough on his own was the best strategy for a man of his skill and resources.

In spite of being brothers, Diksi (O24) and Abraham (O22) did not plough together as they should have according to the ideally stated norm. Both would have lost had they done so. If Abraham had joined his brother, Diksi would have gained additional labour which he did not need. In return he would have had to have ploughed Abraham's fields, thus decreasing the amount of land which he was able to plough for himself when ploughing alone. By joining Diksi, Abraham would have had his fields ploughed at the cost of working the whole season with untrained and stubborn oxen. By joining another team he had his fields ploughed in a much less strenuous way, with experienced oxen. In following their respective strategies, it suited both Diksi and Abraham to disregard the rule that, as brothers, they should plough together.

I mentioned before that the direct goals, in the process of whose attainment the ploughing teams crystallise, are both long-term and short-term ones. Abraham's (O22) strategy is directed towards the achievement of the short-term goal of having his fields sown every year. Although only a few men aim systematically at the long-term goal of ever-increasing wealth, everybody pursues this short-term goal, as everybody's nourishment depends on its attainment. Those who lack one of the necessary resources pursue this strategy by forming a ploughing team with somebody who lacks the other. But only if a simultaneous attainment of other goals has no bearing on the fulfilment of the economic goal of having the field ploughed and sown, and only if no social obligations, of whatever kind, have to be taken into consideration in recruiting the team members, is the distribution of resources the decisive factor in deciding with whom to plough.

Team G (1969–70) is the result of decisions in which the distribution of resources was the main consideration and so is, to a great extent, Team H (1970–1). The latter team would have been economically more viable had it consisted only of members of Konrad's (O36) and Siyalwindi's (N4) households. It would have had more than sufficient labour and would have had only the fields of two households to plough. With Abraham (O22) as its member, it has more labour than it needs and it has to plough the fields of three households instead of two; Abraham's participation is thus more a loss than a gain for Konrad (O36) and Siyalwindi (N4). He was recruited because of their obligation towards him resulting from their previous interactions. After Siyalwindi (N4) had returned to the village, he had kept his cattle in one kraal together with Konrad's (O36) and Abraham (O22) was looking after them. When it had become obvious that Lameck (O40) would be ploughing with his brother, Lorenz (O38), who was back in the village, Abraham (O22) had made it known that he was looking for a team to join as a ploughman. When he could not find one, Konrad (O36) and Siyalwindi (N4) had asked him to join them.

Similar agreements are reached at beer parties, where, with the ploughing season approaching, ploughing arrangements become a prominent topic of conversation. Surprisingly little competition for labour is manifest in these discussions. It is assumed that those who have ploughed together in the past will do so again unless they announce that this is not the case. I have never witnessed or heard of a man trying to persuade another to join him, rather than somebody else, once the other has declared his commitment. At the same time, it is expected that a man will plough with his kinsman if the latter is not in a position to plough on his own and it is recognised that a kinship obligation overrides any previous commitment. A case in point here is that of Abraham (O22) mentioned above. Similarly, Siyandindi (N2) made it known that he was available as a ploughman after Davidson (O7) had returned to the village and Bulawayo (N8) casually mentioned at a beer party that he was going to plough with his son. Unlike Abraham (O22), Siyandindi (N2) could not find anybody to plough with in Mujalanyana, and at one beer party he made an arrangement with Reuben's (P4) brother from a neighbouring village, with whom Muntanga (P6) had ploughed previously.

There are two culturally recognised ways of sowing a field – hoeing or ploughing – and the strategy of most people is directed towards having their fields ploughed as this is quicker and less strenuous than hoeing. The only man in Mujalanyana who neither ploughs nor has his fields ploughed for him is Thomas (O21), a divorcee in his forties who has never remarried. It is impossible to relate this fact to his position within the structure of social relations in the village or within the structure of resources, for his position in these structures is in no way unique. It is true that he does not own oxen but for that matter most people in the village do not. He is, however, still a strong man, fully capable of ploughing and, as such, should be welcome to join any team short of labour, particularly as, being single, he cultivates only a little land and his contribution to the ploughing of the fields of other team members would therefore outweigh their contribution to the ploughing of his field. This is generally the case with bachelors or divorcees living either alone or with only one or two small children, and it is on the whole much easier for them to become members of ploughing teams than it is for men with large families (and in consequence large fields) but no oxen of their own. Of the three people in Mujalanyana who, as youngish bachelors or divorcees, were potentially ideal recruits in 1969–70 – Abraham (O22), Thomas (O21), Muntanga (P6) – Thomas (O21) was much more closely related to one potential recruiter, Bulawayo (N8), than either of the other two, and he stood in a somewhat less distant affinal relationship than Abraham (O22) to another recruiter, Lameck (O40). Still, it was Muntanga (P6) who was recruited by Bulawayo (N8) and Abraham (O22) who was recruited by Lameck (O40).

It is impossible to explain this situation in terms of a structural model. An important aspect of such a model is that social actors enter into it as occupants of statuses and that it is the collection of rights and duties comprising each actor's status (i.e. the jural or moral rules) which are treated as determining his social behaviour. All an individual's attributes apart from the collection of rights and duties pertaining to his status, i.e. his individual personality characteristics, etc., are non-social, non-structural, and, as such, non-admissible in the explanation of social behaviour. In fact, this non-admissibility of factors of individual personality has become one of the most important boundary-maintaining mechanisms of sociology and anthropology in their relation to psychology. The decision model, unlike the structural one, does not dismiss from consideration the personality characteristics of particular actors on purely theoretical grounds. As far as they are sociologically available for analysis, they have to be incorporated into the model. What makes them so available is the fact that the actors themselves attribute meaning to them and take them into consideration in the course of their decision-making. If we did not take them into consideration to the same extent, the explanation of Thomas's course of action would not be possible.

By Toka standards Thomas (O21) is peculiar. He does not have the same kind of ambitions as other men. He has, of necessity, to pursue the short-term goal of securing his nourishment, like everybody else, but he pursues it in a way which is not recognised as proper by Toka cultural standards. He is quite happy to scrounge a meal, beer or tobacco here and there. He enjoys fishing and trapping animals but he dreads the prospect of ploughing several hours a day for two months on end. He has never shown an interest in joining a ploughing team and nobody has ever asked him to. Everybody knows that he would probably soon abandon the plough or come up every day with all possible kinds of excuses as to why he cannot work. To ask Thomas what kind of arrangements he has made for ploughing is a standard joke at every beer party at which ploughing is being discussed. Anybody would become a laughing-stock himself should he ask a similar question seriously; consequently nobody does.

I mentioned that the rule stipulating that kinsmen should plough together is a derivation of a more general rule of mutual obligations among kinsmen. Although this rule is merely one of the factors on which the decisions that lead to the formation of ploughing teams are based, the two biggest teams in Mujalanyana – in terms of the number of households whose members unite in ploughing – are composed of kinsmen: these are Teams F and E. The composition of Team F is the result of decisions in which the distribution of resources and the normatively stated rights and obligations of kinship were factors of equal weight which neatly complemented one another. Mukaswana's (O11) husband is away from the village working on the railway and Mukaswana depends on her brother, Joseph (O9), for having her fields ploughed. Her daughter, Cile (P3), is in a similar position as her husband (P4) is away from the village for most of the time. When Cile's daughter, Malita (Q1), returned to her mother, the number of Joseph's female dependants increased. On the other hand Joseph (O9) lacks sufficient labour in his own household. He himself is an old man for whom ploughing is already too much of a strain and, as co-wives do not work in one another's fields, neither of his households is alone able to muster sufficient labour. He needs the labour which the households of his sister (O11) and his sister's daughter (P3) provide.

The composition of Team E is again the result of decisions in which the distribution of resources and the normatively stated rights and obligations of kinship were the main factors considered. All the team members are bound together by ties of familial kinship, which are those culturally recognised as the most binding. As a result of their full recognition the team became much stronger on labour than its economic viability alone would require. It would effortlessly have achieved a higher degree of economic efficacy had it consisted of the members of the remaining households after Amos (O15) had left the village in 1970, and had it relied on Malake (O20) and Eni (O17) as its ploughmen. But instead, Ilumbela's brother's son, Siyakuwa (O29), and his wife (O28), who moved into Mujalanyana that year, joined the team and provided labour. Until then Siyakuwa (O29) had lived in his wife's village. When he was contemplating a move to Mujalanyana, whose founder had been his father and where his mother (N21) still lived, his main worry was how he would plough there as he had no oxen. Ilumbela (N14) is the headman of Mujalanyana; as such he is interested in attracting as many people to his village as he possibly can, for the bigger his village, the bigger his prestige as a headman. When Siyakuwa (O29) was contemplating the move, Ilumbela (N14) encouraged him by suggesting that he could plough with him, as his son, Amos (O15), was going back to town.

Divorced daughters figure prominently as members of both ploughing teams composed of close kinsmen (O18, O17, O16, Q1). Their cooperation with their parents is, however, usually of a temporary nature. Once they remarry, they go to their husbands' villages and drop out of the team. The attachment of uxorilocally residing sons-in-law (O20, P4) to the team is usually more permanent. But even they might eventually return with their wives to their own villages (as Siyakuwa (O29) returned to Mujalanyana) and drop out of the team.

Due to the prevalence of virilocal residence, the parent–son relationship is the most important for recruiting members of different but mutually related households into a joint team. The cooperation of the households of parents and sons in ploughing is in a way a natural outcome of the developmental cycle of both households. The son has been recruited into his parents' team from the age of nine or ten onwards. Since that age he has been able to lead or drive the oxen with which his father ploughs while his mother sows behind the plough. Joseph's, Konrad's, Lameck's and Reuben's sons (P1, P2, P12, P13, Q2) are in this way members of their parents' teams. If there is no son of a suitable age in the family, the daughter becomes a member of her parents' team (O26, P11). But her attachment to it is less enduring than the son's. After her marriage she is likely to go with her husband to his village and to drop out of the team unless she resides uxorilocally, in which case she continues to be a member of her parents' team if her husband has no oxen to muster his own team (O19, P3). The son's attachment to his parents' team is less likely to be affected by marriage than is the daughter's attachment. After his marriage he is likely to build his house next to that of his parents and his cooperation with them continues. A man is usually ready to retire as ploughman about the time when his children marry, and a son replaces his father as ploughman. He then ploughs while his wife leads or drives the oxen and his mother sows. The father supervises his oxen and occasionally lends a hand (N14 and O15). The cooperation of the parents and their virilocally residing sons and uxorilocally residing daughters is not only the outcome of the recognition of the normative rights and obligations of family kinship, but also the perpetuation of previously established cooperative ties. The Toka attribute a binding force to such ties by assuming that, all things being equal, those who have ploughed together in the past will plough together again, and by refraining from interfering with these established relations even if such interference might seem to be in their immediate economic interest.

The cooperation of parents and their sons in ploughing can also profitably be seen as an outcome of their respective economic strategies. By securing the continued cooperation of his son in the most crucial agricultural work, the father secures for himself the provision for his old age. From the point of view of this long-term goal of the father and his strategic behaviour leading to its attainment, the father's household is obviously more dependent on the assistance of the son's household in ploughing than vice versa. In actual fact, the son's continuing cooperation with his father after he has established his own household might interfere with the pursuit of his own economic strategy.

The son usually has several ways open of establishing his economic independence from his parents' household which would enable him to pursue a strategy leading to his becoming a *muvubi*. From the money which he earns as a labour migrant he might buy his own cattle and soon have his own oxen; instead of ploughing for his parents, he might start pursuing his long-term strategy while his father is still alive. Or he may borrow oxen for training and pursue the same strategy in this way. However, all this would seriously interfere with the father's own strategy. Having his own oxen, he could easily recruit labour into his ploughing team, from which his son had dropped out. However, his control over the team and over the way in which it is employed would then be based solely on his control over the oxen, while if he succeeds in retaining his son as a member of his team, his control is effectively backed by his parental authority and he can manipulate this control more freely, which makes the pursuit of his own economic strategies much easier.

The actual behaviour of fathers and sons who cooperate in ploughing is the result of the interplay of their respective strategies. To be able to pursue his long-term economic goal, the father has to offset any possible centrifugal tendencies of his own. This he effectively does by sharing with him his right of disposal over the oxen. In practical terms it means that the son can use his father's oxen to pursue his own economic strategy by ploughing for money, in the same way as men with their own oxen do. In Mujalanyana, Amos (O15) ploughed for money the fields of Joseph's wife (O10), Musoe (N20) and Jameson (O2). Having his father's oxen at his disposal, the son has no need to procure his own; for all practical purposes he can behave as if he already had his own oxen. All the money which he has earned as a labour migrant and by ploughing for others he can use for gaining the objective by which he wants to become known as a *muvubi*. The mutual cooperation of a father and son in ploughing thus represents for both men the most feasible way of pursuing their respective strategies.

The restructuring of the relations of production, which has been described in this chapter, affected both directly and indirectly the cognitive or cultural order of the people in Ngwezi. The newly emerged relations of production directly affected the notions concerning the norms of inheritance and succession; this process is analysed in the next chapter. Apart from directly affecting the norms to which people subscribe and which they themselves recognise as guiding their behaviour, the restructuring of the relations of production had serious consequences for the inter-village mobility of individuals, and ultimately for the social composition of villages in Ngwezi; these consequences are described in Chapter 4. In their turn, they affected other notions that the Ngwezi Toka hold about their society and the newly emerged notions reinforced the norms of inheritance and succession whose formulation was triggered off by the economic strategies which the Ngwezi Toka pursue. The analysis of the process through which the concepts and categories which form part of these newly emerged notions have been generated, is the subject of Chapter 5.

3
Changing norms of inheritance

An important part of the cognitive or cultural order are the standards or rules which state what people should or should not say or do under given circumstances; they are usually spoken of by anthropologists and sociologists as norms (Homans 1950: 124; Blake and Davis 1964: 456).

The relationship between the 'norms to which the actors subscribe or which they recognise and the social transactional processes in which they engage is rarely one of neat congruence; it is characteristically dialectical' (Keesing 1971: 126). This dialectical relationship can be dissected by considering it as two analytically distinguishable processes. The first is the process through which the norms that the actors recognise enter into the events and transactions in which they engage; the second is the process through which the ongoing transactions affect the norms to which they subscribe and which they are themselves able to quote as guiding their interactions. In the study of the first process, it is the observable interactions that are treated as problematic, in the study of the second one, it is the proclaimed norms. The generalisations about the first process can always be formulated in terms of the actors' strategies and above all in terms of the goals which they pursue in the course of their strategic behaviour. Such a generalisation was suggested in the preceding chapter.

This chapter is concerned with analysing the process of the emergence of a new norm of inheritance. In some situations, like for example in Luapula, where the inheritance practice is a major political issue (Poewe 1981: 96, 102, 121), it is possible to envisage the formulation of a new norm of inheritance as a consciously held individual goal; the generalisations about the process of its emergence could then again be formulated in terms of the actors' strategies. The situation among the Toka, however, is different. Unlike in Luapula, the impact of Christianity upon them is limited and no counterpoint ideology (Poewe 1981) is readily available. Under these circumstances, the formulation of a new norm of inheritance cannot be seen as a result of strategic behaviour specifically aimed at bringing about a change in socially shared notions, and the empirical investigation of the process whereby the new norm is generated has of necessity to take the form of a logical reconstruction of a concrete historical process, the aim of such a reconstruction being to provide an *ex post facto* explanation of this process.

In an empirical situation where the actors justify their transactional processes by reference to the existing moral and jural norms, and quote these norms as the inner motivations for their behaviour, the point that it is the transactions which generate the norms and not vice versa can be argued only on logical grounds. The emergence of norms from recurrent transactions can be empirically deduced in situations where new transactions, spurred by men strategically seeking advantages for themselves, have emerged in defiance of the existing normative notions in whose terms they could not have been justified or explained. Such a situation arose among the Toka when the introduction of the plough created a necessity for regular cooperation between households, which had not existed previously. The fact that it was the members of the father's and son's households who regularly started to cooperate in ploughing, was an outcome of the developmental cycle of both households under the given pattern of post-marital residence. In the traditional kinship ideology, as it still exists in Guta and Cifokoboyo, there is nothing which could possibly justify or explain this cooperation. Although this ideology takes cognisance of the emotional tie between fathers and children, it specifically stipulates that the man's obligations towards the members of his own *mukowa* jurally override his emotional attachment to his own children, who are not his *basimukowa*. The inheritance norms, according to which a man's *basimukowa* all have a claim to his estate and one of them is his main heir, are a clear jural expression of the existing kinship ideology.

Had they persisted in Ngwezi, the norms of matrilineal inheritance would have made the prolonged cooperation of fathers and sons unfeasible. A man who pursues his own economic strategy by ploughing with his father does so only because he can be sure that, after his father's death, his own efforts will not be frustrated by his father's *basimukowa* depriving him of the wealth which he himself has helped to build up in cooperation with his father. He does not invest his savings in owning oxen, and does not pursue his economic strategy independently of his father, only because he knows that after his father's death he himself will inherit the oxen with which he has hitherto been ploughing and his father's cows, which will bear him new plough animals with which he can eventually replace the original ones. In other words, his economic strategy is based on his knowledge that it will not be interrupted, and his efforts frustrated, by his father's death, and that he can continue in its pursuit even after his father has died. To be able to continue, the cooperation which evolved as a result of the adoption of the plough had to be accompanied by a change in the existing inheritance system which would enable a son to become his father's main heir.

Changing norms of inheritance

Although the widest possible distribution of the dead man's estate among his kinsmen is still fully observed in Ngwezi, his main heir is very often not one of his matrilineal kinsmen, but his son. It is quite often the latter who inherits his father's personal effects and a considerable part of his estate, particularly the plough and a large proportion of his herd.

A change similar to that which took place in Ngwezi, or a growing tendency to such a change, has been observed among many matrilineal peoples affected by economic development (Colson 1958: 347; Colson 1961: 95; Meek 1957: 179; Cardinal 1931: 84; Fortes 1950: 272). Economic development everywhere means increased wealth. It has been implicitly assumed that once a man accumulates individual wealth, he holds on to it and transmits it through inheritance to his son, to whom he is bound by strong emotional ties. Colson's explanation of the shift from matrilineal inheritance among the Plateau Tonga is a typical illustration of this assumption:

New economic possibilities emphasize the importance of the household working team, and give rise to clashes between the interests of its members and the interests derived from membership within a matrilineal group. The development of cash-crop farming, with the possibility of accumulating wealth either in the form of savings or in capital goods, is creating tensions in a system based on a male-centred household combined with matrilineal inheritance. More and more the Tonga are demanding, where a clash occurs between the interests of the two groups, that the matrilineal group should give way (Colson 1958: 346–7).

Similarly, Gough points out that 'as soon as individuals begin to acquire private earnings, violent tensions occur between conjugal and paternal ties on the one hand and matrilineal ties on the other' (1961: 649).

Affective bonds between father and son exist of course in all matrilineal systems, and these systems everywhere have to devise mechanisms for 'segregating and limiting the father's authority over his child so that it does not, and is not likely to, supersede the authority of the child's descent group' (Schneider 1961: 21). The hypotheses linking the shift to familial inheritance with the increase in individual wealth do not explain why these mechanisms suddenly fail to operate under the conditions created by economic development. Why should sons benefit from the wealth of their own fathers instead of from the wealth inherited from their own matrilineal kinsmen? The mere fact that there is suddenly more wealth to be inherited does not in itself explain why the norm of inheritance changes. The hypothesis that the wealthier the father is, the more inclined he is to provide for his own sons instead of fulfilling his jural obligation towards his uterine heirs rests on an unexplicated psychological assumption that the affective bond between the father and son becomes more binding if there is more wealth to be transferred than before. Goody avoids this pitfall of psychological reductionism and he ascribes the loosening of ties between the wide range of matrilineal kinsmen to the rise of property differentiation which upsets the reciprocity of the matrilineal inheritance pattern:

Among the LoDagaba the transfer of wealth outside the living-together group of distant uterine kin is based upon recognition of reciprocity, so that what is lost in one transaction can be regained in the next. Large inequalities of fortune render such a mode of inheritance difficult to work, because they upset the operation of equal exchange; and nowadays people are more likely to hold on to wealth, since they can do more with it (Goody 1962: 348).

Douglas suggests that Goody's emphasis is not entirely right in implying that differential access to wealth puts a strain on the system of matrilineal inheritance. She argues that 'it is not differentiated wealth, in itself, that causes rich men to favour their sons so much as scarcity in the basic resources' (Douglas 1969: 130):

On my view the enemy of matriliny is not the cow as such, not wealth as such, not economic development as such, but economic restriction. Many societies changing from production for subsistence to production for exchange find themselves entering a very restricted field. Economic restriction ... produces a movement to close the ranks and resist encroachment by other people. The emphasis is less on finding men to exploit resources than on an equitable sharing of a fixed amount within a limited group (Douglas 1969: 131).

However, economic restriction and a necessity to tighten the control of a narrow group over scarce resources do not have to lead inevitably to the shift from uterine inheritance. There are other means by which matrilineal systems can 'close the ranks and resist encroachment by other people' for which the hypothesis of the decline of matriliny under the conditions of economic restriction does not account: the generation depth and span of the effective matrilineage may narrow, and the resources may be transmitted through inheritance only to the nearest uterine kin. Colson reports that among the Tonga, with the development of cash-crop farming and the increasing scarcity of fertile land, there is a tendency for matrilineal groups to break down, especially for purposes of inheritance, into small groups composed of uterine siblings and their immediate descendants through females (Colson 1961: 95; see also Colson 1958: 253). Fortes writes of the Ashanti that, as a result of intensive cash-crop farming, the maximal matrilineage or a major segment of it lost its significance for the inheritance of property; there emerged a tendency to pass the wealth on to the immediate descendants of the deceased's own mother (Fortes 1950: 261). A similar narrowing of the span of the matrilineage appears to have taken place among the Yao, among whom there seems to have been a change from adelphic succession to a straight system of matrilineal primogeniture which indicates a man's eldest sister's first-born son as the rightful successor and heir (Mitchell 1956: 157).

Goody's claim that wide distribution of wealth through a matrilineal system of inheritance to close as well as distant kinsmen is compatible only with a poor, egalitarian economy, has been confirmed by comparative research (Aberle 1961). However, it does not follow from this that an increase in wealth and the emergence of property differentiation are sufficient conditions for the change in the system of inheritance. They are relevant only insofar as they upset the basic principle of reciprocity which underlies all ongoing social transactions. Accumulation of wealth which can be put to use, and particularly the emergence of considerable property differences, are incompatible with a wide distribution because any group which has produced the wealth through the joint efforts of its members, opposes its transfer to those who have not contributed to its production. It tries to secure at least a greater portion, if not all of it, for the group members. I suggest that it is this tendency, for the members of the productive group to keep the fruits of their own labour for themselves, which works against the principle of a wide distribution. In some societies this tendency has been explicitly expressed in the statements of informants. Among the Ashanti, Fortes noted severe criticism 'of the tendency of matrilineal heirs to eject their predecessor's widows and children from the enjoyment of properties in the building up of which they have often assisted' (Fortes 1950: 272).

Each division of inheritance is an outcome of the often conflicting interests of particular people whose decisions result from a multiplicity of varying considerations. The actors' reasons which lead to the division of a particular estate in a certain way could be the same as those which lead to the division of another estate in a completely different way, whereas the reasons behind the division of two estates in the same way could be completely different. When this is taken into consideration, there are, in consequence, rather complex methodological difficulties involved in citing actual cases as evidence of the actors' reasons where the reasons have not been specifically verbalised by all concerned and accepted by them as meaningful in the given situation. During my fieldwork I either witnessed, or was given adequately detailed descriptions of, the transmission through inheritance of the estates of seventeen men in Ngwezi who had sons at the time of their deaths. Although I have no detailed knowledge of the reasons leading to the selection of the main heir in some of the cases, on the whole, they nevertheless clearly indicate that the principle that those who have contributed through their efforts to the production of wealth have a right to it after the death of the holder, is either fully accepted and taken for granted, or at least held as an ideal.

In eight of the seventeen cases the son had ploughed with his father; he became his father's main heir in five of these, in two cases the deceased was succeeded by his younger brother, and in one case by his brother's son. In all these three cases, when, for various reasons, some other kinsman than the son succeeded the deceased and became his main heir, most of the cattle were distributed among the deceased's children and the oxen and the plough were given to the deceased's son who had been ploughing regularly with his father during the latter's life.

In the remaining nine cases the son did not plough with his father, either because he was too young (two cases), or because he was absent from the village as a labour migrant (one case), or because the father had no oxen (six cases). In only two of these nine cases did the son succeed his father and become his main heir. In one of these two cases the son's succession was, moreover, a compromise solution in a complicated situation in which there were two strong contenders for succession and various kinsmen were alternatively accused or suspected of having killed the deceased by sorcery.[1] In seven out of these nine cases in which the son did not plough with his father, some kinsman other than the son succeeded and became his main heir (younger brother in four cases, sister's son in two cases and sister's daughter's son in one case).

In none of the three cases in which the father had oxen but none of his sons ploughed with him, did the division of the estate proceed smoothly. In one case (mentioned above) a young son eventually succeeded his father and became his main heir. It was a normative solution which, as such, was acceptable as a compromise to the two contenders for succession and their supporters. In the second case, the younger brother succeeded the deceased and kept for himself the deceased's plough, four oxen and all the other cattle without giving anything to the deceased's young son. The deceased's widow strongly objected to this way of dividing the estate, which she considered to be a clear breach of the norm which had been revalidated many times before in the cases in which the son had become his father's main heir. In the third case, a sister's daughter's son succeeded. The dead man's son was a labour migrant and for several years the deceased's wife's son from her former marriage had been ploughing with the deceased (Davidson (O7) in Mujalan-yana village). When he did not receive a share of the estate, he alluded to the successor's sorcery and expressed his dissatisfaction with the way the estate had been divided. He felt quite strongly that, as one who had helped to build up the deceased's wealth through his cooperation with him, he was entitled to a share. When what he took to be his just demands were not met by the dead man's kin, he left the scene of the division of the estate in rage.

The cases of sons succeeding their father, as well as the conflicts manifest in the first two of the three cases in which the father had oxen but did not plough with his sons, clearly indicate that the new inheritance norm has been established to the extent that it can be positively invoked without any opposition to it or that its breach may be considered to be a deviation. The conflict manifest in the last case indicates that one's entitlement to the wealth one has helped to produce is part of the existing notions. In other contexts, I have often heard men refer to their father's cattle as their own, pointing out the fact that, by ploughing their father's fields, they helped to raise the money with which the cattle were purchased. Such remarks also indicate the existence of the same notions.

The transmission of wealth from father to son thus seems to occur when they have produced it through their joint cooperative efforts. If the production group consists of matrilineally related kinsmen, however rich any male member may be, no tendency will arise towards the transmission of the wealth to his own sons instead of his matrilineal heirs (Hill 1963: 82). A change from uterine to agnatic inheritance can only be generated by the emergence of previously non-existent conditions which bring fathers and sons into close cooperation and into the formation of joint productive teams.

In his analysis of the LoDagaba system of inheritance, Goody stresses a similar point when he argues that the mode of uterine inheritance is disharmonic with the residential pattern in which the domestic group is formed around an agnatic core (Goody 1962: 423) and the productive unit consists of agnatically related men (Goody 1958). He suggests that 'in societies in which residence is agnatically based, uterine inheritance produces a flow of property between local units which, like the passage of women between exogamous groups, widens the whole area of significant social relationships, but between kin rather than between affines' (Goody 1962: 423). He sees in the maintenance and creation of these wider social relationships one of the main functions of the given system of inheritance (ibid.: 346, 423).

Insofar as the residential pattern and the composition of productive groups are concerned, the Ngwezi Toka are similar to the LoDagaba. But among the Toka, the wide distribution of part of the deceased's estate among his kin has always been practised irrespective of whether the main heir is the deceased's matrilineal kinsman or his son. The reciprocal claims of a wide range of kinsmen upon one another have been maintained in spite of the changes which otherwise occurred in the system of inheritance; the existing notions of kinship have been sustained as a result of the persistence of people's behaviour relating to the transmission of property on the death of the holder.

Goody interprets the various mechanisms which the LoDagaba have adopted to circumvent their system of inheritance, as a means of achieving a man's goal of ensuring that at least part of his wealth remains within the compound in which he lives, while the advantages of the uterine system of inheritance for the maintenance and creation of wider social relationships remain preserved (ibid.: 422ff).

The problem I am dealing with here is, in a way, opposite to that of Goody. His problem was: 'Why should a society continue with a particular mode of inheritance when it apparently spends so much of its energy in circumventing its provisions?' (ibid.: 423). Considering that the 'function' of the transmission of property on the death of the holder has not changed among the Toka, the problem dealt with here is rather why the norm of inheritance has changed instead of circumventing mechanisms being adopted. The two problems are similar in that they both concern the question of the emergence of culturally normative responses to the problems facing the actors. I would suggest that, in dealing with the problem of why a certain normative response has emerged in a given society, an analysis in terms of existing groups and categories and in terms of the institutionalised behaviour appropriate for their members is inadequate. Both among the LoDagaba and traditionally among the Toka, property has been inherited according to uterine ties. When, among the Toka, the domestic group started forming around the agnatic core and the productive group started to consist of members of fathers' and sons' households, different normative notions were generated than those of the LoDagaba, where the domestic and productive groups are also formed around the agnatic core. I would suggest that the variable determining the norm concerning the transmission of property is not so much the structure of the productive group (ibid.: 337), but rather particular individual goals which the group members try to attain and the strategies which they employ to that end.

One of the strategies which the LoDagaba have adopted to circumvent the system of uterine inheritance is for a man to encourage his sons to farm on their own so that when he dies there will be less common property for the matrilineal heir to take out of the compound (ibid.: 326–7). A similar strategy is not feasible for the Toka. Although it would be to the son's advantage, as it would enable him to pursue more effectively his own economic goals, it would jeopardise the father's attainment of his goal of securing provision for his old age. I would suggest that it is precisely because it would conflict with the father's long-term strategy, that even gifts *inter vivos* – one of the principal strategies employed to circumvent the system of uterine inheritance in almost all matrilineal systems – do not take place among the Toka. This certainly applies to gifts of oxen, of which I have not recorded a single case. If a father alienated the oxen to his son during his lifetime, the most important reason for the son's cooperating with him would be removed. The father would have to depend solely on the strength of the son's moral obligation towards him. As a son's loyalty lay – at least initially – with his own matrilineal kin, in the case of divorce, when his wife would leave him for her natal home and her son would follow her there, the father would ultimately be left, not only without the desired provision for his old age, but also without oxen. It is strategically advantageous for a man to cling to his property until he dies. It is also fully consistent with his main economic strategy that, although he cannot prevent his son from procuring his own oxen from his savings, he certainly does not encourage him to do so.

The crucial variable accounting for the reasons why the restructuring of the relations of production among the Toka led to an outright change in the system of inheritance, instead of to a development of mechanisms circumventing the traditional system, lies in the fact that both father and son pursue their respective strategies by utilising the same resources. This in itself is the result of the father's knowledge that he can pursue his strategy only if he makes it possible for his son to pursue his own at the same time, and the son's knowledge that he will be able to continue in the pursuit of his own strategy, utilising the same resources, even after his father's death. For the cooperation between them to be, and to remain, to the advantage of them both, not only do the resources which they utilise have to remain indivisible, they also have to remain available to whichever one of them survives the other. The oxen belong to the father and he is not deprived of them in the case of his son's death: the son, if he inherits them, is not deprived of them in the case of his father's death.

Analytically, at least three processes can be distinguished through which the ongoing social transactions affect the normative rules which the actors conceive of as guiding or regulating these transactions: the process of norm revalidation, the process of norm adaptation and the process of norm replacement.

Revalidation of the norm takes place where no discrepancy arises between an action and the norm which the actors conceive of as determining, guiding or regulating it.

Adaptation of the norm takes place where the actors recognise a certain norm as determining, guiding or regulating a given action but, through the mode of its invocation during the events and transactions in which they engage, they have actively modified the scope of the norm's applicability or validity by widening or narrowing the range of situations in which it is legitimate to invoke it, or by altering the ideal behaviour contained in it.

Replacement of the norm takes place where a certain norm disappears from the cultural repertoire through a repeated lack of revalidation and a new norm is generated through being recognised by the actors as determining, guiding or regulating their behaviour (Holy 1979: 100–1).

With regard to this analytical distinction, the normative changes which have occurred among the Ngwezi Toka have the character of the adaptation of the norm which stipulates the relationship of the main heir to the deceased; the norm has been broadened to include the deceased's son, who was normatively excluded from being his father's main heir before. The trend of this change could lead one to predict that eventually the rights of uterine kinsmen to inherit will be completely disregarded, and a new norm specifying the son as the main heir will be formulated. Only then will it be possible to speak of the disappearance of an old norm and the emergence of a new one and to conceive of the process of the alteration in the Toka normative system as completed. It follows that the processes of norm adaptation and of norm replacement are not two empirically distinct processes, but should rather be viewed as a single process through which the ongoing social transactions affect the norms through time. The disappearance of an old norm and/or the emergence of a new one are the result of this process; at any given moment in time, before being completed, the process will necessarily appear as norm adaptation.

The adaptation of the norm stipulating the relationship of the main heir to the deceased has been justified by the notion that those who help to produce a man's wealth are entitled to inherit it after his death. This notion, which has always been part of the traditional Toka culture, and in Guta and Cifokoboyo is invoked to justify inheritance by the deceased's children, has itself the character of a norm in that it stipulates what should be the ideal behaviour under given specific circumstances. Since mutually incompatible norms, provided they are applicable to, and can be invoked in, the same situation, obviously cannot exist side by side, it follows that the norms will be affected not only by the transactions in which people engage, but also by other norms. Although, ultimately, the norms derive from the transactions, the relationship between any given transaction and a norm which is conceived of as determining, guiding or regulating it does not necessarily have to be a direct one. A norm behind any given transaction can emerge, not only as a direct cultural response to an ongoing social process, but also as the result of an overall adjustment of the whole normative system to events taking place on the transactional level.

The relationship of the revalidation of a norm to the process of norm adaptation and replacement is rather different from the relationship obtaining between the two latter processes. The cases in which a son became his father's main heir, as well as conflicts which have arisen when there were oxen to be inherited and neither a son nor a man who ploughed with the deceased inherited them, indicate that the norm providing for a son as his father's main heir, as well as the norm stipulating one's entitlement to the wealth one has helped to produce, are fully established and taken for granted. The reason for this is that previous cases when the son became his father's main heir were considered by the actors as having proceeded according to these norms. As such, all the previous cases known to the actors have revalidated them. It is not the existence of the norm as such which is affected by the events and transactions in which the actors engage, but rather its recognised validity and applicability for them. An action performed in congruence with the norm reaffirms the legitimacy of the invocation of the norm in the given situation; it reaffirms its recognised applicability.

Norm revalidation is an important part of the perpetual recreation of social reality through actors' practical accomplishments. Expressed in more traditional jargon, it is a part of the maintenance of the given social order. As such, it is a process, the notion of which is already contained in the theory of culture as an ongoing process (Shibutani 1955: 564; Scheffler 1964: 802–3).

Changing norms of inheritance

The revalidation of a norm is thus an inherent part of the overall relationship between the transactions in which the actors engage and the normative notions which they hold about them. Each norm has to be perpetually revalidated through actions to be perceived as such. This applies irrespective of whether it is part of a stable normative system, whether it is in the process of adaptation, or whether it has only recently emerged. Ultimately, it is its revalidation in the ongoing social transactions which ascribes to a given notion its normative value; on the other hand, it is its continual lack of revalidation which leads to its disappearance.

The invocation of a norm by actors in actual transactions, and its revalidation through these transactions, are two aspects of the dialectical relationship between actions and norms. In this chapter, I have dealt only with that aspect of this relationship which concerns the way in which norms are affected by actions. The action in which the norm has been enacted affects this norm in that it revalidates it and thus makes it invocable and enactable in a future action. As far as the other aspect of the relationship is concerned, I have already pointed out in Chapter 2 that norms enter into action only through being invoked and enacted by specific individuals. As far as the norm of inheritance by sons is concerned, it is not the father who invokes it. As in Guta and Cifokoboyo, it is the deceased's *basimukowa* who choose the successor in Ngwezi and who decide about the inheritance of the deceased's property. But unlike in Guta and Cifokoboyo, in Ngwezi the son belongs to his father's *basimukowa*, for not only has the norm of inheritance and succession changed, but the concept of the *basimukowa* has changed as well. As a result, the son is not disqualified from succeeding his father and from becoming his main heir on account of not belonging to his *basimukowa* as he is in Guta and Cifokoboyo.

I shall return to the question of succession and inheritance in Chapters 7 and 8 where I discuss in detail how and by whom the recognised norms of inheritance and succession are invoked and enacted. This discussion presupposes an understanding of the way in which the category of the *basimukowa* is conceptualised in Ngwezi. Thus, before embarking on this discussion, I describe, in the next chapter, the consequences of the restructuring of the relations of production for the social composition of villages in Ngwezi, and in Chapter 5 the way in which their altered composition has affected the way in which descent and descent categories are conceptualised.

4

The structure of local groups

One of the important consequences of the introduction of new agricultural technology and the resulting restructuring of the relations of production in Ngwezi has been a decrease in the inter-village mobility of the male population. This has led to considerable changes in the social composition of existing villages.

Individual mobility

My study of individual mobility in Ngwezi is based on a census of 119 married, divorced, or widowed men and 134 married, divorced or widowed women in twelve villages. To indicate the changes which have occurred, I compare it with individual mobility in Cifokoboyo, whose analysis is based on a census of 114 married, divorced, or widowed men and 120 married, divorced or widowed women in eleven villages in that area.

At the time of the census, sixteen women in Ngwezi resided in their natal villages. Nine of them had never left the village in which they were born and another seven returned to it after they had temporarily established residence elsewhere. (In Table 2 women who had moved back to their natal villages appear as residing in their third or fourth village.) It is quite typical that a divorcee returns to the village of her parents, which does not necessarily have to be her natal village. It is sometimes a village into which her parents (or her mother) have themselves moved from the village in which she was born. Not only divorcees return in this way to their parents' villages; sometimes widows do likewise or a woman returns with her husband.

At the the time of my census, fifty-four men in Ngwezi resided in their natal villages. Fifty-two had never left it, and two had returned to it, with their wives, after a spell of uxorilocal residence.

The percentage of Ngwezi women who have never left their natal village is precisely the same as that of women in Cifokoboyo (6.7% in both areas; see Table 2) and the percentage of Ngwezi women actually residing in their natal villages at the time of the census is only slightly smaller than in Cifokoboyo (11.9% as against 14.9%). While the basic pattern of mobility

Table 2. Individual mobility of married, divorced and widowed women

Age	Living in natal village		Living in 2nd village		Living in 3rd village		Living in 4th village		Living in 5th village		Living in 6th village		Total	
	Cifo-koboyo	Ngwezi	Cifo-koboyo	Ngwezi	Cifo-koboyo	Ngwezi	Cifo-koboyo	Ngwezi	Cifo-koboyo	Ngwezi	Cifo-koboyo	Ngwezi	Cifo-koboyo	Ngwezi
under 19		2 / 33.3%	3 / 42.9%	2 / 33.3%	4 / 57.1%	2 / 33.3%							7	6
20–9	3 / 9.4%	2 / 7.4%	22 / 68.7%	17 / 63.0%	4 / 12.5%	6 / 22.2%	3 / 9.4%	2 / 7.4%					32	27
30–9	1 / 2.5%	1 / 4.2%	21 / 52.5%	10 / 41.6%	13 / 32.5%	6 / 25.0%	4 / 10.0%	5 / 20.8%	1 / 2.5%	1 / 4.2%		1 / 4.2%	40	24
40–9	2 / 8.3%	2 / 6.2%	9 / 37.5%	15 / 46.9%	11 / 45.8%	10 / 31.2%	2 / 8.3%	4 / 12.5%		1 / 3.1%			24	32
50–9	1 / 11.1%	1 / 6.2%	5 / 55.6%	7 / 43.7%	1 / 11.1%	4 / 25.0%	2 / 22.2%	3 / 18.7%				1 / 6.2%	9	16
60–9	1 / 16.7%	1 / 4.0%	3 / 50.0%	7 / 28.0%	1 / 16.7%	12 / 48.0%	1 / 16.7%	5 / 20.0%					6	25
over 70				2 / 50.0%	1 / 50.0%	1 / 25.0%	1 / 50.0%	1 / 25.0%					2	4
Total	8 / 6.7%	9 / 6.7%	63 / 52.5%	60 / 44.8%	35 / 29.2%	41 / 30.6%	13 / 10.8%	20 / 14.9%	1 / 0.8%	2 / 1.5%		2 / 1.5%	120	134

Table 3. *Individual mobility of married, divorced and widowed men*

Age	Living in natal village Cifo-koboyo	Ngwezi	Living in 2nd village Cifo-koboyo	Ngwezi	Living in 3rd village Cifo-koboyo	Ngwezi	Living in 4th village Cifo-koboyo	Ngwezi	Living in 5th village Cifo-koboyo	Ngwezi	Living in 6th village Cifo-koboyo	Ngwezi	Total Cifo-koboyo	Ngwezi
20–9	7 30.4%	17 77.3%	13 56.5%	3 13.6%	3 13.1%	2 9.1%							23	22
30–9	3 10.3%	17 56.7%	21 72.4%	9 30.0%	5 17.2%	3 10.0%				1 3.3%			29	30
40–9	5 17.9%	13 40.6%	14 50.0%	14 43.8%	8 28.6%	5 15.6%	1 3.5%						28	32
50–9	2 10.0%	2 10.0%	12 60.0%	12 60.0%	4 20.0%	6 30.0%	2 10.0%						20	20
60–9	2 18.2%	3 37.5%	6 54.5%	2 25.0%	3 27.3%	2 25.0%						1 12.5%	11	8
over 70			1 33.3%	5 71.4%	1 33.3%	2 28.6%	1 33.3%						3	7
Total	19 16.7%	52 43.7%	67 58.8%	45 37.8%	24 21.1%	20 16.8%	4 3.5%			1 0.8%		1 0.8%	114	119

of women in both areas is thus virtually the same, the mobility patterns of men differ considerably. Whereas only 16.7% of men in Cifokoboyo have never lived elsewhere than in the village in which they were born, 43.7% of men in Ngwezi have never left their natal village (Table 3).[1]

Residence of men in Ngwezi is thus much more stable than in Guta and Cifokoboyo. The social structure of the latter areas depends on high individual mobility, which eventually brings men back to villages in which many of their uterine kinsmen live. At the same time, it is the relations of production which make this mobility possible. A family household is a viable unit of production and a move to a different village does not mean a breaking-off of any regular cooperative relations and a gradual establishing of new ones. In Ngwezi, the tendency of men to stay in villages in which their parents live is a direct consequence of the restructuring of the relations of production, and of the emergence of regular cooperation between the households of fathers and sons. If the men in Ngwezi had the same pattern of mobility as in Guta and Cifokoboyo, and if they eventually followed their mother to her natal village, they would have to break off their cooperation with their father or some other member of their village and establish new cooperative relations with uterine kinsmen in their mother's village. This might be difficult as such kinsmen are regularly cooperating with other households in their own village and might be unwilling to follow their kinship obligations towards the newcomer as it would again mean breaking off some already firmly established relations. The difficulties which the newcomers to Mujalanyana village – Muntanga (P6), Siyandindi (N2), Jameson (O2), Siyakuwa (O29) – experienced when trying to join some of the existing ploughing teams there, clearly indicate that, unlike before, to change village membership is inconvenient, particularly for those who do not have their own oxen.

The continuous cooperation of households in ploughing is, however, not the only factor which makes inter-village moves undesirable and which prevents men from moving unless witchcraft accusations, bitter quarrels with neighbours or other strong reasons compel them to. In Guta and Cifokoboyo, ecological conditions and the mainly subsistence-oriented mode of production put little constraint on spatial mobility. Land is abundant and a new field can easily be founded by clearing a piece of uncultivated bush. Houses are simple wattle and daub structures which are easily built within a few days. Material possessions are few and can easily be moved from one village to another. In Ngwezi, the situation is different. The ploughing of the fields has spurred on an increased production of crops for the market, which for most people means more wealth. Men who have more material possessions and possibly a dry brick house with a zinc roof are even more reluctant to move to another village and start from scratch there, than are those for whom such a move would mean only the establishing of new cooperative relations.

The structure of local groups

The increased cultivation of maize, the only cash crop grown, which ploughing has made possible, has led to an increased exploitation of the rich loamy soil on which maize thrives. Although in Ngwezi, as in Guta and Cifokoboyo, there is enough land for growing sorghum and peanuts, the land suitable for growing maize is becoming increasingly scarce. Its shortage is another factor militating against inter-village mobility; a man moving from his natal village to another might find it difficult or impossible to get hold of a piece of land there suitable for growing maize, as all such land might already be under cultivation.

In Ngwezi, as in Guta and Cifokoboyo, the higher proportion of men, as against women, who have never left their natal villages is primarily due to the fact that, ideally, women and not men change their residence upon marriage. The predominance of virilocal over uxorilocal residence accounts also for the fact that more women than men change their residence as a result of divorce or widowhood. The pattern of inter-village mobility caused by marriage, divorce or the death of the spouse is analysed in Appendix 2.

However, the Ngwezi Toka change their residence not only following marriage, divorce or widowhood, but often even before marriage. Men in my sample moved from one village to another thirty-two times while still single (34.0% of all registered men's moves). The lower percentage of men changing their residence before marriage in Ngwezi, than in Cifokoboyo, where changes of residence before marriage represent 58.9% of all men's moves, again clearly indicates the increased residential stability in Ngwezi. In seventeen cases out of the thirty-two (53.1%), men in Ngwezi moved from one village to another with their parents, in seven cases (21.9%) with their father (in five cases the father was divorced, in two cases he was a widower), and in five cases (15.6%) with their mother (in two cases the mother was divorced, in three cases she was a widow). These figures indicate clearly the strong bond by which men in Ngwezi are bound to their fathers. Whereas in Cifokoboyo the ratio of men residing with their divorced fathers to those residing with their divorced mothers is 1:3, in Ngwezi it is 5:2. In three cases out of thirty-two (9.4%) the men in Ngwezi moved from one village to another to take up residence with their kinsmen (in two cases a brother, in one case a mother's brother) because both their parents were dead.

Women in my Ngwezi sample changed residence thirty-four times prior to their marriage (15.4% of all registered women's moves). In nineteen cases out of the thirty-four (55.9%) they moved from one village to another with their parents (in ten of these nineteen cases the move was to a newly founded village); in eight cases (23.5%) they followed their mothers (in four of those cases the mother was a divorcee, in the other four she was a widow), and in five cases (14.7%) they followed their fathers (in three of these cases the father was a divorcee, in another two a widower). Compared with Cifokoboyo,

92

where no woman moved with her father after her mother had died or been divorced, these figures again indicate an increased attachment of children to their fathers in Ngwezi. However, women residing with their divorced mothers still outnumber women residing with their divorced fathers by 2:1. The fact that more men follow their divorced fathers than their divorced mothers, whereas more women follow their divorced mothers, is not only due to a stronger emotional attachment of daughters, as against sons, to their mothers, but also due to the different roles of sons and daughters in economic cooperation with their fathers. In two cases of the thirty-four (5.9%) women moved from one village to another to live with their kin after the death of their parents.

My Ngwezi sample yielded forty-two cases of a husband and wife moving together from one village to another. In nineteen cases the move was connected with the fission of the village and the couple left their village for a newly founded one. In the remaining twenty-three cases, they moved for various reasons from one already existing village to another. In five out of these twenty-three cases the couple moved into the village of the husband's parents after a spell of uxorilocal residence, in one case they joined the husband's widowed father, and in another case the husband's divorced mother, also after a spell of uxorilocal residence. In two cases the move was to the village of the husband's mother's brother. If, for various reasons, a man does not want to live in his own village, his wife's village is the preferred alternative place of residence. In four cases the couple moved from the husband's village to join the wife's parents in their village, in three cases to join the wife's widowed or divorced mother, in two cases to join the wife's son, and in one case her divorced father. Four couples moved from the village in which they first established their residence to a village in which neither of them had any close kin.

Residential arrangements of men and women at the time of the census are summarised in Tables 4 and 5, which indicate that virilocal residence is an important structural principle of village affiliation and is reflected in the pattern of individual mobility in Ngwezi in the same way as in Guta and Cifokoboyo. In Ngwezi, 88 out of 119 men (73.9%) reside in villages in which either both or one of their parents live or have died (the figure for Cifokoboyo is 72.8%), while only 53 out of 134 women (39.5%) do so (the figure for Cifokoboyo is 40.8%). Within this broad framework of the unaltered effects of virilocal residence, there exist considerable differences in the pattern of individual mobility between Ngwezi and Cifokoboyo. Tables 4 and 5 bear this out clearly. Only 24 women in Ngwezi (17.9%) and 23 in Cifokoboyo (19.2%) reside in villages in which both their parents live or have died. While there is no significant difference in these percentages, there are many more men in Ngwezi who reside in villages in which both their parents live or have

Table 4. *Residence of married, divorced and widowed men*

Age	Living in a village where both parents live or have died		Living in a village where father lives or has died		Living in a village where mother lives or has died		Living in a village where neither parent lives or has died				Total	
							Living in wife's village		Living in a village of some close kin			
	Cifo-koboyo	Ngwezi	Cifo-koboyo	Ngwezi	Cifo-koboyo	Ngwezi	Cifo-koboyo	Ngwezi	Cifo-koboyo	Ngwezi	Cifo-koboyo	Ngwezi
20–9	11 47.8%	15 68.2%	5 21.7%	3 13.6%	5 21.7%	1 4.5%		3 13.6%	2 8.7%		23	22
30–9	12 41.4%	18 60.0%	3 10.3%	3 10.0%	7 24.1%	5 16.7%	3 10.3%	4 13.3%	4 13.8%		29	30
40–9	9 32.1%	15 46.9%	2 7.1%	5 15.6%	8 28.6%	6 18.7%	2 7.1%	4 12.5%	7 25.0%	2 6.3%	28	32
50–9	7 35.0%	5 25.0%	1 5.0%	2 10.0%	6 30.0%	6 30.0%	2 10.0%	3 15.0%	4 20.0%	4 20.0%	20	20
60–9	1 9.1%	1 12.5%	1 9.1%	1 12.5%	4 36.4%	1 12.5%	2 18.2%	3 37.5%	3 27.3%	2 25.0%	11	8
over 70					1 33.3%	1 14.3%	1 33.3%	1 14.3%	1 33.3%	5 71.4%	3	7
Total	40 35.1%	54 45.4%	12 10.5%	14 11.8%	31 27.2%	20 16.8%	10 8.8%	18 15.1%	21 18.4%	13 10.9%	114	119

Total for Cifokoboyo: 83 (72.8%)
Total for Ngwezi: 88 (73.9%)

Total for Cifokoboyo: 31 (27.2%)
Total for Ngwezi: 31 (26.0%)

Table 5. *Residence of married, divorced and widowed women*

Age	Living in a village where both parents live or have died		Living in a village where father lives or has died		Living in a village where mother lives or has died		Living in a village where neither parent lives or has died — Living in husband's village		Living in a village where neither parent lives or has died — Living in a village of some close kin		Total	
	Cifo-koboyo	Ngwezi	Cifo-koboyo	Ngwezi	Cifo-koboyo	Ngwezi	Cifo-koboyo	Ngwezi	Cifo-koboyo	Ngwezi	Cifo-koboyo	Ngwezi
under 19	1 14.3%	1 16.7%	1 14.3%			1 16.7%	4 57.1%	4 66.6%	1 14.3%		7	6
20–9	8 25.0%	7 25.9%	1 3.1%		6 18.8%	3 11.1%	16 50.0%	17 63.0%	1 3.1%		32	27
30–9	8 20.0%	7 29.2%		1 4.2%	6 15.0%	2 8.3%	25 62.5%	12 50.0%	1 2.5%	2 8.3%	40	24
40–9	5 20.8%	5 15.6%	1 4.2%		6 25.0%	11 34.4%	8 33.3%	15 46.9%	4 16.7%	1 3.1%	24	32
50–9		2 12.5%			2 22.2%	3 18.7%	5 55.6%	10 62.5%	2 22.2%	1 6.2%	9	16
60–9	1 16.7%	2 8.0%		4 16.0%	3 50.0%	4 16.0%		9 36.0%	2 33.3%	6 24.0%	6	25
over 70							1 50.0%	1 25.0%	1 50.0%	3 75.0%	2	4
Total	23 19.2%	24 17.9%	3 2.5%	5 3.7%	23 19.2%	24 17.9%	59 49.2%	68 50.7%	12 10.0%	13 9.7%	120	134
	Total for Cifokoboyo: 49 (40.8%) Total for Ngwezi: 53 (39.5%)						Total for Cifokoboyo: 71 (59.2%) Total for Ngwezi: 81 (60.4%)					

When a woman resided in the village which was both the village of her husband and that of her parents (or one of her parents), her residence was classified as that with her parents or parent. The village in which she resided could actually have been her husband's village into which her parent or parents had moved to join her.

died (54 out of 119, i.e. 45.4%) than there are in Cifokoboyo (40 out of 114, i.e. 35.1%). This again indicates an increased stability of residence in the male population of Ngwezi.

Table 4 indicates that, of the thirty-four men in Ngwezi who reside in villages in which only one of their parents lives or has died, twenty reside matrilocally and fourteen patrilocally. The ratio of men residing patrilocally to those residing matrilocally is thus about 2:3. This again is indicative of an increased importance in father–son ties as a basis of village affiliation in comparison with Cifokoboyo, where the ratio of men residing patrilocally to those residing matrilocally is about 2:5. This increase in the importance of father–son ties is obviously the result of the restructuring of the relations of production in Ngwezi, and, like the general decline in male mobility, it is a consequence of the established regular cooperation of households of fathers and sons in ploughing. Of the twenty-nine women in Ngwezi residing in villages in which only one of their parents lives or has died, twenty-four reside matrilocally and five reside patrilocally, the ratio of patrilocal to matrilocal residents being 1:5 (as against 1:8 in Cifokoboyo). Although the proportion of women residing patrilocally has increased in Ngwezi in comparison with Guta and Cifokoboyo, the increase is smaller than the increase in the proportion of patrilocally residing men. This is clearly due to the fact that women are less affected by the restructuring of the relations of production: as I mentioned in Chapter 2, the cooperation of uxorilocally residing daughters with their fathers in ploughing is of a less enduring nature than the similar cooperation of virilocally residing sons.

The increased stability of residence of the male population, coupled with the increased importance of the father–son relationship as a basis of village affiliation, has strongly affected the social composition of villages in Ngwezi, which differs considerably from that in Guta and Cifokoboyo.

The social composition of the village

My analysis of the social composition of Toka villages is based on a house-to-house census of 260 hut owners in twelve villages in Ngwezi and 64 hut owners in four villages in Guta and Cifokoboyo. Married people apart, I include as 'hut owners' divorcees and widows or widowers who have their own households. In the case of married couples, the 'hut owner' is the one who represents for the other his or her link with the village. Thus if the couple live virilocally, the husband is the 'hut owner', if they live uxorilocally, the wife is classified as such. The concept of the 'hut owner' is different from that of the 'household head'. If a married couple inhabit their own household, the man is always its head irrespective of whether he resides in his 'own' village or in the village of his wife. Moreover, the concept of the 'hut owner' as applied here is not a Toka concept but my own. Among the

Toka, a man and his wife who have built a hut for themselves after their marriage, own it jointly; but in the case of divorce one of them forfeits the ownership rights in it. If the marriage of a couple residing virilocally ends in divorce, the woman moves with her belongings to her own village, in which her close kinsmen live, and her husband continues to occupy the hut. In the case of an uxorilocal marriage, the man moves back to his own village and the hut remains as his former wife's property. Thus in the case of divorce, the spouse who resides in the village in his or her own right becomes the sole owner of the hut. If, strictly speaking, neither husband nor wife is its sole owner during their marriage, one of them is at least a potential sole owner of it. This, I believe, justifies the use of the concept of 'hut owners' in my analysis.

Of the four villages in Guta and Cifokoboyo in which I did my census, two were founded by their present headmen; in the remaining two the present incumbent is the second headman of the village. Six of the twelve villages in Ngwezi were founded by their present headmen; another village has so far also had only one headman; he died and the village, which diminished considerably after his death, is without a formal head. In two villages, the present incumbent is the second headman of the village. Another village in my sample has also had two headmen; after the death of the last one, it split into four hamlets, which exist without a formal head. In one village, the present incumbent is the fourth headman. I have no information about the age and history of one village in my Ngwezi sample. My census in all three areas is biased towards newly established villages and the older villages are considerably underrepresented. This, however, does not distort the principles of village affiliation but in fact facilitates their elucidation. Many inhabitants of a long-established village live in it because one of their ancestors lived there; but they are not always aware of why he resided in the village and which of his kinship ties to its other inhabitants were decisive in his joining it. This uncertainty does not obtain in newly established villages. Their inhabitants can always point out the kinsmen whom they joined or because of whom they live there.

Following the observation that 'the inhabitants of a particular village are not merely a random grouping of unrelated individuals but that the majority of village members are linked to the village headman by varying ties of kinship and affinity' (Turner 1957: 61; similar observations were made by Mitchell and Barnes 1950; Gluckman 1951: 64; Colson 1951: 112; Watson 1954: 7), to which the Toka are no exception, the analyses of the social composition of villages among Central African peoples usually take the village headman as their starting-point (Turner 1957: Chapter 3). Such an analysis could be misleading and possibly obscure the actual principles of village affiliation.

One hamlet in the village is always the headman's own, others are headed by men who either have a kinship relationship to the village headman or are strangers whom the headman provided with building-space and a piece of village territory for their fields. In the following analysis, I focus my attention on hamlet heads instead of village headmen, mainly for two reasons.

As far as the actual day-to-day behaviour of their inhabitants is concerned, individual hamlets operate as independent units. The village, composed of several hamlets, emerges as a unit only in the political sphere by recognising the authority of a single headman. This authority manifests itself most strikingly in the hearing of disputes within the village but it is effectively challenged by the hamlet heads, particularly when they are ambitious men who try to sever their ties with the headman and thus gradually to become recognised as headmen in their own right. Generally, the hamlet head himself hears the disputes within his hamlet, referring to the village headman only those which he has failed to settle; he does so reluctantly and tries by all means to avoid it as this means the recognition of his subordination to the headman, which he is otherwise disputing. The village headman's own judicial authority applies, in most cases, to the hearing of disputes between the inhabitants of his own hamlet, and in this respect it does not differ from the authority of any other hamlet head. It surpasses it, however, in that it also applies to the hearing of disputes between the inhabitants of different hamlets within the village, and in that the village headman has the authority to hear disputes which the hamlet head has failed to resolve. But the difference between the authority of the two is only one of degree, and in this respect it is equivalent to the difference between the authority of a village headman and that of the senior headman in the area. In the same sense in which the headman has his own village while recognising the superior judicial authority of the senior headman, the hamlet head has his own 'village' while recognising the superior judicial authority of his village headman.

There is yet another important reason for focusing on hamlet heads in the analysis of the social composition of a village. The inhabitants of a hamlet stay in it, not because of their ultimate kinship tie with the village headman, but because of their kinship relationship either with the hamlet head himself or with some other member of the hamlet. Unless they are strangers who 'only asked the village headman for a place to live' and had enough followers to start their own hamlet instead of joining some existing one, all heads of hamlets within a village lived originally as members of the headman's hamlet. They seceded from it and started their own hamlets because they had, or felt themselves to have, qualifications for becoming village headmen. They founded only hamlets instead of villages for one or both of two reasons: either they did not have enough followers to start their own villages or they could not find a suitable piece of unoccupied land on which to build and start fields. In the first case the hamlet head usually hopes to attract more followers in the future and either to find a suitable piece of unoccupied land

The structure of local groups

or to secede formally from the original village and thus eventually to become established as a proper village headman. In the second case, he hopes that his village headman will eventually recognise the hard and, for him, unpleasant facts of the situation, and agree to the formal secession and the consequent division of the original village territory into two, whereupon the hamlet head will be recognised by the chief and by the administration as an independent village headman in his own right.

The emergence of independent hamlets within a village usually follows the death of the village headman; the kinship relationship of the hamlet head to the original headman qualifies the former to become the latter's successor. If another kinsman succeeds to the headmanship, the hamlet head realises his genealogically given right to become a village headman himself, by seceding from the successor's village. If, when analysing the principles of village affiliation, we concentrated only on the relationships of the inhabitants of a village with the village headman, the kinship relationship of the hamlet head and his followers to the headman would be considered as one of the relationships of village affiliation. This would be a serious distortion of the facts, as it is actually a relationship along which the fission of villages occurs. This means that if the ties of village affiliation are not to be confused with those along which the fission of villages proceeds, the hamlet head and not the village headman has to be treated in the analysis as the ultimate point of attraction of people to a village.

If, however, the analysis of the relations taken into account by the actors in their decisions about their residence, were to concentrate solely on the relationship of the inhabitants of a hamlet to its head, the relations which affiliate people to a particular village would also be considerably obscured if not completely distorted. Among the Toka, it is not, in most cases, the actual kinship link to the hamlet head which is relevant to the residence of a particular individual, but his or her kinship ties to some other individual. The latter then becomes the link between a particular resident and the hamlet in which he lives. We may say, in other words, that each Toka hamlet is composed of small kin groups attached to the hamlet head in various ways through one of their members. For other members of the group, this particular individual is their link with the hamlet.

I analyse first of all the composition of the kin groups of which every Toka hamlet and village consist, and later the relations of these kin groups to the hamlet head. In analysing the composition of kin groups I concentrate on the relations of the members of the group to whichever one among them represents their link with other inhabitants of the hamlet or with its head.

Altogether, 136 individuals represent such a link in Ngwezi; 76 of them were men and 60 were women. Of 21 individuals constituting the link of the kin group to the hamlet head in Guta and Cifokoboyo, 11 were men and 10 were women. More people in Ngwezi than in Guta and Cifokoboyo are

Table 6. *Composition of kin groups in Toka villages*

Category of the relation to the link	Actual relation of the link to the hut owner		No. of households	
			Guta and Cifokoboyo	Ngwezi
	B (the link is the hut owner's brother)		2	5
	Z			1
	ZD			1
	ZH		1	2
	ZDH			1
	S		1	2
	SWM		1	
	D			1
	DH		1	2
	DHM			2
	DD			1
	DDH			1
	MB		1	3
	MMB		1	1
	MM		1	
			8	24
Uterine	M	Father dead or divorced and residing in a different village from the mother	Mother's matrilocality	8	13
			Mother's patrilocality	1	1
			Mother's virilocality		6
			Mother's link to the village is affinal	2	4
			Mother has no link to the village		8
		Mother and father both alive and residing in the same village	Mother's matrilocality		8
			Mother's patrilocality		1
			Mother's link to the village is affinal		4
				11	45

Parental	F & M			Both father's and mother's link to the village is affinal	Neither father nor mother have any link to the village
					Father and mother both alive and residing in the same village — Father's own village (father is the hamlet head) / Father's matrilocality / Father's patrilocality / Father's link to the village is affinal
					(F) Mother dead or divorced and residing in a different village from the father — Father's own village (father is the hamlet head) / Father's link to the village is affinal
				34	**145**
			Both father's and mother's link to the village is affinal		1 } 7
			Father's own village (father is the hamlet head)	8 } 10	6
			Father's matrilocality	2	29 } 47
			Father's patrilocality		6
			Father's link to the village is affinal		1
			Father's own village (father is the hamlet head)		1
			Father's link to the village is affinal		8
					2
Agnatic	FM				1
	FB				1
	FBW				1
	Fpathalf BWS				1
	S				1
	DH			1 } 2	
	Z				2 } 20
	pathalf Z				1
	ZH				4
	B				6
	pathalf B				1
	BS				1
	BDH			1	
	FM				1
Ambivalent, mixed and affinal	DHFM				1 } 2
	W			1 } 3	1
	ZH			1	
	HZH			1	
Total				**34** 34	**145** 145

The 'agnatic' and 'uterine' categories include agnatic and uterine kinsmen and cases of residence with affines of these kinsmen. The 'ambivalent, mixed and affinal' category includes cases in which a relationship is ambivalent or is traced in a mixed line, and cases of residence with a hut owner's own affines.

thus affiliated to the villages through a male, and the relations between men within a village are much more important than the relations between women, or between men through women, in the former area than in the latter two. The existing variety of the relations of members of kin groups to whichever one of them represents their link with other inhabitants of their hamlet is shown in Table 6.

A number of inferences may be drawn from the table. The first is that in Guta and Cifokoboyo the uterine ties outnumber the agnatic ties as factors governing village affiliation by three to two (19:12), whereas in Ngwezi both uterine and agnatic ties are of equal importance (69:67).

In Ngwezi, as in Guta and Cifokoboyo, the most important of all uterine ties is that between the mother and her children; unlike in Guta and Cifokoboyo, it is, however, no more important than the tie between the father and his children. Fifty-seven hut owners in my Ngwezi sample were residing in a particular hamlet because it was the one in which both their parents lived. The parents of six of them had no kinship link to other inhabitants of the hamlet, in which 'they only asked for a place to live'. The parents of one hut owner both had affinal links to another inhabitant of the hamlet. In these seven cases it is impossible to decide whether the children actually followed their mother or their father in their residential arrangements. From the remaining fifty cases in which children resided in the same hamlet as both their parents, they followed the mother in their residential arrangements in thirteen cases and the father in thirty-seven cases. It is significant that in twenty-nine cases out of the thirty-seven, the father was a hamlet head. In total, children in Ngwezi, like those in Guta and Cifokoboyo, reside as often matrilocally as they do patrilocally: I encountered forty-five cases of matrilocal and forty-seven cases of patrilocal residence in Ngwezi. As in Guta and Cifokoboyo, it is quite common in Ngwezi for children whose father has died, or who has divorced his wife and has been living in a hamlet different from hers, to reside with their mother. In my Ngwezi sample, I encountered thirty-two hut owners residing in the same hamlet as their mother after their father's death or after their parents' divorce. But unlike in Guta and Cifokoboyo, I also encountered ten hut owners who lived in the same hamlet as their father after their mother had died or been divorced. Only two of them had resided with their father while their mother was still alive; the mothers of the remaining eight were all dead. This considerably limited their choice of residence. Moreover, in all these eight cases the father was a hamlet head, which gave his children an additional incentive to stay with him. The proportion of hut owners in Ngwezi who follow their divorced mother in residence is considerably higher. Of the thirty-two hut owners residing matrilocally after the death or divorce of their father, twenty-six lived with their widowed mother and six with their divorced mother. It follows that children residing with their divorced mothers outnumber children residing with their divorced fathers by three to one (6:2). This does not in itself necessarily indicate a stronger preference for residence with the mother than with the father. At least in some of the cases in which children were residing with their divorced mother, the couple had actually been divorced when their children were still very young. They followed their mother not because it was their choice but because it was so arranged by other people. They grew up among their mother's kin in a village different from their father's; their relations with their father had necessarily been severed, and their eventual residence with their mother has to be seen more as an outcome of their life history than of their conscious evaluation of the strength of the maternal as opposed to the paternal bond.

To be able to appreciate more fully the strength of the mother–child bond in relation to the father–child bond as a factor affecting residential arrangements, we have to take into account that a person's matrilocality is not necessarily his or her mother's matrilocality. It can be the latter's patrilocality, virilocality, a hamlet to which she is tied by affinal links, or a hamlet to which she is bound by ties of neither kinship nor affinity. In Guta and Cifokoboyo, 72.7% (eight out of eleven) hut owners residing matrilocally (in the strict sense of residence with their own mother) lived in their mother's matrilocality. This indicates not only that the mother–child bond and the coherence of the matricentric family are the most important principles of village affiliation, but also that the perpetuation of this bond from one generation to another, or cumulative matrifiliation, is a factor which distinctly relates to the social composition of the village. The situation is quite different in Ngwezi. Out of forty-five hut owners residing matrilocally, only twenty-one (46.7%) lived in their mother's matrilocality; two resided in their mother's patrilocality, six in her virilocality, eight in a hamlet to which she was bound by ties of affinity and another eight in a hamlet in which she was a stranger. Cumulative matrifiliation thus relates to the social composition of villages in Ngwezi to a much lesser extent than it does in Guta and Cifokoboyo, and the matricentric family is a less coherent unit in Ngwezi than it is in the northern Toka areas. The figures from the three areas suggest that, in Ngwezi, in contrast to Guta and Cifokoboyo, matrilocal residence is largely a manifestation of personal ties with the mother herself, and also that many more of the uterine ties which form the basis of village affiliation are personal ties with the mother. In Ngwezi, 53.3% (24 out of 45) of hut owners residing matrilocally lived in a hamlet to which their mother was not bound by ties of uterine kinship at all. In Guta and Cifokoboyo, only 27.3% (3 out of 11) of hut owners residing matrilocally lived in a hamlet in which their mother had no kinship links; the remaining 72.7% (8 out of 11) of them resided in a hamlet to which she was bound by ties of uterine kinship. Out of sixty-nine hut owners in Ngwezi who were bound to the hamlet in which they lived by some recognised tie of uterine kinship, twenty-two (i.e. 31.9%)

Table 7. *Relation of the hamlet head to the links with kin groups in his hamlet and to the hut owners in his own kin group*

Category of the relation to the hamlet head	Actual relation of the hamlet head to the link with the kin group or to the hut owner in his own kin group	Guta of Cifokoboyo		Ngwezi	
		No. of relationships	No. of hut owners attached through the relationship	No. of relationships	No. of hut owners attached through the relationship
	B (head is the owner's B)	4	8	11	19
	mathalf BWMZS			1	2
	ZS	5	10	1	3
	ZDH	1	3	1	4
	S	1	1	5	9
	DS	1	1		
	DH	1	1	2	3
	DHF			1	2
	DDH			1	1
Uterine	M (F dead; M's virilocal.)				
	MB	2	3	3	3
	MZS	1	2	8	16
	MZH			4	6
	MZHZS			1	1
	MMZS			2	4
	MMZHZS			1	1
	MMMBS			1	1
	MMMZDS	1	1	1	1
		17	30 (54.5%)	44	76 (32.3%)

Agnatic		**(33)**	**(55)**	**(152)**	**(235)**

Category	Kin type	(33)	(55)	(152)	(235)
Agnatic	B			12	12
	pathalf B			6	16
	BS			1	1
	BDH				1
	BWF				1
	BWMB				3
	pathalf BWS				1
	pathalf BWMZS				2
	ZHF				1
	S			1	1
	DH			1	1
	F			37	37
	FB	8	8	7	9
	FBS	1	2	6	12
	FFB			1	1
	FZH			1	2
	(subtotal)	9	10 (18.2%)	79	101 (43.0%)
Ambivalent, mixed and affinal	ZH	1	3	1	1
	MBS			1	2
	MBSWH				3
	MFB			2	1
	MFZS				3
	MMBS			1	2
	FZS	3	3	3	1
	FMBWZS				
	WZH	1	3		
	HZS	1	3		
	(subtotal)	6	12 (21.8%)	8	13 (5.5%)
Virilocal	H			1	3
	HB			3	9
	(subtotal)			4	12 (5.1%)
None (strangers)		1	3 (5.5%)	17	33 (14.1%)
Total		33	55[a]	152	235[a]

[a] Another 9 hut owners in Guta and Cifokoboyo and 25 hut owners in Ngwezi are the hamlet heads themselves. This gives a total of 64 hut owners in the four villages in Guta and Cifokoboyo and 260 hut owners in the twelve villages in Ngwezi.

resided in it merely because of their personal ties with their mother, who herself was not bound to it by any kinship ties at all. In Guta and Cifokoboyo only three out of nineteen hut owners (i.e. 15.8%) were in the same position.

Just as a person's matrilocality need not to be his or her mother's matrilocality, a person residing patrilocally (again in the strict sense of residence with his or her own father) may again be residing in his or her father's matrilocality, or patrilocality, or in a hamlet to which the father is bound by ties of affinity, or in a hamlet where he is a stranger, or in a hamlet of which he himself is the head. In Ngwezi, where patrilocal residence is as frequent as matrilocal residence, out of forty-seven hut owners residing patrilocally, thirty-seven lived in their father's own hamlet, six in their father's matrilocality, one in their father's patrilocality and three in a hamlet to which their father was bound by affinial ties.

The tendency of the hamlet head's children to reside patrilocally is one of the factors affecting village affiliation in both Guta and Cifokoboyo and in Ngwezi. In the former two areas, 80% (8 out of 10) of all individuals residing patrilocally were the children of a hamlet head. In the twenty-five hamlets in Ngwezi, thirteen hamlet heads had children who were married. Thirty-seven of these children lived in their fathers' hamlets, which means that 78.7% (37 out of 47) of all individuals residing patrilocally in Ngwezi were children of hamlet heads. The actual number of hamlet head's own descendants residing with him varies from one to eight in Ngwezi and from one to three in Guta and Cifokoboyo; in Ngwezi the median is three and in Guta and Cifokoboyo it is two. The comparison of the Ngwezi figures with those from Guta and Cifokoboyo indicates that a Ngwezi hamlet head relies more on his own children in building up a hamlet than does his Guta or Cifokoboyo counterpart. The strategies employed by men in building up their hamlets are reflected in Table 7, which summarises the hamlet heads' kinship relations to the links with kin groups in their hamlets and to the hut owners in their own kin groups.

It follows from Table 7 that the villages in Ngwezi have a considerably different composition than those in Guta and Cifokoboyo. In the latter areas households related through ties of uterine kinship to the hamlet head represent 54.5% and those related to him agnatically represent 18.2% of all households in the census. The remaining 27.3% are households related to him through ambivalent, affinal or mixed ties, and households of strangers. In Ngwezi, 32.3% of all households are related through ties of uterine kinship to the hamlet head, 43.0% are related to him agnatically, and 24.7% are the households of strangers, and households related to the hamlet head through ambivalent, affinal and mixed ties. Considering that almost the same proportion of households in Guta and Cifokoboyo and in Ngwezi are either households of strangers or households related to the hamlet head through ambivalent, mixed and affinal ties, the different proportions of households related through ties of uterine and agnatic kinship are significant. It is also significant that in Guta and Cifokoboyo the agnatic ties are largely personal ones with the father himself (80% of all agnatic ties), whereas in Ngwezi only 36.6% (37 out of 101) of all agnatically related households were those of the hamlet head's own children; the majority of these were attached to the hamlet head through varying ties of agnatic kinship. This means that, in Ngwezi, the hamlet head aims at attracting to his hamlet his own children and both his uterine and agnatic kin, with households related to him agnatically outnumbering by four to three those related to him through ties of uterine kinship.

As a result, it is not so much the men related through ties of uterine kinship as those related to one another through ties of agnatic kinship who are kept in spatial proximity in Ngwezi. Out of the 191 married, divorced or widowed men there[2] 37 were residing with their uterine kin while 56 lived with their agnatic kin.

Fission of villages

Village fission is always instigated by politically enterprising men who manipulate their kinship ties in an effort to achieve village headmanship. This is the reason why fission usually takes place after the headman's death when the question of his successor has been settled and the politically ambitious men who do not succeed to the office have to take an alternative course to achieve their goals. In Ngwezi, the range of men who may legitimately succeed the deceased (including deceased village headmen) has been widened to include his son, and in consequence the whole pattern of village fission has changed in spite of the fact that the basic reasons for its occurrence have remained unaltered. In Guta and Cifokoboyo, the main contestants for village headmanship are typically matrilateral parallel cousins or sons of two female matrilateral parallel cousins – e.g. Kamenyani (H15) and Matongo (H12) in Guta. Whichever one of them does not succeed aims at fulfilling his political ambitions by rallying the support of his close uterine kinsmen and his own children, and founding his own settlement. In Ngwezi, the main contestants for village headmanship are typically the son and the sister's son of the previous headman. Again, the one who does not succeed rallies the support of his own kinsmen and, with them, founds his own settlement. The fission of Mujala village illustrates this process (Diagram 10).

When Cabakani (M2), the headman of Mujala, died in 1938, the three main contestants for the headmanship were his son, Naamu (N22), his 'grandson', Jeke Siyanusiya (O51), and his sister's son, Kandela (N36), who at that time lived in a different village into which his mother (M6) had married. Although Naamu (N22) had the support of most people in the village, among whom his siblings and his paternal half-siblings figured prominently, Kandela (N36)

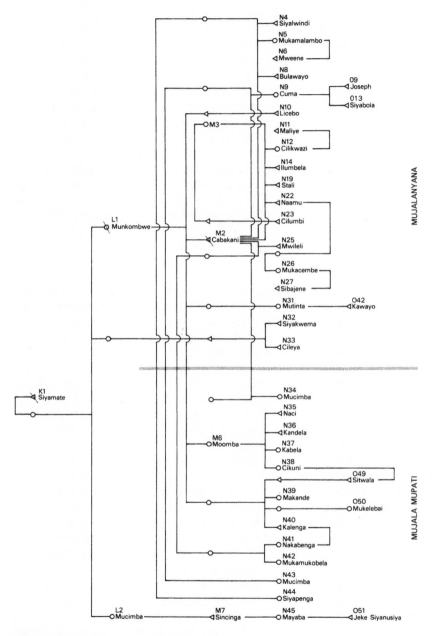

Diagram 10. The fission of Mujala village

eventually succeeded to the headmanship and moved his household to Mujala. The following year the village split and Naamu (N22) became the leader of the break-away faction, whose members built their houses on the bank of the Ngwezi river, 43 km north-west of Mujala. Their move was justified by a story according to which Cabakani (M2) himself had visited the new site, liked it very much, and decided to move his village there. He had told his children that, should he die in the old village before having had a chance to move it, they themselves should move to the new site.

The settlement on the bank of the Ngwezi river became known as Mujalanyana (the small Mujala) to distinguish it from the original Mujala village, which is nowadays commonly referred to as Mujala Mupati (the big Mujala). Naamu (N22) became the first headman of Mujalanyana. With the exception of Mucimba (N34), all his siblings and paternal half-siblings and their spouses and children left the old village with him – Stali (N19), Cilikwazi (N12), Ilumbela (N14), Mwileli (N25), Bulawayo (N8), Mukamalambo (N5), Siyalwindi (N4) and Cuma (N9) and her two married sons, Siyabola (O13) and Joseph (O9). The core of the new village was thus formed by Cabakani's children and their descendants. Attached to this core were some of their kinsmen who left the old village with them – Cileya (N33), Siyakwema (N32), Licebo (N10) and Mutinta (N31) with her son, Kawayo (O42) – and some of their affines who had been living in the old village – Sibajene (N27), the husband of Naamu's wife's sister, and Cilumbi (N23), the son of Cabakani's wife's brother.

Although some of the children of Cabakani's own siblings – Mutinta (N31) and Licebo (N10) – left the old village with Naamu, most of them remained there with Kandela (N36) and formed the core of what remained of the original settlement – Kalenga (N40), Makande (N39), their sister's son, Mukelebai (O50), and their brother's son, Sitwala (O49). Kandela (N36) himself was joined in Mujala Mupati by his brother, Naci (N35), and his sister, Kabela (N37). His other sister, Cikuni (N38), had already been living in Mujala as Sitwala's (O49) wife before Kandela (N36) moved his household there. Also Jeke Siyanusiya (O51) remained in Mujala Mupati in spite of his unsuccessful bid for headmanship. The remaining households in Mujala Mupati were those of the kinswomen of Cabakani's various wives – Siyapenga (N44), Mucimba (N43), Mukamukobela (N42) and Nakabenga (N41).

Whereas in Guta and Cifokoboyo it is the establishment of a matricentric family as a local unit which lies at the very heart of village fission, in Ngwezi the process of fission is rather triggered off by a patricentric family – like that of Cabakani (M2) – or a group of siblings and paternal half-siblings, which is a remnant of such a family, establishing itself in its own settlement. When a son's children mature and establish their own families, new patricentric families come into existence, headed by sons of the founder of the original family. The son's family may very often now start to exert its own unity

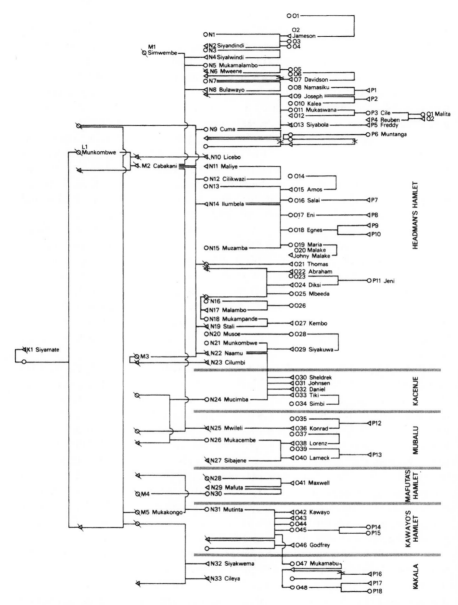

Diagram 11. Master genealogy of Mujalanyana village. (Only the people mentioned in the book are indicated in the diagram.)

against the unity of the original family. If its unity receives territorial expression by the family establishing itself as a local unit, the members of the original patricentric family are inevitably pulled apart and the original territorial unity of the group of siblings starts to fade away. The fission of the village whose core was formed by members of one patricentric family then becomes a territorial expression of the new phase in the development of this family. The emergence of separate hamlets within Mujalanyana village clearly illustrates this process (Diagram 11).

The original settlement which Naamu (N22) and other immigrants from Mujala founded on the bank of the Ngwezi river in 1939 consisted of eighteen households. The descendants of most of the original settlers still live in Mujalanyana; some of the original settlers, however, subsequently left the village, or their descendants did so. Cileya (N33), Licebo (N10) and Cilumbi (N23) died in Mujalanyana, and their children either married away or left the village as labour migrants and never returned. Cilikwazi's husband, Maliye (N11), who had been living uxorilocally in Mujalanyana, left in 1953, together with his children, and founded his own village, to which he also succeeded in attracting some of his brothers and sisters and other more distant kin. During the period of my fieldwork, Mujalanyana consisted of between fifty-four and fifty-nine households consisting of the descendants of the original settlers together with their kinsmen who had joined them during the three decades of the village's existence, and their descendants. The village consisted of six, and at one time seven, hamlets.

The first hamlet split off from the main body of the village in the mid-1950s when Naamu (N22), who had three wives and wanted to keep their households fairly separate to avoid quarrels among them, built a house for his senior wife, Mucimba (N24), some hundred metres east of the main body of the village. This hamlet is known as Mubalu (new village). Mucimba (N24) was later joined there by her younger widowed sister, Mukacembe (N26), and her two sons Lameck (O40) and Lorenz (O38), and their wives and children. Another resident of Mubalu is Mwileli's son, Konrad (O36). During his father's lifetime, he had lived with him and his siblings and their descendants in the headman's hamlet. After his father's death, he left Mujalanyana and moved to the village of his older brother. After this brother had been killed in a car crash in Lusaka and another of his brothers had died, he moved to the village of his wife. He had disputes with its inhabitants and moved back to Mujalanyana. First he stayed in a vacant house in the headman's hamlet, and later he built his own house in Mubalu.

About 1.5 km east of Mubalu is a hamlet called Kacenje. It is inhabited by Naamu's sons, Daniel (O32), Sheldrek (O30), Johnsen (O31) and Tiki (O33); with them lives their mother, Mucimba (N24), who moved there from Mubalu. Naamu's sons moved to Kacenje after their father, the first headman in Mujalanyana, died in 1965 and the headmanship went to

Naamu's younger brother, Ilumbela (N14), in 1966. Daniel (O32), who was one of the contestants for headmanship, expressed his right to become a village headman by establishing his own settlement, in which he was joined by his brothers. In a way similar to that in which Mujalanyana was founded by Cabakani's descendants emigrating from Cabakani's village, Kacenje came into existence as a settlement founded by Naamu's descendants breaking away from Naamu's own village. Its establishment was at the same time an expression of the unity of Naamu's children against the unity of the group of Cabakani's children and their descendants.

Unlike Naamu (N22), who had enough followers to have the settlement which he founded recognised as a village by the Native Authority and to be, himself, officially recognised as a headman, his son, Daniel (O32), having a much smaller following, could not found his own village right away. Like the founders of most hamlets, he hopes, however, that his hamlet will eventually grow in size and be officially recognised as an independent village. Although this is the final ambition of most hamlet heads, it has very little significance outside the political power structure. As far as the day-to-day conduct of their affairs and the day-to-day behaviour of their inhabitants are concerned, most hamlets operate as independent units. The degree of their independence depends primarily on their size, their kinship composition, their spatial distance from the headman's hamlet and, above all, on the reasons which led to their emergence.

Kacenje, which came into existence after Daniel's ambitions to succeed to the headmanship in Mujalanyana had been frustrated, is more independent of the headman's hamlet than is Mubalu. The fields of the inhabitants of Mubalu are situated in one block together with those of the members of the headman's hamlet, and there exists quite close cooperation between the members of the two hamlets. On the other hand, hardly any economic cooperation exists between the inhabitants of Kacenje and any other hamlet in Mujalanyana: the fields of the inhabitants of Kacenje are located in one block separate from the fields of the inhabitants of other hamlets, and Kacenje has its own well in the riverbed so that its inhabitants do not meet the people from the headman's hamlet even when drawing water. The members of the two hamlets meet virtually only when attending the cases which are heard by the headman in his hamlet, and when attending the beer parties. A beer party in one of the hamlets is attended by people from the others in exactly the same way as it is attended by inhabitants of other villages. Although nobody from the headman's hamlet conceives of Kacenje as an independent village, it actually acts as such in many respects, as the following episode illustrates.

Mushoke [a distant kinsman of Ilumbela (N14), the headman of Mujalanyana], from Siyamujale village, married Margret, who was staying with Simbi [O34], paternal half-sister of her father, in Kacenje. Ilumbela's daughter, Salai [O16], acted as

The structure of local groups

Mushoke's representative during the wedding. The night before the final wedding ceremony, Margret was taken from Kacenje to Salai's house in the headman's hamlet to spend the night there with the bridegroom. When the bride's procession was leaving Kacenje, the payment called *mali ecigwisya munzi* [money for leaving the village] was demanded by the bride's party from Salai, as the bridegroom's representative. Before the procession entered the headman's hamlet, a payment for entering the village [*cinjiziyo co munzi*] was demanded. These payments are not asked for if the bride and bridegroom are from the same village.

After Kacenje came into existence, the core of the inhabitants of the headman's hamlet was reduced to members of Ilumbela's own patricentric family and their children. Attached to them were still some of Ilumbela's siblings and paternal half-siblings, as well as some of Cabakani's (M2) more distant kinsmen, but several of these later made attempts at establishing their own settlements. The most important of these attempts, and the most successful one, was that of Kawayo (O42). Like Jeke Siyanusiya (O51) in Mujala Mupati, Kawayo (O42) is Cabakani's 'grandson' and, as such, he is in line of succession to the headmanship originally held by Cabakani. He was, however, still a very young man when Cabakani (M2) died and, as such, he did not stand any chance of succeeding him. He moved with his parents to the new village founded by Naamu (N22). When Ilumbela (N14) succeeded Naamu (N22) as the headman of Mujalanyana, Kawayo (O42) realised that the headmanship of the village would now pass from Ilumbela (N14) either to his son or to one of his brothers, and that he himself would not stand a chance in the contest, being a too distant collateral kinsman of Ilumbela. To be able to fulfil his ambition of becoming a headman in his own right, he rallied the support of his own siblings, most of whom had been living in Mujalanyana, and founded his own settlement. The rural council is conscious of the difficulties involved in providing adequate water supplies and educational and medical facilities for the small, scattered and isolated village settlements, and tries to prevent their proliferation, which it sees as detrimental to its development plans. It requires a man who wants his settlement to be officially recognised as a village to produce a letter from his previous headman justifying the establishment of the new settlement. Overpopulation of the former village and the consequent scarcity of land around it are usually accepted by the rural council as adequate reasons, provided that the new settlement is sufficiently large to be recognised as a village in its own right. The opinion of the chief on the matter is sought and his approval is necessary for the settlement being recognised as a village by the council.

Kawayo (O42) knew that he would never receive a letter from Ilumbela (N14) in which the latter would approve of his move, as such a move would diminish the size of Mujalanyana and thus run contrary to Ilumbela's own ambitions of being the headman of a large village. Kawayo (O42) and his siblings had their fields in a place called Cuulu (a place of anthills) over 3 km north of the headman's hamlet. Other inhabitants of the headman's hamlet had their fields there as well but stopped cultivating them in the late 1950s. Kawayo (O42) and his siblings never stopped cultivating their fields in Cuulu and, in 1967, Kawayo (O42) told Ilumbela (N14) that the fields were too far from the village and that he and his siblings would build a temporary camp there to stay near them. They moved to Cuulu at the beginning of the cultivating season in November 1967, and they started to build what looked to everybody, not like a seasonal camp in the fields but very much like a permanent village. These suspicions were confirmed when Kawayo (O42), his siblings (O43, O44, O45, O46) and his mother (N31) abandoned completely their houses in the headman's hamlet and willingly put them at the disposal of anybody who was interested in using them, and when, in the following year, they founded additional fields round the new settlement and completely abandoned their other fields near the headman's hamlet.

Kawayo's hamlet behaves in every respect like an independent village and it is also usually referred to as Kawayo's village. The fields of its inhabitants are located around it and separated from the fields of other inhabitants of Mujalanyana by uncultivated bush. The men from Kawayo do not even attend the cases which the headman of Mujalanyana hears in his hamlet and do not maintain any ritual links with Mujalanyana, as I shall discuss in Chapter 6. They meet the other inhabitants of Mujalanyana exclusively at beer parties, which they attend in exactly the same manner as do the inhabitants of other villages.

Like the emergence of Kacenje, the founding of Kawayo's hamlet followed the same pattern as the process of village fission through which Mujalanyana itself came into existence. In all three situations, the men who either did not succeed or had no chance of succeeding to headmanship in the original village became leaders of break-away factions that founded their own settlements. The core members of Naamu's (N22) and Kawayo's (O42) factions were the members of the patricentric families of their fathers, i.e. their full and paternal half-siblings. The significance of the patricentric family as a group whose spatial coherence underlies the village fission, is not so clearly obvious in the case of Daniel's (O32) faction, which established itself in Kacenje and which consists only of his full siblings.

Within two years of its being founded, Kawayo's hamlet grew rapidly into a sizeable settlement consisting of fifteen households. Apart from having attracted his own three siblings (O43, O44, O45), two daughters of his sister (P14, P15) and his paternal half-brother (O46), Kawayo (O42) also has his own mother (N31) living with him. There are also several strangers residing in his settlement. He did not succeed, however, in attracting all his siblings. His sister, Mukamabu (O47), resides, together with her husband's sister (O48), her husband's son (P16) and her husband's sister's son and daughter (P17, (P18), in a hamlet called Kakala. Another resident of Kakala is Siyakwema (N32), one of the original founders of Mujalanyana. Kakala is situated about 1.5 km west of Kawayo's hamlet. Its inhabitants do not consider it to be part of Kawayo's settlement but regard it as a hamlet of Mujalanyana village; their contact with other members of Mujalanyana is much closer than that of the inhabitants of Kawayo's settlement.

At about the same time that Kawayo (O42) founded his hamlet, Siyalwindi (N4) attempted to start his own settlement about 800 m west of Kawayo's hamlet. After Naamu's (N22) death, Siyalwindi (N4) was one of the contestants for the headmanship of Mujalanyana, and his later attempt to found his own hamlet was generally interpreted as an attempt to achieve the headmanship which he had missed after Naamu's death. He moved to his new place together with his sister (N5), her daughter (O5), and the sister of his wife's mother. But his hamlet never grew beyond these four households. Siyalwindi (N4) has three sons working in town and he went to see them to find out what the prospects were of them moving, together with their families, into his new village. None of his sons, however, showed any interest and, before the rains started in 1970, Siyalwindi (N4) abandoned his hamlet and returned to his old house in the headman's hamlet.

In Siyalwindi's case, as in all previously mentioned cases of village fission, the line of cleavage parallels the relationship between the contestants for headmanship.[3] These men are typically the son, the brother, or the sister's son of the previous headman. At the same time, it is the sons and the siblings of the leader of the break-away faction who form the core of his followers. Siyalwindi (N4) did not succeed in establishing his own hamlet, not because his right to it had been disputed, but because he was not able to muster the support of his own sons as he had originally hoped to do. While it is the relationship between the father and his sons which constitutes, in this way, the main structural principle of village affiliation in Ngwezi, the relationships between brothers or paternal half-brothers, between the father's brother and brother's son, and between patrilateral parallel cousins, are as much principles of village affiliation as they are principles of village fission (Diagram 12). Whether they will be one or the other depends on the phase of the development of the families of both men concerned as well as on their size. Due to a stronger bond between father and sons and the resulting coherence of the patricentric family, men are perpetually pulled away from their matrilateral kin and consequently the relationship between the mother's brother and the sister's son, between cross-cousins, or between matrilateral parallel cousins is, in comparison with Guta and Cifokoboyo, more often a principle of village fission than of village affiliation. Relationships of agnatic kinship thus have a different significance in the processes of village

The structure of local groups

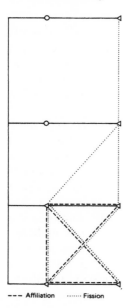

--- Affiliation   ...... Fission

Diagram 12. Relationships of village affiliation and fission

affiliation and fission than genealogically equidistant relationships of uterine or cognatic kinship, and it is due to this differing significance that more men in Ngwezi reside with their agnatic than with their uterine kin.

The inhabitants of a village meet together when the village headman hears disputes concerning some of them, at beer parties, and on certain ceremonial and ritual occasions. Apart from the cult connected with spirit possession and the occasionally performed rain-making ritual, ceremonial and ritual occasions are all connected with various stages of an individual's life cycle (girls' puberty ceremonies, weddings, funerals, final mourning ceremonies). Beer parties and most of the ceremonies and rituals are attended, not only by the inhabitants of one village, but by many people from other villages as well. A Toka village therefore hardly emerges as a distinct unit in any other than the political context.

A hamlet, on the other hand, is a distinct unit in many social contexts. The members of most ploughing teams, of groups of men who keep their cattle jointly in a common kraal, of most work parties mobilised through beer, and of groups of women jointly performing various domestic tasks, are all recruited from among the inhabitants of the same hamlet. The spatial borders of individual hamlets, including those closely bordering on one another like Mubalu and the headman's hamlet in Mujalanyana, represent clear cleavages in mutual economic cooperation and daily face-to-face

116

contact of individuals. The people with whom one lives in the same hamlet are not only one's neighbours but also one's kinsmen. Most of them are agnates or paternal kin. The fact that it is typically one's agnates or paternal kinsmen whom one sees most often, with whom one regularly cooperates in a whole range of activities, and in whose company one spends one's leisure time, affects the growing tendency to stress one's genealogical links with them and to stress the genealogical links with forebears one has in common with them, when reckoning one's *mukowa* membership. A description of the way in which this membership is conceptualised in Ngwezi is the subject of the next chapter.

5

The changing concept of the *basimukowa*

I have mentioned that in Guta and Cifokoboyo the people collectively referred to as *basimukowa* are the most important category among one's kin. They are conceptualised as uterine kinsmen, or, more specifically, as descendants in the matrilineal line of a common ancestress. This conceptualisation is sustained because most of them usually do not live further apart than in several neighbouring villages. Being spatially close together, they can attend one another's funerals and final mourning ceremonies, they can inherit one another's property and one of their members can become the deceased's successor and main heir, and they can assemble for the performance of rituals. Because of the spatial distribution of the *basimukowa*, individual villages can be conceptualised as being owned by particular *mikowa*, fission of villages can be understood as a territorial expression of *mukowa* segmentation, succession to village headmanship can be seen as determined by the relations between *mukowa* and village, and the status of particular residents of the village can be differentiated on the basis of their *mukowa* membership. A considerable range of actual social transactions can thus be interpreted as being determined or affected by the *mukowa* membership of their participants. There is either no discrepancy between the notional level and the level of actual social transactions for which the existing notions provide an adequate meaning, or, wherever there is a discrepancy (e.g. the succession of sons to village headmanship), it can still be explained, and thus made meaningful, within the framework of existing notions.

In Ngwezi, the people collectively referred to as *basimukowa* are also considered to be the most important category among one's kin and are conceptualised as members of the same *mukowa*. But unlike in Guta and Cifokoboyo, they are not necessarily uterine kinsmen. It is rather the cognatic descendants of a common ancestor who are counted as one's *basimukowa* and a *mukowa* is consequently a cognatic descent category. As in Guta and Cifokoboyo, each *mukowa* has its recognised head and it is called either after him, or after its founder, or is referred to by the name of the clan of which it is taken to be a subdivision. Diagram 13 shows the members of the *mukowa wa* Cileya, known also as the Bancindu, of which it is held to be a subdivision.

The changing concept of the basimukowa

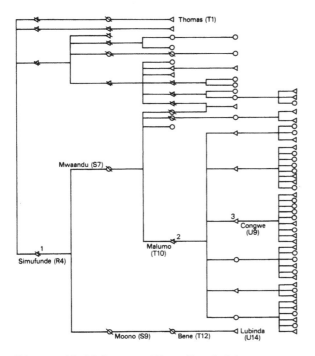

Diagram 13. *Mukowa wa* Cileya (Bancindu)

Figures indicate the order of succession of the heads of the *mukowa*. Simufunde was the founder of the village called Cileya and was referred to by the name of his village. All other *mukowa* heads were also headmen of Cileya village and Cileya was their honorific title: hence the name of the *mukowa*.

Not all the ideally distinguished *basimukowa* are represented in the diagram, but only those whom Congwe (U9), the present head of the *mukowa*, considered to be important. Including the putative founder of the *mukowa*, Simufunde's (R4) parent, whose name is no longer remembered, the *mukowa* has a depth of five generations counted from the youngest adult generation. All *mikowa* in Ngwezi, like those in Guta and Cifokoboyo, are of a similar genealogical depth of five or six generations.

Apart from the norms of inheritance and succession, the tracing of descent for the purpose of reckoning *mukowa* membership is thus another notion which has changed in Ngwezi. While several specific hypotheses about the change of the norms of inheritance in matrilineal systems affected by modern economic development have been advanced so far, there exists basically one very general hypothesis about the influence of such development on groups or categories whose members are recruited on the basis of common

119

matrilineal descent: as 'the institutionalisation of very strong, lasting or intense solidarities between husband and wife is not compatible with the maintenance of matrilineal descent groups' (Schneider 1961: 16–18), the latter cannot be maintained under conditions of economic development, which invariably leads to the strengthening of familial ties at the expense of ties of wider kinship (Smelser 1963: 39; Lewis 1955: 14; Bauer and Yamey 1957: 66).

The theory which causally links the decline of matriliny with the increased importance of the individual family can be taken to account adequately for changes in notions about descent only under two specific conditions. The first obtains when the membership of the individual family, or interpersonal kinship relationships which spread from it bilaterally, become the principle of recruitment into all those activities into which people were recruited before because of their membership of a matrilineal descent category. The second one obtains when these activities cease to be performed altogether; the theory is adequate as long as their cessation can be shown to be causally linked to the emergence of the individual family as the main kinship group. Expressed differently, the theory can be judged to provide an adequate explanation for a change in the conceptualisation of descent only when the individual family (or possibly personal kindred) controls the behaviour of its members in all spheres of activity in which it was controlled before by their descent group. Such a situation arises when the individual family takes over all the functions formerly discharged by a descent group, or when such functions cease to be performed after the family has emerged as the main kinship group and their demise is directly caused by its emergence.

That the former notions about descent cannot persist under these conditions is readily understandable. If groups whose members were recruited on the basis of their descent from a common ancestor or ancestress cease to be relevant in any sphere of activity, it is to be expected that the very notion of descent as such will cease to be relevant and will eventually disappear. Its disappearance is the inevitable consequence of the dialectic relationship between specific cultural notions (in this particular case the notion of descent) and the social interactions whereby, on the one hand, the interactions become endowed with meaning by the invocation of appropriate notions, and on the other hand, the notions themselves are kept in existence by being brought to bear on actions. The action in which a specific cultural notion has been enacted affects this notion in that it revalidates it and thus makes it invokable and enactable in a future action. If a situation arises in which a specific notion cannot for practical reasons be invoked or enacted, it ceases to be continually revalidated and it is eventually bound to disappear. As it is the very notion of descent which becomes practically irrelevant when groups of people recruited on the basis of their membership of a descent category cease to crystallise in action, the need to replace the notion of matrilineal descent with a different mode of descent reckoning does not arise.

Although the conditions outlined above empirically obtain in some matrilineal societies,[1] they do not obtain in all of them. At least three other ways, or their various combinations, in which matrilineal descent will be affected under the conditions of modern economic development, can be envisaged.

(1) The range of activities performed by groups whose members are recruited on the basis of matrilineal descent narrows down, or, expressed differently, the range of functions discharged by matrilineal descent groups diminishes. The notion of matrilineal descent becomes affected in that the range of situations in which it is seen as a valid principle of recruitment decreases: matrilineal descent becomes a less embracing organising principle than before, but unlike under the conditions outlined above, it does not disappear altogether; it merely becomes invoked less frequently. For example, among the Gwembe Tonga resettled after the construction of the Kariba dam, daily interaction among the lineage members within a neighbourhood declined and the notion of common matrilineal descent ceased to be invoked in claims to land. Fellow members of the lineage ceased to respond to demands for assistance with elopement damages and bridewealth payments made by young men who were not able to find employment in towns; their requests for assistance were usually heeded only by their own fathers, brothers and mother's brothers (Colson 1971: 90–1).

Such a diminishing importance of matrilineal descent as a principle of recruitment into groups which crystallise in various interactional contexts may well be just a stage in the development leading to its total demise, and Gough (1961) consistently treats it as such in her explanation of the disintegration of matrilineal descent groups upon the society's entry into the capitalist market system. The fact remains, however, that while the tracing of descent in a matrilineal line became obsolete in many societies following their exposure to the capitalist market economy, in other societies the importance of matrilineal descent as an organising principle has merely diminished, but not altogether disappeared, even after a long period of the society's exposure to a market economy. This would seem to indicate that the theory which sees the decline of matriliny as a universal process and which causally links it with the society's absorption into the capitalist economy is too crude to account satisfactorily for all the observable differences in the pattern of change; other factors which affect this pattern have obviously to be brought into the explanation.

(2) The size of groups whose members are recruited on the basis of matrilineal descent decreases. When this happens, the notion of matrilineal descent is affected in that it again becomes a less embracing organising

principle than before. But instead of being seen as applicable to a diminished range of situations, it becomes seen as a principle of recruitment into specific activities applicable to a narrower range of people than before; only matrilineal descent from closer ancestors is now given recognition as a criterion defining membership of a culturally recognised category. In consequence, the generation depth and span of effective matrilineage narrows. This process has taken place for example among the Tonga (Colson 1961: 95; 1958: 253), the Ashanti (Fortes 1950: 261) and probably the Yao (Mitchell 1956: 157).

Gough (1961) treats the narrowing of the generation depth and span of the effective matrilineage as a stage in the gradual establishment of the individual family as the key kinship group, which spells out the ultimate demise of matriliny. Given that the individual family has in many cases existed for long periods alongside groups organised on the basis of the matrilineal principle (albeit reduced in size), this would appear again to be an unwarranted generalisation. Obviously factors other than the emergence of the individual family as the key kinship group have to be taken into account in explaining why the importance of matrilineal descent as a principle of recruitment into groups which crystallise in various interactional contexts diminishes in some cases, why the narrowing of the generational depth and span of the effective matrilineage occurs in others, and why the notion of descent as such becomes obsolete in yet others.

(3) The range of activities performed by groups whose members are recruited on the basis of descent does not change, or at least not dramatically, but matrilineal descent ceases to be recognised as a valid principle of recruitment into such groups. The notion of descent as such does not become obsolescent but the mode of tracing descent through females becomes replaced by tracing descent through males or through both sexes. This is what happened among the Toka.

Presumably, the significance of the individual family has increased, and the father–son bond strengthened, in all matrilineal societies absorbed into the capitalist market economy. To treat this general factor as a cause of all the particular changes in descent conceptualisation is thus clearly inadequate: the particular cannot be explained by reference to the general. There must obviously be other factors which influence the way in which matrilineal descent becomes affected when the society is exposed to modern development and it is the differing strength of these factors which determines the particular way in which the conceptualisation of descent changes. If this is so, the explanation of the change in the conceptualisation of descent must consist in stipulating the practical reasons for which the existing notions of descent can no longer be invoked in action and in consequence cease to be revalidated and gradually disappear.

Following Lowie (1920: 70–6, 122–37, 157–62, 166–85), Murdock (1949) and Fox (1967: 109–11) stress the role of residence rules in the process of social change. According to Murdock, it is patrilocal residence which inevitably leads to the decline of the matrilineal mode of tracing descent as 'patrilocal residence involves a man in a lifelong residential propinquity and social participation with the father's patrilineal kinsmen' (Murdock 1949: 202). It follows for him that 'bit by bit, ties with patrilineal kinsmen are strengthened and ties with matrilineal relatives undergo a diminution in importance' (ibid.).

In his analysis of the Suku residential arrangements, Kopytoff criticises Murdock's evolutionary model for equating the concept of 'residence' with a specific point in physical space. He makes a valid point that the concept of residence should concern 'a person's relationship to various social fields' and in consequence should not refer to 'the *spot* at which one lives but the *zone* within which one resides' (Kopytoff 1977: 555). A man can 'reside' patrilocally in his father's locality and at the same time his 'residence' is still avunculocal in the residential zone, within which his relations to its other inhabitants are important principles of recruitment into various activities. Patrilocal residence does not then need to pose a threat to matriliny as Murdock's model predicts.

It has to be noted, however, that the avunculocal residence within the residential zone is the product of the in-gathering process by 'which lineage members drift "back" directly into the lineage center or, indirectly, to the subsidiary loci as they grow older' (ibid.: 549). Such an in-gathering process is at work in traditional Toka society in Guta and Cifokoboyo as well as in other Central African matrilineal and virilocal societies like, for example, the Ndembu (Turner 1957) or the Tonga of Malawi (van Velsen 1964). In none of them is matriliny threatened by patrilocal residence, for men have not been brought into '*lifelong* residential propinquity and social participation with the father's patrilineal kinsmen' (emphasis added) which Murdock's model stipulates as the initial condition for the diminution in importance of ties with matrilineal relatives. In all of them, matrilineally related men are kept in spatial proximity within individual villages because of their inter-village mobility.

Among the Ngwezi Toka, this mobility has decreased considerably and village residence has become stabilised. The main mechanism through which men related to one another through the ties of uterine kinship were kept in spatial proximity was thus removed. The social composition of villages in Ngwezi hinders the tracing of descent in a matrilineal line for the simple reason that people related by the ties of uterine kinship live dispersed in different villages and areas, and the spatial distance between them prevents them from being jointly recruited into groups which crystallise in various situational contexts. When this becomes empirically the case, i.e. when the membership of a descent category which defined an individual's entitlement to membership of various social groups (Keesing 1971: 128) can no longer do so because the individual cannot, for practical reasons, activate his entitlement, his membership of the descent category becomes, for all practical purposes, meaningless and consequently the descent which defined his membership of the category also becomes meaningless.[2] For just as norms are kept in existence only by being perpetually revalidated in action, so are other notions, including notions of descent and descent categories.

This interpretation subscribes to Murdock's view (*pace* Fortes 1958: 3) 'that an alteration in the prevailing rule of residence is the point of departure for nearly all significant changes in social organisation' (Murdock 1949: 202) in that it stipulates the spatial distribution of people resulting from particular residential arrangements as the most important restraint on the practical possibility of the invocation of the existing notions of descent.

Once cognates instead of uterine kin start to live in spatial proximity, descent will change, rather than the descent category disappearing completely, only when certain necessary conditions are fulfilled:

(1) Descent categories must continue to be used in defining entitlement to membership in social groups which crystallise in the context of economic, political, ritual or other activities.
(2) They have to be localised in the sense that their members, or the majority of them, live in a more or less clearly defined territory and that their rights in it are recognised.
(3) Social relations into which people enter in their social identities (Goodenough 1965) defined on the basis of descent have to be defined, not only as relations among the members of the descent category, but at the same time as relations among the residents of the territory in which the category members have recognised rights; in other words, territorial ties have to parallel descent ties in the framework of a certain sphere, or spheres, of social relations.

All these three conditions have to be fulfilled simultaneously. If condition (2) is not fulfilled, condition (1) cannot obtain, as members of the descent category, being widely dispersed, cannot for practical reasons assemble for action and thus activate their entitlement, which will consequently cease to be revalidated. If condition (3) is not fulfilled, the entitlement to membership of social groups previously defined in terms of descent, would simply be defined in terms of territorial ties and the action of co-residents in a given territory which was formerly conceptualised as the action of members of a descent group, would now, if enduring, simply be conceptualised as the action of co-residents.

All three conditions have been fulfilled in Ngwezi. The same range of actual social transactions as in Guta and Cifokoboyo is conceptualised as being the affairs of the *basimukowa*. The *mikowa* in Ngwezi are also seen as being localised in specific areas over which they have recognised rights, and the territorial ties between co-residents parallel their descent ties in the sphere of social relations into which people enter in their social identities defined on the basis of descent.

The people whom Congwe (U9) distinguishes as his *basimukowa* (Diagram 13) live mostly in his own and in three neighbouring villages. There is, however, no context in which *all* these people would act in their social identity relationships defined on the basis of their *mukowa* membership, i.e. on the basis of their cognatic descent from Simufunde's (R4) parent. In this respect, *mukowa wa* Cileya, and any other *mukowa* for that matter, is not a cognatic descent group that could be defined on the basis of interaction, but a cultural category (Oliver 1955). I shall discuss later in what situations and to what extent this category is used in defining entitlement to membership of social groups. For the time being, I limit myself to a discussion of the *basimukowa* as a cultural category distinguished in the Toka notional realm.

In Guta and Cifokoboyo, where only descendants in a matrilineal line from a common ancestress count as *basimukowa*, it is descent alone which defines the boundaries of this category. In Ngwezi, where membership of the category is defined on the basis of cognatic descent from a recognised ancestor, any Toka can be simultaneously a member of several such categories.

Although it is not unusual for a *mukowa* to have a depth of six or seven generations, its average depth is about five generations. Basing the calculation on a five-generational depth, and taking into account that it is usually male forebears who are recognised as the apical ancestors of *mikowa*, any individual may ideally trace his descent back to eight different ancestors and thus potentially exercise a choice of affiliation with eight different *mikowa*. In practice, however, his choice is much more limited.

First of all, the number of *mikowa* with which he can affiliate himself is effectively reduced because not all of the eight potentially recognisable forebears will in fact be remembered. It is usually only the founders of villages, particularly of large villages, who are remembered and who have become apical ancestors of existing *mikowa*. Although many men try to found their own villages, only a few succeed and hence the number of forebears who are recognised as *mukowa* ancestors is extremely limited. It can happen that an individual can affiliate himself with only one *mukowa* through his father and with only one *mukowa* through his mother. In that case, he has no choice of affiliation and his situation is no different than it was when descent was traced matrilineally. Usually, however, there is some choice and an individual can be affiliated through his father to either his father's mother's or father's father's *mukowa*, and through his mother either to the *mukowa* of his mother's mother or to that of his mother's father. If such a choice obtains, it is usually the place of residence of the individual's forebears that becomes decisive. If the individual's paternal grandmother resided virilocally in his father's natal village, the individual will affiliate himself with his father's father's *mukowa*. If, on the other hand, she resided uxorilocally in his father's natal village, the individual will affiliate himself with his father's mother's *mukowa*. Similarly, the residence of his maternal grandparents determines his affiliation to either his mother's mother's or his mother's father's *mukowa*.

The fact that only some of an individual's forebears are recognised as *mukowa* founders and that their place of residence determines to a great extent his actual *mukowa* affiliation, makes it possible for Ngwezi Toka to talk about an individual's *mukowa* membership in terms similar to those in which Toka in Guta and Cifokoboyo talk about it. The same factors also make it possible to distinguish an individual's affiliation with his father's father's, his father's mother's, his mother's father's and his mother's mother's *mukowa* in spite of the fact that, theoretically, an affiliation with more than four *mikowa* is possible.

An individual whose maternal *mukowa* is Munkombwe and whose paternal *mukowa* is Moono, refers to his membership of these two *mikowa* by saying *kuli bamaama ndili Munkombwe* (I am Munkombwe to my mother) and *kuli bataata ndili Moono* (I am Moono to my father). As in Guta and Cifokoboyo, through his two remaining grandparents he is linked to two other *mikowa*, of which he is a grandchild (*muzikulu*).

It is not only an individual's forebears' residence which affects his *mukowa* affiliation, but his own residence as well. Thus it will primarily depend on a person's own residence whether he will consider himself and be considered by others as a member of his father's or mother's *mukowa*. It is, for example, Thomas's (T1) cognatic descent from Simufunde's (R4) parent (Diagram 13) which substantiates his membership of *mukowa wa* Cileya, which is his maternal *mukowa* and a *mukowa* whose members are owners of the area in which his village is located. Had he lived in an area owned by the members of his paternal *mukowa*, he would most certainly not affiliate himself with the *mukowa wa* Cileya. Provided that a specific individual considers himself, and is considered by others, to be a member of a particular *mukowa*, his own descendants will also consider themselves in most cases to be members of that *mukowa*, irrespective of where they are actually living. In this way all Malumo's (T10) descendants (Diagram 13) consider themselves members of the *mukowa wa* Cileya, irrespective of whether or not they live in the four villages inhabited by its members. Their genealogical distance from Malumo (T10) is close enough to override their actual residence as the chief factor determining their affiliation. Thus, unlike in Guta and Cifokoboyo, in Ngwezi it is an individual's cognatic descent from a specific ancestor, and his own and his direct ascendants' actual place of residence, that jointly determine his *mukowa* affiliation.

Obviously, not all members of a cognatic *mukowa* can live in residential proximity; but the core of each *mukowa* is anchored in a specific village or area. For the members of this residential core, the choice of *mukowa* affiliation is virtually as firmly determined as it was traditionally when only descent in the matrilineal line counted. The choice is wider for those who live in settlements 'owned' by *mikowa* from whose founding ancestors they are not themselves descended in any line; given that the number of recognised *mikowa* is limited, even their choice of affiliation is substantially circumscribed (for a discussion of a similar limitation of the number of recognised cognatic descent groups by the number of established villages among the Goba, see Lancaster 1981: 276).

The territorial distribution of people not only determines to a great extent their *mukowa* affiliation. It is at the same time virtually the sole factor determining the relative importance of the attachment of every individual either to his *mukowa kuli banyina* (*mukowa* on the mother's side) or his *mukowa kuli baisi* (*mukowa* on the father's side). For, as in Guta and Cifokoboyo, every individual in Ngwezi claims membership of these two descent categories and thus recognises two sets of *basimukowa*: *basimukowa kuli banyina* and *basimukowa kuli baisi*. Both are not of equal importance to him and his knowledge of both his sets of *basimukowa* is, as a rule, not equally extensive. Whereas in Guta and Cifokoboyo the primary attachment of every individual is to his mother's *mukowa*, in Ngwezi the primary attachment can be either to his mother's or to his father's *mukowa*, with the attachment to the latter prevailing numerically over the attachment to the former.

The figures in Diagram 14 depict the paternal and maternal *mikowa* of three individuals as they themselves have conceptualised them. *Basimukowa* below the level of the informant's generation are omitted in the figures for simplicity. Even so, the figures clearly indicate that the range of people recognised as *basimukowa* on the father's and the mother's side is not equal and symmetrical. Whether an individual has a more extensive knowledge of the *basimukowa* on one side or the other, depends on whether he considers as primary his attachment to his father's or to his mother's *mukowa*.

Both Munkombwe's (Diagram 14, Fig. 1) and Siyamwaanja's (Fig. 2) primary attachment is to the *mikowa* of their fathers. When, for example, Munkombwe's daughter was to get married, it was Siciyako, the head of Munkombwe's and her daughter's *mukowa*, who was informed about the prospective marriage and whose formal approval of it was sought. Nobody from Kambole's *mukowa* was informed. While both Munkombwe and Siyamwaanja count the siblings of their grandparents and their descendants as members of their paternal *mikowa*, they recognise only their mothers' nearest kinsmen as their maternal *basimukowa*. The only distant maternal relative whom Siyamwaanja includes in the category of his *basimukowa* on his mother's side is the head of the *mukowa* himself.

Unlike Munkombwe's and Siyamwaanja's attachment, Donald's (Fig. 3)

The changing concept of the basimukowa

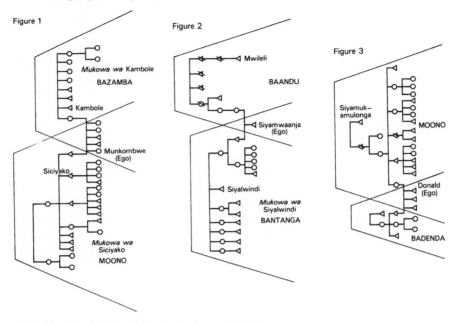

Diagram 14. Affiliation with the father's and mother's *mikowa*

primary affiliation is with his maternal *mukowa*. His knowledge of the *basimukowa* on his father's side is again considerably narrower than his knowledge of his maternal *basimukowa*. He does not even know who is the head of his paternal *mukowa*.

The factor determining an individual's primary attachment to either his paternal or his maternal *mukowa* is again his place of residence. Both Munkombwe and Siyamwaanja live in a village into which their mothers married and to a number of whose other inhabitants they are agnatically related. A number of their paternal *basimukowa* live in that village and most of the remaining people whom they count as their paternal *basimukowa* live in neighbouring villages. They are in daily face-to-face contact with most of them and they meet the others frequently. The people whom they recognise as their maternal *basimukowa* live mostly in their mother's natal villages, with whose inhabitants they have only infrequent contact. Similarly, all the people whom Congwe (U9) counts as his paternal *basimukowa* (Diagram 13) live in his own and in three neighbouring villages. Congwe's village is that in which his father was born and into which his mother married. She was of the Moono *mukowa*, which is Congwe's maternal *mukowa*. Most of its members live in the natal village of Congwe's mother. It is quite distant from Congwe's own village and his contact with his maternal *basimukowa* is very

128

infrequent. Donald (Diagram 14, Fig. 3), on the other hand, lives in his mother's natal village, in which his father lives in uxorilocal residence; to quite a number of its inhabitants he is related through ties of uterine kinship and he counts them and their own near kinsmen as members of his maternal *mukowa*. His father is from a different, quite distant, tribal area and most of his own kinsmen live there. Donald has hardly ever seen them.

In a situation in which residential affiliation is a chief factor affecting an individual's primary attachment to his *mukowa*, it can be expected that a change of residence will eventually be accompanied by a change of affiliation, or, alternatively, that the primary affiliation with one of the two *mikowa* will be altered to tally with the social composition of the area in which an individual lives without a change of residence necessarily being involved. Such a change of affiliation can simply involve stressing cognatic descent through one parent instead of the other. There is some indication that this is precisely what Malumo (T10) (Diagram 13) did. An important natural resource on the territory of Cileya's village are six pools in the Ngwezi river which are collectively fished every year towards the end of the dry season. The people from the whole Ngwezi area can take part in the fishing, which lasts for about two weeks, and every year about four hundred people do so. The fishing is organised by headman Cileya, who informs all other headmen in Ngwezi about its date. Headman Cileya possesses a medicine for chasing the crocodiles away from the pools and he ritually cleans every pool before it is fished. He receives a tithe from everybody's catch which he then shares with Chief Musokotwane. The members of Cileya's *mukowa* are exempt from the tithe as the pools are located in the territory of which they are the 'owners' and in this sense are their collective property.

There is a story according to which Malumo's father, Sibulo, as the possessor of the appropriate medicine, ritually cleaned the pools of crocodiles before they were fished. This would suggest that the pools were then not the property of the *mikowa wa* Cileya (Bancindu) but of Sibulo's *mukowa*. Sibulo had two wives, of whom Malumo's mother, Mwaandu (S7), of the Bancindu *mukowa*, was the senior one. He had a son, Mongolo, by his junior wife, who was older than Sibulo. The story goes that Sibulo, when he was very old, gave his medicine to Malumo (T10). Mongolo asked: 'I am your oldest son. Why did you give the medicine to Malumo instead of me?' Sibulo replied: 'Your mother was not related to Cileya; that is why I gave the medicine to Malumo.'

This story might be taken as an explanation of how the control of the pools passed from one *mukowa* to another. The transfer was achieved through Malumo (T10), the organiser of the collective fishing and the possessor of crocodile medicine, claiming his primary attachment, not to his paternal *mukowa*, in which the control of the pools had been hitherto vested, but to his maternal *mukowa* whose members were in the majority in the area. It was thus ultimately through the shift in Malumo's *mukowa* allegiance that the change in the control over the pools was accomplished. Malumo's descendants nowadays trace their *mukowa* membership through his mother, Mwaandu (S7), without having any idea what Sibulo's *mukowa* affiliation could have been.

As a result of similar adjustments in *mukowa* affiliation, as well as of the residential patterns discussed before, the primary attachment of a considerable number of men in Ngwezi is to the *mukowa* of the head of their hamlet. Of the 194 married, divorced and widowed men in the twelve villages in Ngwezi in which I carried out my census, 73 (37.6%) were members of their hamlet head's *mukowa*. For 40 of them this was their paternal *mukowa* and for 21 their maternal *mukowa*. Twelve men shared the same paternal and maternal *mukowa* with the head of their hamlet. As in Guta and Cifokoboyo, it is again the high incidence of uxorilocal residence which prevents the villages in Ngwezi from consisting predominantly of the male members of one *mukowa*. Out of the 194, 44 men (22.7%) were married to women of a hamlet head's *mukowa* and resided uxorilocally in their villages. The remaining 77 (39.6%) were members of other *mikowa* than their hamlet head's, and their wives were not affiliated to their hamlet head's *mukowa*.

6

Mukowa and ritual

In spite of the frequent fission of villages and the perpetual emergence of new hamlets, it is not unusual for a large hamlet to be inhabited by members of a *mukowa* three or four generations deep. The core of the inhabitants of the headman's hamlet in Mujalanyana (Diagram 11) consists of cognatic descendants of Cabakani (M2) who consider themselves to be members of his *mukowa*, Cabakani (M2) being an ancestor three generations removed from the youngest adult generation of the inhabitants of the hamlet. Equally, with the exception of Godfrey, the inhabitants of Kawayo's hamlet in Mujalanyana (Diagram 11) are all cognatic descendants of Mukakongo (M5) and they all consider themselves to be members of the *mukowa* of which she is the apical ancestress. Mukakongo (M5) is again three generations removed from the youngest adult generation of the inhabitants of the hamlet. Most of the inhabitants of the headman's hamlet in Mujala Mupati (Diagram 10) are cognatic descendants of Munkombwe (L1) and consider themselves to be members of the *mukowa* of which she is the apical ancestress; Munkombwe (L1) is four generations removed from the youngest adult generation of the inhabitants of the hamlet.

It has been mentioned in Chapter 4 that hamlet boundaries represent important and significant cleavages in the field of social interaction and everyday face-to-face contact between individuals. In spite of this, the boundaries of recognised *mukowa* categories do not coincide with hamlet boundaries. The *mukowa* is a category which, from the point of view of any individual Toka, does not contain only those members of his hamlet or village who trace their descent cognatically from the same ancestor as he does, but also numerous other individuals outside his own settlement. The awareness of common *mukowa* membership across hamlet and village boundaries manifests itself in two ways. First, people are aware that they and other inhabitants of their hamlet who are cognatic descendants of the same ancestor, are at the same time members of a *mukowa* of a wider span and genealogical depth than that of which this ancestor is the apex. In this sense, there is an awareness of the majority of the inhabitants of Mujala Mupati and Mujalanyana sharing membership of the *mukowa* of six generations' depth of which Siyamate (K1), the founder of Mujala village, is the apical ancestor. Secondly, people are aware that not only inhabitants of their hamlet who are cognatically descended from the same ancestor are members of their *mukowa*, but also many other people who live in other hamlets, villages, or areas of the tribal territory.

These notions exist only because they have a bearing on specific actions. At the same time, it is only through being invoked in specific actions that they emerge and maintain their existence. Two interactional situations are in this respect significant in relation to the two ways in which the awareness of common *mukowa* membership across hamlet and village boundaries manifests itself: the rain-making rituals and the final mourning ceremonies. In this chapter I discuss how the awareness of membership of a *mukowa* of a wider generational depth and span than the immediate *mukowa* segment localised in a given hamlet or village is maintained through the performance of the rain ritual.

I used the example of the *mukowa wa* Cileya (Diagram 13), known also as Bancindu, of which it is held to be a subdivision, to illustrate how the *mukowa* is conceptualised in Ngwezi in contrast to Guta and Cifokoboyo. The core of the Bancindu live in the western part of the Ngwezi area. Cileya, the oldest village there, was founded by Simufunde (R4; Diagram 15), who was born in his mother's brother's village in the Nyawa chieftainship. Probably some time at the beginning of this century, Simufunde left his natal village, together with his brother, Manyepa (R1), some descendants of his two other brothers, Kuname (R3) and Simwingani (R2), and his paternal half-brother, Siyabemba, and founded his own village in the western part of the Ngwezi area in a place called Mulele. He was referred to as *maleya wa kaleya siminziakwe* (one who deserted his mother's brother) and from his nickname derives the name of the village (Cileya) and the honorific title of its headman. Simufunde (R4) and his brother (R1) both died in Mulele and are buried there. Simufunde was succeeded as headman by his daughter's son, Malumo (T10), who moved the village to its present site some 4 km west of Mulele in 1933. Three villages split from Cileya during Malumo's time.

The first is Mangulwani, which is situated about 3 km south-east of Cileya and was founded some time in the late 1920s by Mangulwani (T7), the son of Mulombwe (S6), and a woman who was brought as a slave to Cileya's village. The second headman of the village was Mangulwani's son, who, after his death in 1966, was succeeded by his younger brother, who had been living in another village and, at the time of my fieldwork, had not taken up residence in Mangulwani as was generally expected of him. An overwhelming majority of the inhabitants of Mangulwani consist of the descendants of Mangulwani's father, Mulombwe (S6), the descendants of Simufunde's and Manyepa's brother, Kuname (R3), and the descendants of Malumo's sister, Mudenda (T9).

Mukowa *and ritual*

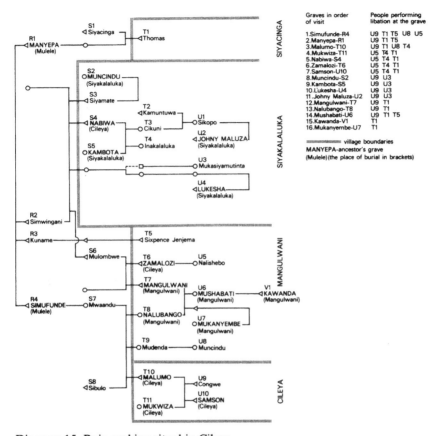

Diagram 15. Rain-making ritual in Cileya

Another village which split off from Cileya is Siyacinga, situated about 2 km south-west of Cileya. Its founder was Siyacinga (S1), who married Manyepa's (R1) daughter, and before founding his own village had been living uxorilocally in Cileya. After Siyacinga's death his son, Thomas (T1), succeeded to the headmanship of the village, the core of whose inhabitants is formed by descendants of Manyepa's daughter.

The last village to split off from Cileya was Siyakalaluka, situated about 1 km south of Cileya and founded by its present headman, Kamuntuwa (T2). He is a Lozi who married Nabiwa's daughter, Cikuni (T3), from Cileya, and had been living uxorilocally in her village before founding his own. Most inhabitants of his village are his wife's kinsmen: cognatic descendants of her paternal grandfather, Simwingani (R2).

133

Mukowa *and ritual*

The inhabitants of the four villages participate in a common rain-making ritual whose principal organiser is Congwe (U9), the present headman of Cileya and the *mupati* of the Bancindu *mukowa*. The ritual is clearly conceptualised as that of the Bancindu.

Below I give a description of the ritual as performed in December 1971 when a prolonged drought after the first onset of rains seriously threatened the planted crops (Diagram 15).

The day before the ritual, a shrine (*kasanza*) of peeled sticks was built in Cileya's village and at night people danced around it till about midnight. At dawn the next day people started bringing seeds from every house in the village, which were put into a gourd and into two pans placed on the *kasanza*. Hoes, axes and spears were also placed on it.

Unlike in Guta, no libation was performed at the *kasanza* in the morning. The people from Mangulwani, Siyakalaluka and Siyacinga assembled in Cileya, and the ritual was started by Congwe (U9) leading the procession to Mulele, the original site of Cileya's village, where Simufunde (R4) and Manyepa (R1) are buried. The march was accompanied by singing special songs. In Mulele, Congwe (U9) poured a libation of water, beer and milk at Simufunde's (R4) grave. As in Guta and Cifokoboyo, all libations were accompanied by incantations asking for rain.

During this and other libations, the people sat down on the ground and slowly clapped their hands rhythmically. This was occasionally accompanied by the beat of a drum. After Congwe (U9), Thomas (T1) poured a libation and made an offering of snuff on Simufunde's grave; he was followed in turn by Muncindu (U8).

The libation at Simufunde's grave was followed by a song, as were the libations to all the prominent ancestors.[1] When singing, the participants in the ritual occasionally looked up and moved their hands and arms in a way depicting the pulling of rain from the sky.

From Simufunde's grave, the procession moved to Manyepa's (R1) grave, marked by a big stone, where Congwe (U9) was again the first one to pour a libation of water and beer. He was again followed by Thomas (T1), who was in turn followed by Sixpence Jenjema (T5).

After several songs had been sung, the procession moved from the graves to a large baobab tree which used to stand in the middle of Cileya's original village. Those who had lived there used to perform libations and offerings to their own forebears at this tree. It is a shrine to which the ancestral spirits come to drink the offerings. Congwe (U9) and Muncindu (U8) made a libation at the tree, pouring water and beer into a large opening in its trunk.

From the baobab tree the procession moved back to another tree growing at a place where women from the original village used to gather to perform their domestic tasks.[2] Only Muncindu (U8) and Nalishebo (U5) made a libation at this tree.

134

Mukowa *and ritual*

On the way back from Mulele to Cileya, the procession passed through the village founded by Bandama, the son of Malumo's (T10) sister, Mukatundwe. A rain-making ritual was also being held there that day and people were singing and dancing round a shrine. The procession joined them for a while in song and dance. Moono, from Mangulwani, one of the women participating in the ritual led by Congwe (U9), poured water on the shrine. For her the libation was justified by the fact that Mukatundwe, the mother of the founder of Bandama's village, was her 'grandmother' (her FMZ). But Congwe (U9) told her that she should not have done it, as the ancestors honoured at the shrine were not Bancindu as was Mukatundwe and the other people participating in the ritual led by him. He did not think that the ancestors would punish anyone because of this mistake but they would laugh and would think that people were stupid not to know who their ancestors were and to offer libations indiscriminately to everybody everywhere. He thought that this might offend them and that they would then not respond to the libations offered to them.

The Toka believe that the ancestors know their descendants better than the latter remember their ancestors. But the ancestors do not like to be forgotten or neglected by their descendants. If people other than the *mukowa* members should pour libations to the *mukowa* ancestor, or if the *mukowa* members should pour libations to those who were not their own ancestors, the ancestors would take this as an indication of their descendants being confused about their ancestry. They would feel that their descendants did not really care about them (because if they did they would know better) and they would be likely to withhold their powers over rain.

The incident in Bandama clearly indicates that the rain-making ritual is conceptualised in *mukowa* terms. It also indicates that, although the *mikowa* in Ngwezi are conceptualised as discrete units, as are the descent categories in Guta and Cifokoboyo, their boundaries are blurred to a much greater extent by existing ambiguities and are consequently open to different, and in a way easier, manipulation. I shall return to this point later.

From Bandama the procession continued back to Cileya, stopping first at the graves near this village. The most important grave there is that of Malumo (T10), who succeeded Simufunde (R4) as the village headman and the head of the *mukowa*. Congwe (U9), Thomas (T1), Muncindu (U8) and Inakalaluka (T4) poured libations on his grave. This was followed, as were all libations to prominent ancestors, by a dance on the grave immediately around the offering. At times people danced on their knees and put their hands on the ground with their palms up. This is part of the request for the ground not to be hard but soft from the rain. When dancing, people also spewed water and beer out of their mouths to the left and right, imitating the falling rain. In the same way they also sprinkled water on each other.

After the libation at Malumo's grave, Nalishebo (U5) and Inakalaluka (T4)

135

Mukowa *and ritual*

poured water and Thomas (T1) poured beer on other graves in Cileya – those of Malumo's wife, Mukwiza (T11), Nabiwa (S4), Zamalozi (T6), Samson (U10), and a few other people whom nobody was able to identify any longer.

From here the procession returned to the village itself, where beer and water were poured on the *kasanza*. The libation was followed by prolonged singing and dancing round the *kasanza*, after which the procession, again led by Congwe (U9), set out on the way to Siyakalaluka. There, Congwe (U9) and Mukasiyamutinta (U3) performed libations on the graves of Muncindu (S2), Kambota (S5), Lukesha (U4) and Johny Maluza (U2). Mukasiyamutinta (U3) and Inakalaluka (T4) then poured water and beer very casually on three other graves. From here the procession went to the village of Siyakaluka itself and people danced and sang in front of Kamuntuwa's (T2) house. Water was poured on its roof in imitation of the falling rain and people poured water on each other's heads.

From Siyakalaluka, the procession went to the graves near the village of Mangulwani. The first grave there, on which a libation was poured, was that of Mangulwani (T7), the founder of the village, and this offering was followed by one at the grave of his wife, Nalubango (T8). Congwe (U9), Thomas (T1) and Sixpence Jenjema (T5) then performed libations on the grave of Mushabati (U6), and afterwards Thomas (T1) poured water on the graves of Kawanda (V1) and Mukanyembe (U7).

From the graves the procession went to the village of Mangulwani, where the ritual ended with dancing around the *kasanza*, over which water and beer was poured and under which was placed a branch of the *munga* shrub cut in Mulele and pulled into the village. Branches of this shrub are a rain-medicine, *kaunga mayoba*. They are pulled from the grave into the village to make sure that the rain will not fall only on the grave where the libation was made, but will be carried from it into the village.

As in Guta and Cifokoboyo, it is through the performance of its own rain-making ritual that a *mukowa* in Ngwezi becomes recognised as such and gains and maintains its own identity in relation to other *mikowa*. The successful manipulation of their kinship ties by politically enterprising men in their effort to achieve village headmanship, leads to the perpetual fission of existing villages and the emergence of new settlements. As a rule, the core of the inhabitants of each settlement is formed by the descendants of an ancestor or ancestors who are genealogically nearer to the living people than is the apical ancestor of the *mukowa*. Thus the core of the inhabitants of Cileya's village, after Mangulwani, Siyakalaluka and Siyacinga have split from it, is formed by the cognatic descendants of Malumo (T10). The majority of people living in Siyacinga are descended from Simufunde's brother Manyepa (R1), the majority of people living in Siyakalaluka are descended from Simwingani (R2), another of Simufunde's brothers, while most of the inhabitants of Mangulwani are descended either from

136

Mukowa *and ritual*

Simwingani's son, Mulombwe (S6), or from Malumo's sister, Mudenda (T9), or from Simufunde's brother, Kuname (R3), with the descendants of Mulombwe (S6) being clearly dominant both in the sense of being numerically the strongest and in the sense of holding the village headmanship. In strictly genealogical terms, the descendants of Malumo (T10), Manyepa (R1), Simwingani (R2) and Mulombwe (S6) represent segments of the Bancindu, the Bancindu being conceptualised as cognatic descendants of Simufunde's (R4) parent. With regard to those segments, the significance of village fission is that it spatially isolates them and thus gives them their very existence. It is only through the process of village fission that each segment gains its identity in relation to another segment of the *mukowa*.

Congwe (U9), Thomas (T1), Inakalaluka (T4), Nalishebo (U5), Muncindu (U8) and Sixpence Jenjema (T5) took a much more prominent part in the Bancindu rain-making ritual than anybody else: they were the most important people who performed the libations, particularly at the graves of the prominent ancestors of the *mukowa*. Taking into account the position of these people in the Bancindu genealogy, it would be possible to analyse the ritual as a manifestation in action of the internally divided *mukowa*. This could be seen as neatly expressed in libations offered at the graves of Simufunde (R4) and Manyepa (R1), the two most important Bancindu ancestors buried in Mulele, and in libations offered at the shrine there. Assuming that Congwe (U9), apart from being the head of the *mukowa*, acted as a representative of Malumo's (T10) segment, and that Thomas (T1) acted as a representative of Manyepa's (R1) segment, Sixpence Jenjema (T5) as a representative of Kuname's (R3) segment, Nalishebo (U5) as a representative of Mulombwe's (S6) segment and Muncindu (U8) as a representative of Mudenda's (T9) segment, the unity of the Bancindu could be seen as symbolically enacted through all the segments participating in a joint ritual, clearly conceptualised as that of the Bancindu as a whole. Some sort of segmentary model of the *mukowa* would result. For the picture to be complete, Inakalaluka (T4) would have to have taken part in the libations in Mulele. She told me that had it not been for the fact that she was late and joined the procession only when it was back on its way to Cileya, she would have done this. The segmentary model of the *mukowa* could then represent the segments localised in the hamlets and villages of which their members are the 'owners', thus expressing their independence *vis-à-vis* other segments of the *mukowa* in the sphere of political relations, while the unity of the whole *mukowa* is expressed in its ritual.

Such an interpretation of the role of the *mukowa* in political and ritual action would, however, be defective if it ascribed to the concept of the segment an importance which it does not have in reality as it is known and experienced by the Toka. They do not conceive of someone performing a libation during the rain-making ritual as a representative of a specific segment of the *mukowa*. To perform libations to ancestors is the prerogative of the senior members of the *mukowa*, their seniority being defined in terms of their age as well as in terms of their genealogical position. Most libations at the graves of the Bancindu ancestors were performed by Congwe (U9), Thomas (T1), Nalishebo (U5) and Inakalaluka (T4). They are all senior members of the *mukowa*; all of them performed libations at the graves of the prominent ancestors (or would have done so, had they not been late in coming as Inakalaluka (T4) was) like Simufunde (R4), Manyepa (R1) or Malumo (T10), the head of the *mukowa* preceding Congwe (U9). This they did, not only because of their seniority (many less senior members of the *mukowa* like Muncindu (U8), Sixpence Jenjema (T5) or Mukasiyamutinta (U3), abstained from performing libations on many graves), but also because they acted at the same time as representatives of the four villages jointly participating in the ritual. It is normally men who act as such representatives. Thus Thomas (T1), the headman of Siyacinga, was the main representative of his village, and Congwe (U9), apart from being the main organiser of the ritual as the head of the *mukowa* acted at the same time as the representative of Cileya. As I mentioned before, the village of Mangulwani was without a resident headman at the time and Nalishebo (U5), the genealogically senior member of the Bancindu in Mangulwani, acted as their main representative. At times she shared this role with Muncindu (U8), another woman from Mangulwani whose genealogical position in the Bancindu *mukowa* is equivalent to that of Nalishebo (U5). The situation in Siyakalaluka was different. The village was started by Kamuntuwa (T2) with the support of the various kinsmen of his wife, who form the majority of its present inhabitants. Although Kamuntuwa (T2) is recognised as the village headman and its political representative, he is not of the Bancindu *mukowa* and cannot perform libations and offerings to its ancestors. During the ritual, it was Inakalaluka (T4), the elder sister of Kamuntuwa's wife, Cikuni (T3), who acted as the main representative of the village. Mukasiyamutinta (U3) is in a genealogically similar position to that of Inakalaluka (T4); she is, however, younger than Inakalaluka (T4), so the libations to prominent ancestors of the Bancindu were left for the latter to perform. It is generally expected that Kamuntuwa's son will succeed him as headman in Siyakalaluka. Being a member of the Bancindu *mukowa*, he will be able, unlike his father, to act as the representative of Siyakalaluka in the ritual sphere, particularly should his mother and her elder sister be dead by then.

The Toka recognise a distinct connection between the *mukowa* and the territory in which its members first settled and in which the *mukowa* ancestors are buried. It can either be the territory of a single village or a territory comprising several villages which, as a rule, are offshoots of one single village. The connection between the *mukowa* and its territory is a crucial element in the Toka cognitive picture of the rain-making ritual.

Mukowa *and ritual*

The Toka conceptualise the *mukowa* as a community of the living and the dead who are all 'owners' of the territory with which they are associated. This notion is clearly expressed in Congwe's (U9) and Thomas's (T1) incantations during the libations on Manyepa's (R1) grave:

Manyepa, here is water. This is your country. Do not fear these people; even if the UNIP rules[3] do not fear. It is your country. What we want is water; we want rain. Because UNIP cannot give us rain, we pray to you, our ancestors. You ask God to give us rain. We are asking this through someone who is ruling the country. You give us power today. We have come to you today to ask for the rain from God through you. We do not want someone to cause us to forget you. We do not want to be cheated by the people saying that there are no *mizimu*.[4] We know that there are *mizimu* and we do not want to be stopped by anybody. Then lead us to know our *mizimu*. If we do not have rain, we shall not be able to keep cattle and we shall not be able to plough. When you left us, you left us with rain. Thus we do not know why the rain is giving us trouble. This is why we have come for the libations. Do not forget us. We are also keeping people as you were keeping them.[5]

Sure do not say bad things to us [i.e. do not reject us]. Here is plenty of beer for you. We have come because we want to pour beer on you. Do you not want us to have water in order that we can plough and drink? Do you want us to die from hunger? If you want beer, here is beer and water. We pour on you because you are hot. This will make you feel cold. We want water today. You give us water in order that each one of us can know that you are the owners of the land and people will think that we are also the owners of the land. We ask God through you. If the rain comes, people will think that we are liked by you, our ancestors. They will know that we are the true men of the soil. I am praying to you that the rain should rain continuously for two days. Then we will dress in *milamba*.[6] Pray to the one who gives good things to the people.[7]

The ancestors do not have power over rain everywhere but only in the territory of which they are the owners, provided that their association with it has been maintained after their deaths through their being buried there. For this reason, the spouses of the Bancindu ancestors, although buried in Cileya, Mangulwani, Siyakalaluka, or Siyacinga, have no power over rain there. Equally, they do not have power over rain in the villages of which their own *mikowa* are the owners, for their association with them has been interrupted by their being buried in Bancindu villages. By the same token, the Bancindu ancestors buried elsewhere than in Mulele, Cileya and the neighbouring villages which split off from Cileya, have no power over rain anywhere. It is from the uninterrupted association of the *mukowa* with the land that the power of the *mukowa* ancestors over rain derives. And it is the length of this uninterrupted association which defines the degree of power of each particular ancestor. The more generations removed he is from the living members of the *mukowa*, the greater are his powers. The connection of ancestors with land does not bring rain in itself, but only when it is sustained by the actions of their living descendants, who, by pouring libations to them, indicate that they are aware of this connection.

Naturally, not only the members of the *mukowa* which owns a specific territory profit from the rain sent by the *mukowa* ancestors, but all the people who live in that territory; they too need and want rain. For this reason it is not only the members of the *mukowa* who take part in the rain-making ritual, which is conceptualised as a *mukowa* affair, but all the inhabitants of the territory. Those who are not members of the *mukowa* performing the ritual, bring their seeds and implements to the shrine built in their village and take an active part in all the singing and dancing. The rain-medicine (*kaunga mayoba*) is placed under the shrine of each village to ensure that every village gets the rain. Although all the inhabitants of the territory take part in the ritual in this way, it is only the *mukowa* members who can perform libations at the graves of the ancestors.

The ancestors do not act singly, but as an undifferentiated body. Although they are approached individually at particular graves, it is perpetually made clear that people are not addressing their request only to the particular ancestor at whose grave they are performing the libation at that moment. In the incantations, frequent requests are made to an ancestor to summon all others to come and share in the offering. The libations are made to all the ancestors as a body and are meant to be shared by all of them alike.

Besides being approached directly, the *mukowa* ancestors can also be approached through their spouses. Thus, in the Bancindu rain-making ritual, libations were performed at the graves of Mukwiza (T11), Muncindu (S2), Kambota (S5), Lukesha (U4), Johny Maluza (U2) and Mukanyembe (U7). None of these was of the Bancindu *mukowa* but all were married to Bancindu. Unlike the Bancindu ancestors, they cannot produce rain in the territory in which they are buried for they are not its 'owners', but they can exert their influence on the Bancindu with whom they were associated during their lifetime and whose descendants they bore or fathered, and in the libations offered to them they are requested to do so:

Give us water, Muncindu [S2], we want heavy rain. You will see us people who remained on the earth. Give us water. We want water, Muncindu. Go to those who died and ask for water. Here is beer; we want maize, we want food; we want food and grazing for our cattle. Muncindu, go and tell your husband. Come all of you with your husbands and drink.

Although it is not the apical ancestor of the *mukowa* alone who produces, or is instrumental in producing, rain, but all of them as a body, and although they can be approached through any one of their number and even through their spouses, it is not sufficient to approach the apical ancestor or the prominent ancestors of the *mukowa* through only those who are genealogically their juniors. They have to be approached directly lest they would feel offended and would not use their powers. One informant metaphorically explained this by saying: 'The chief can summon the headman but a headman cannot summon the chief.' This is the reason why every rain ritual starts with libations to the apical ancestor and other prominent ancestors of the *mukowa*, and why the ritual would be thought ineffective if they were not approached directly through libations on their graves.

The internal division of the *mukowa* into segments plays no part in the conceptualisation of the relations between the ancestors, their living descendants, and the land of which both the dead and the living members of the *mukowa* are owners. This is not to say, however, that the *mukowa* segment, which can be distinguished analytically, is not part of the Toka notions. The relation between the *mukowa* and a specific territory is a crucial element not only in the Toka conceptualisation of the rain-making ritual, but also in their conceptualisation of the *mukowa* as such. The *mukowa* for them is not simply people cognatically descended from any ancestor who is sufficiently removed, but only people descended from that ancestor or ancestors who have the power to provide rain. They are aware that a *mukowa* segment, or a branch of the *mukowa* localised in its own settlement, as they themselves put it, is the nucleus of a potential new *mukowa*. They see the new *mikowa* as coming into being through the process of village fission, which spatially separates the segments, some of which then acquire the status of new independent *mikowa*. This happens when a segment has been associated for several generations with a particular locality, so that its ancestors can provide rain, and when its members start to perform their own rain-making ritual.

Just as village fission is not an automatic process simply put into motion when the settlement reaches a certain size, it is the same with the emergence of a new *mukowa*. Both processes are instigated by ambitious men manipulating the existing relations to their own personal advantage. Similarly, just as village headmanship is endowed with prestige and is sought by most men who think that they have a chance to achieve it, so is the headship of a *mukowa*. Parallels between these two positions can be extended yet further. To succeed to the headmanship of an established big village is always seen as preferable to establishing one's own new village; for those who, however, fail to succeed to an existing headmanship, founding their own village or even hamlet is preferable to forfeiting their ambitions for ever. Equally, to succeed to the position of the head of an existing *mukowa*, which performs its own rain-making ritual, is definitely preferable to starting a new *mukowa* and becoming its first head. But again, failing the former, to become recognised as the head of any *mukowa* is preferable to forfeiting all hopes of ever being a leader of a rain-making ritual. Like the fission of villages, the fission of *mikowa* is also instigated by enterprising men who manipulate their kinship ties to achieve a desired status for themselves; unlike in Guta and Cifokoboyo, it is not only ties of uterine kinship, but ties of cognatic kinship as well which can be skilfully manipulated. This gives a specific form to the process of *mukowa* fission in Ngwezi and in its turn ultimately enables the *mikowa* to be conceptualised for all practical purposes as exclusive categories in spite of the fact that, due to their cognatic nature, they cannot by definition be exclusive.

On his mother's side, Lubinda (U14) is a member of the *mukowa wa* Cileya (Bancindu; see Diagram 13) and his membership is recognised by Congwe (U9) and other members of the *mukowa*. Lubinda (U14) is the headman of his own village, Siciyako, which is located on the Ngwezi river, almost 30 km west of Cileya's village. It was founded by his father, Munjila, whom Lubinda succeeded as headman in the early 1940s. The village had moved its site several times before it moved to its present location in 1933. It was the first village built there and since then four other villages have been established nearby with the permission of the headman of Siciyako. By virtue of this fact he has the status of a senior headman in relation to the headmen of the other four villages. During the lifetime of Malumo (T10), the head of the *mukowa wa* Cileya who preceded Congwe (U9), Lubinda (U14) used to attend the rain-making rituals in Cileya and there poured libations to the Bancindu ancestors before pouring libations to Munjila in Siciyako. When Malumo (T10) died, Lubinda (U14) was already a headman and he could not have succeeded to the headmanship in Cileya. Being a descendant of Simufunde (R4), he could, however, have inherited Simufunde's *muzimu*, held by Malumo (T10), and become the head of the *mukowa wa* Cileya. This is, in fact, what he was bidding for. His idea, for which he tried to gain support, was that one of Mwaandu's (S7), Moono's (S9) or Malumo's (T10) descendants could succeed to Malumo's name and to the village headmanship while he should succeed to Simufunde's (R4) name and to the headship of the *mukowa*. He was convinced that, being matrilineally descended from Simufunde (R4), he was better qualified to become the head of the *mukowa* than Congwe (U9), who traces his membership through his father.[8] He is also older than Congwe (U9), which according to him should have given him preference. But his plans were effectively frustrated by other members of the *mukowa wa* Cileya. When a final mourning ceremony for Malumo was to be held, Lubinda (U14) and Moono's (S9) other descendants were not informed about it. It was Congwe's paternal half-brother, Nongolo, who had the main say in suggesting Congwe (U9) as Malumo's successor, to both Malumo's (T10) and Simufunde's (R4) names. According to Lubinda (U14), the ownership of the pools in Ngwezi river (see p. 129) was Nongolo's main consideration in making this suggestion. Sibulo (S8), the father of Nongolo and Malumo (T10), passed his crocodile medicine to Malumo (T10), who in this way gained control over the pools. Nongolo, when suggesting Congwe (U9) as Malumo's successor, hoped that Congwe (U9) would share the fish from the pools with him.

Congwe (U9) himself denies that Lubinda (U14), and Moono's (S9) other descendants, were not informed about the final mourning ceremony for Malumo (T10): all Bancindu were informed. According to him, Lubinda

(U14), had he been living in Cileya, could have succeeded Malumo (T10). But because he was living in his own village, which is far away from Cileya, nobody even considered his succession; it was not practical: a head of the *mukowa* who lives far away from the *mukowa* members is not of much use to them.

There is no need to reconstruct the events surrounding Malumo's death and Congwe's succession to his position. What is significant about them for our present discussion is that Lubinda (U14) tried to achieve the position of the head of the *mukowa wa* Cileya, and when he failed he opted for the best alternative left open to him. Since Congwe (U9) succeeded Malumo (T10) as the headman of Cileya village and the head of the *mukowa wa* Cileya, Lubinda (U14) has not attended any rain-making ritual in Cileya. Since then, he has performed his own ritual in Siciyako, of which the main part is the pouring of a libation on the grave of his father, Munjila. No Bancindu ancestors are mentioned in his ritual. In the incantation accompanying the libation to his father during one rain-making ceremony, Lubinda (U14) only asked Munjila to call his sons and to invite all his people who were buried with him to share in the drink. Mwali, Lubinda's FZDD, who poured a libation on Munjila's grave after Lubinda had done so, asked Munjila to call everyone, his sisters, brothers, sons and daughters, to come and share in the drinks of water, beer and milk; she also asked him to bring his wife and mother as they should also come and drink with him.

These references indicate that the libations at the graves in Siciyako are conceptualised as libations to Munjila, Lubinda's father, and to other ancestors of a descent category which is referred to by Lubinda (U14) and other people in his village as *mukowa wa* Siciyako. Although Lubinda's mother, Bene (T12), is buried in Siciyako, Lubinda (U14) does not pour libations on her grave. She is of the Bancindu *mukowa* and one of Lubinda's aims is to sever any links with this *mukowa*. He obviously feels that a libation on her grave might jeopardise his aim. It is his father, Munjila, who is instrumental in conceptualising Lubinda's *mukowa* as the *mukowa wa* Siciyako, and for this reason Lubinda makes offerings only at his grave. After one such offering, a discussion followed about what should be done with the beer that remained and one woman suggested that they should pour it on all the graves. Lubinda declared: 'Anyone of you can pour on any other graves. Thank you, father, I have nothing else to ask you.'

Refraining from pouring libations at his mother's grave is in line with Lubinda's overall underplaying of his membership of the *mukowa wa* Cileya. He consistently does not activate it in any way. This necessarily involves a neglect on his part of his maternal *basimukowa*, which the Toka normally view with disapproval. Lubinda is, however, able to refute any possible resentment against him and to present Congwe (U9) as the man responsible for the severing of his relations with the Bancindu *mukowa*. Lubinda's legs are partly paralysed and he walks with the utmost difficulty. It is impossible for him to go to Cileya, where most of his maternal *basimukowa* live, and it should be up to Congwe (U9) to come and see him when the need arises. But he never does, for, as Lubinda says, he is too concerned with his own ambitions and the only thing he wants is to be a big chief. And when it comes to any dealings with him they are anyhow pointless, as Lubinda readily demonstrates by reference to various previous encounters, mostly concerning their joint hearing of cases.

Lubinda's strategy is not only aimed at severing his relations with his maternal *mukowa* and establishing primary affiliation with his paternal *mukowa* for himself and other people in his village. His main goal is to establish the *mukowa wa* Siciyako as an independent *mukowa* in its own right, of which he himself is the head. To be a *mukowa* head is important for him for maintaining and substantiating his status as a senior headman, which derives from the fact that his ancestors were the first to settle in the area in which his village is located. By performing his own rain-making ritual at the graves of his ancestors buried there, Lubinda effectively demonstrates the long-lasting connection of his ancestors with the area. Were he not able to perform his own ritual, and were he to depend on the head of the *mukowa* living in the area where the Siciyako village was formerly located to officiate, his claim to the antiquity of his village on its present site would become questionable.

I mentioned before that the Toka consider it important for the apical ancestor and other prominent ancestors of the *mukowa* to be as many generations removed from the living members of the *mukowa* as possible, because the ancestors' powers over rain increase with the length of their association with the territory of which they and the living members of their *mukowa* are the owners. It is not, however, this notion itself which determines the time when the members of a *mukowa* resident in a particular village will start to consider themselves a *mukowa* independent of that of which they have hitherto been a part. In other words, a new *mukowa* does not automatically come into being when an ancestor, buried in the village in which his descendants are domiciled, is considered sufficiently removed from his living descendants to be able to apply effectively his powers over rain.

The ascendants of at least one parent of the village headman are, as a rule, well remembered. They are the ancestors who are usually thought to be the most important ones in producing rain. If they are buried, not in the headman's own village, but in that from which it originated, libations have to be poured on their graves by the head of the *mukowa* on behalf of its members resident in the break-away village.

Mujalanyana village (Diagram 10) was started, as I mentioned before, by Naamu (N22), the son of Cabakani, the headman of Mujala. When Naamu (N22) died, he was succeeded as headman of Mujalanyana by his younger brother, Ilumbela (N14). Ilumbela and a number of people in Mujalanyana consider themselves to be members of Cabakani's (M2) *mukowa*. Its head is, however, not Ilumbela but Kandela (N36), the present headman of Mujala Mupati, who succeeded to Cabakani's name. When Ilumbela (N14) is due to perform a rain-making ritual in Mujalanyana, women in the village brew beer, which is first taken to Majala Mupati. There, Kandela (N36) pours it on the graves of Cabakani (M2) and other ancestors of his *mukowa* buried there. Only then does Ilumbela (N14) pour libations on the graves of Naamu (N22) and other people buried in Mujalanyana.

Unlike Ilumbela's father, Cabakani, Lubinda's father, Munjila, is buried in the present-day Siciyako village of which he was a founder. The present headman's father is usually not considered sufficiently far removed from the living members of his *mukowa* to be able to bring rain alone without libations being poured to his ascendants. Lubinda, however, unlike Ilumbela, does not officiate at a rain-making ritual only after the headman of the village from which Siciyako had originated, has performed libations to the ancestors on behalf of the members of his *mukowa* resident in Siciyako. If he did, he would be denying the status he claims, that of head of the *mukowa wa* Siciyako. The origin of Siciyako village and the ancestors of Munjila are, however, still well enough remembered to necessitate the justification of Lubinda's action. At one rain-making ritual in Siciyako, Mwali, Lubinda's FZDD, when pouring a libation on Munjila's grave, justified the fact that no offerings were made to other ancestors by pointing out Lubinda's inability to walk:

All in Zuka [the area from where the village of Siciyako originated] should come together to drink, to smoke, to send away [misfortune]. You who founded the village here, you the big one here. Because to Zuka is very far. Siciyako has no legs to walk. This is why we pour libation to you here.

It is not necessary for the headman himself to approach the head of his *mukowa* with a request to pour libations to the ancestors (cf. Ilumbela's behaviour). In spite of this, the fact that Lubinda's legs were paralysed is used to present his behaviour, not as a deliberate action which is part of his strategy of establishing himself as the head of his own *mukowa* but as something which is forced upon him by circumstances over which he has no control. Although the fission of the *mukowa* is tacitly recognised, it is presented as something which Lubinda did not intend.

As in Guta and Cifokoboyo, the fission of a *mukowa* in Ngwezi can also be seen as complete when the *mukowa* segment starts to perform its own rain-making ritual. However, the fact that in Ngwezi the *mukowa* is conceptualised as a cognatic descent category lends to its fission certain characteristics that this process lacks in Guta and Cifokoboyo.

In the latter areas, the status of every *mukowa* segment is unequivocal and there is never any doubt about which *mukowa* the segment in question is a part of. The affiliation of the segment with a particular *mukowa* can be altered only through the manipulation of the genealogy (see the Bancimba's and Bantanga's genealogical versions in Diagrams 6 and 7). In Ngwezi, the status of a *mukowa* segment localised in a particular village can often be ambivalent without the actual genealogy being questioned or disputed. The status of Bene's (T12) and Munjila's (Bene's husband's) descendants in Siciyako is a case in point. Had Lubinda (U14) succeeded to Malumo's (T10) name, they would have stressed their affiliation with the Bancindu *mukowa* through Bene (T12), and in the ritual sphere they would have acted as Bancindu. The fact that nowadays they stress their affiliation with the *mukowa wa* Siciyako through Lubinda's father, Munjila, is the result of the failure of Lubinda's original plans.

In Guta and Cifokoboyo, the fission of a *mukowa* is the result of competition between politically ambitious men within it. The fission of a *mukowa* in Ngwezi is also the final result of competition between politically ambitious men. But as the case of the emergence of the *mukowa wa* Siciyako indicates, the fission can be triggered off by competition between two men who do not necessarily both have to belong to the *mukowa* which will be ultimately split. In Lubinda's case the *mukowa* which split into two was his paternal *mukowa*, and yet it was not his competition with the headman of the village from which the village of Siciyako seceded, so much as his competition with Congwe (U9), which eventually led to the emergence of the new *mukowa wa* Siciyako.

I have suggested before that to conceptualise the *mukowa* segments localised in the hamlets and villages of which their members are the owners as expressing independence *vis-à-vis* other segments of the same *mukowa* in the sphere of political relations, would be defective if it ascribed to the concept of the *mukowa* segment an importance which it does not have in the Toka conceptual universe. The Toka do not see the relations between hamlets of a village and between villages neighbouring on one another as having anything to do with the *mukowa* and their segments localised in them. They see them as relations between the men who are the heads of these particular settlements; they are political relations operating within a given territorial framework. These relations are, however, not static. The leaders of hamlets and villages try constantly to gain advantages for themselves and to enhance their status, thus perpetually changing the relations which exist between them. The relations between the segments of a *mukowa* become the object of manipulation in an attempt to achieve what are primarily political goals. Ritual activities get as much 'politicised' as do the resolutions of disputes, economic cooperation or any other activity.

The manipulation of the relations between the segments of a *mukowa* is a standard part of the strategies employed by politically ambitious men. Lubinda (U14), in what can be seen primarily as his political strategy, first severed his relations with his maternal *mukowa* and established primary affiliation with his paternal *mukowa* for himself and other people in his village; through performing his own rain-making ritual he then established his paternal *mukowa* as an independent *mukowa* in its own right. He could not have succeeded in establishing the *mukowa wa* Siciyako as an independent *mukowa* of which he is the head, had his father not been buried in Siciyako. The founder of a new village or the founder of a hamlet who aspires to village headmanship is in a different position. His ancestors are not buried in his new settlement and hence the *mukowa* segment of which he is a member can never become an independent *mukowa* during his lifetime. He can, however, still manipulate its affiliation in order to achieve his political objective.

Just as the villages which split off from Cileya participate in the rain-making ritual there, the hamlets of Mujalanyana participate in the rain-making ritual in that village (Diagram 11). The day before the libations on the graves in Mujalanyana, Johnsen (O31) from Kacenje hamlet and Freddy (P5), Malake (O20) and Maria (O19) from the headman's hamlet, went to Mujala Mupati with the beer brewed in Mujalanyana. Ilumbela (N14) sent word specifically to Kawayo (O42) and to Siyakwema (N32) informing them about the ritual. They were supposed to join the people going to Mujala Mupati. But none of them turned up. Although Siyakwema (N32) later attended the libations poured on the graves in Mujalanyana, Kawayo (O42) and other people from his hamlet did not. Their absence was conspicuous and it was widely commented on; Ilumbela (N14) himself clearly displayed his disappointment and he saw Kawayo's action as a deliberate attempt to show that he has nothing to do with what goes on in Mujalanyana. The *mukowa wa* Cabakani is the maternal *mukowa* of the inhabitants of Kawayo's hamlet. Ilumbela (N14) was convinced that, in his attempt to assert his independence of Mujalanyana, Kawayo (O42) would sever all his relations with the *mukowa wa* Cabakani and would demonstrate his primary attachment to the *mukowa* of his father. He clearly declared that in future he expects Kawayo (O42) to take part in the rain-making ritual in his father's natal village in an attempt to demonstrate that his settlement is not a part of Mujalanyana.

Headmen's and hamlet heads' manipulation of their *mukowa* affiliations are clearly meaningful to other headmen and hamlet heads whose statuses are affected through them. They see them as manifestations of their opponents' intentions and they take these intentions into consideration in deciding on their own strategies. Knowing what Kawayo (O42) was up to, Ilumbela (N14) specifically invited him to the rain-making ritual in Mujalanyana, which is conceptualised as that of the *mukowa wa* Cabakani.

Similarly, Congwe (U9; Diagram 15), in deciding on his actions, takes into consideration what he thinks might be Thomas's intentions. Thomas (T1), the headman of Siyacinga, is in a similar position to Lubinda (U14). His father, Siyacinga (S1), is buried in his village and Thomas (T1) could easily start performing his own rain-making ritual by pouring libations to him.

Mukowa *and ritual*

Descendants of Siyacinga and his wife could easily start stressing their attachment to their paternal, instead of to their maternal, *mukowa*, which would considerably diminish the size of the *mukowa wa* Cileya and, consequently, the status which Congwe (U9) enjoys as its head. Congwe is well aware of this. For this reason, he makes it his point to consult Thomas (T1) before he intends to perform the rain-making ritual and to discuss with him in detail all the arrangements. It is also for this reason that Thomas (T1) is allowed to play a prominent part in the Bancindu ritual, during which he clearly ranks as second in importance only to Congwe (U9) himself. By making him deeply involved in this way in the ritual affairs of the Bancindu, Congwe tries to offset any possible centrifugal tendencies on his part and thus to prevent the fission of the *mukowa wa* Cileya, which he clearly sees, if not as being imminent, then at least as being highly likely.

I have mentioned before that the factor determining an individual's *mukowa* affiliation is his place of residence. This statement can now be qualified to give it a meaning which would embrace the complexities of social reality as the Toka know and live it. It is their place of residence which determines the *mukowa* affiliation of the inhabitants of Siciyako, Kawayo and Siyacinga, in the sense that they consider themselves to be members of the same *mukowa*, as are most of their neighbours in their respective settlements. But this alone does not determine which particular *mukowa* that will be. Whether the inhabitants of Siciyako will consider their primary attachment to be to the *mukowa wa* Cileya or to the *mukowa wa* Siciyako, whether the people in Kawayo will stress their attachment to the *mukowa wa* Cabakani through Kawayo's mother or to the *mukowa* of Kawayo's father, or, whether those who live in Siyacinga will trace their *mukowa* membership from Thomas's father, Siyacinga, or from Thomas's mother and, through her, from the ancestors of the *mukowa wa* Cileya, does not depend on their place of residence. It is ultimately determined by the settlement leader's manipulation of his, as well as their, *mukowa* affiliation in the way which best suits his political goals.

7

The role of the *mukowa* in succession

Apart from rain-making rituals, the final mourning ceremonies (*mayobo*), at which the successor of the deceased is chosen and the deceased's estate divided among his survivors, are the main situations which the Toka themselves conceptualise in *mukowa* terms. They say that it is the *basimukowa* of the deceased who decide on his successor and who inherit his property.

Each *mayobo* is organised by a kinsman of the deceased who has been living in the deceased's village. If the deceased was a man, he may be assisted by a kinsman of the deceased's wife. The organiser decides on the date of the ceremony and informs the relatives of the deceased in their villages, his relatives who have been working in towns as labour migrants and who should be present, and the headmen of neighbouring villages. As a rule, the *mayobo* is held over a weekend so that even those kin who work in towns may attend.

A week or so before the *mayobo*, the preparations for brewing beer start. If the deceased was a man, two groups of women brew beer: his kinswomen or affines and kinswomen or affines of his wife. The two groups are widely helped by other women from the village and by the kinswomen of the deceased who have come from other villages to attend the *mayobo*. Quite a number of women from neighbouring villages also take part in the work, particularly if close kinship ties exist between their inhabitants. The work is organised in such a way that young women, both married and unmarried, pound the maize in mortars to the accompaniment of rhythmic songs while the older women sieve the flour. The younger women also bring the water and later do the actual brewing. The men from the village, again assisted by younger kinsmen of the deceased from other villages who have come to attend the *mayobo*, collect the firewood both for the brewing and for several large fires that will be lit on the night of the *mayobo*.

During the week preceding the *mayobo*, the kin of the deceased and his wife who come from distant villages and from towns, arrive in the village. They sleep either in the houses of their relatives or in the open in front of the house of the deceased. Most of the participants arrive only on Saturday night when the *mayobo* starts. It takes place in front of the deceased's house, where several fires are lit which the participants gather around in distinct

149

groups. One group is formed by men who were specifically invited to attend the *mayobo* by its organiser; they are mostly headmen from neighbouring villages. With them are seated older kinsmen and affines of the deceased and older men from the village and neighbouring settlements. The younger kinsmen and affines of the deceased usually sit around another fire together with other younger men who have come to attend. Sometimes the arrangement is more formal: the invited headmen and other older men form one group, the deceased's kinsmen another and the younger men a third. Old kinswomen of the deceased usually sit with other old women round their own fire; they spend the night in singing special songs, accompanying their singing by beating empty tins with reed stalks. Younger kinswomen of the deceased sit round another fire with other younger women from the village of the deceased and from neighbouring villages. Young men and women who come to attend the *mayobo* spend the whole night in dancing to the music of three drums and xylophone, which they accompany by singing. They dance until the early morning, when the successor is ceremonially installed. There is always a large number of young people present at each *mayobo*; they come to dance and drink beer. Older people who do not take part in the dancing, do not stay awake the whole night. They come to the *mayobo* with their mats and blankets and when they eventually make their beds, they sleep in the open round the fire in front of the deceased's house; this is done even by people from the village of the deceased.

As in Guta and Cifokoboyo, the successor is chosen at a secret meeting held during the night of the *mayobo*. When generalising about the composition of these meetings, the Toka say that those who take part in them are the deceased's *basimukowa*, although headmen of neighbouring villages or their representatives may also participate to give an independent opinion about those who come into consideration for succession. The choice of the successor is particularly important when the deceased has small children who have to be looked after by him. The successor's personal qualities are also important when he is succeeding, not only to the deceased's name, but also to village headmanship. The Toka say that the successor is in fact sometimes chosen by one of the headmen present at the meeting and accepted by the deceased's *basimukowa*. I have not, myself, witnessed this happening.

I observed altogether thirteen meetings for choosing the deceased's successor. In ten of these, the deceased was a man, in three of them a woman (Meetings 2, 5 and 8). In all of them, the suggestion about who should succeed, which was later accepted by all present, was forwarded by one of the male *basimukowa* of the deceased.

Only in three of the thirteen meetings were men unrelated to the deceased present, and only in one of them (Meeting 1) were they there for the reasons explicitly stated by the Toka. A large inheritance was at stake, sorcery was suspected and an argument between the paternal and maternal *basimukowa* of the deceased was expected. A headman and another old man from a neighbouring village, who were not related to the deceased, were specifically invited by the *basimukowa* to attend the meeting to ensure that its deliberations would be fairly conducted. Another meeting (13), when a headman from a neighbouring village and his brother, both unrelated to the deceased, were present, was for choosing the successor of a man who had been living in a village and area in which there were very few of his *basimukowa*. Only four of them, including the deceased's own daughter, were present at the *mayobo*. Hardly anybody in the village, including the deceased's own kinsmen, had any idea who his remaining *basimukowa* actually were nor where they lived; consequently, they could not be properly informed. The two unrelated men joined two of the deceased's *basimukowa* to form the meeting. Its deliberations were anyhow easy for there were hardly any kinsmen of the deceased to choose his successor from; he had no sons and only one daughter. Of necessity she had to succeed, although a woman's succession to a man's name and vice versa is quite unusual.

When generalising about the composition of meetings for choosing successors to deceased men, the Toka also mention as a rule that some of the *basimukowa* of the widow attend.

Of the ten deceased men whose final mourning ceremonies I observed, eight were married when they died. However, the *basimukowa* of the deceased's wife took part in only three meetings. Their kinship relationships with her are indicated in Diagram 16.

The widow's *basimukowa* are present at the meeting to look after her interests. The successor has a right to marry the deceased's wife provided she is not his near kinswoman. The widow's representatives can refuse a suggested successor if he would not make a suitable husband for her. Like the successor, who has a right to marry the deceased's wife, the widow is entitled to be offered a new husband. If the successor himself does not want to marry her, his brother or any other near kinsman may be offered to her instead. The widow's representatives can again refuse him if they think he would not make a suitable husband. If the widow has no intention of remarrying, her representatives communicate her decision to the meeting.

In the past, the successor usually married the widow. Early in the morning he was put into the house with her. After having intercourse, he gave a sign to the people waiting outside, who greeted him with cheers. Only then was he formally installed as the successor of the deceased. It seems that to be married to her husband's successor was the widow's duty and that a widower had a similar duty to marry the successor of his deceased wife. Nowadays the widow is always asked whether she wants to marry her husband's successor. If she declines, she receives a small payment (usually 50n or K1)

The role of the mukowa *in succession*

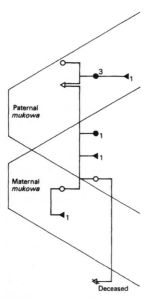

Diagram 16. Deceased's wife's representatives at the meetings for choosing the successors

Wife's representatives present at the meetings are indicated in black and the numbers next to the symbols indicate the number of individuals of each kinship type actually present.

from her husband's kin. She is also entitled to this payment when the successor refuses to marry her and when her husband's kin have nobody to offer her.

The kin of the deceased are not only responsible for providing the spouse of the deceased with a new marital partner (or, if the deceased was a man, for compensating his widow in cash), but also for making sure that the death will not endanger the surviving spouse.

When Cikuni, Siyamukamulonga's wife, died, no diviner was consulted about the cause of her death and it was suspected that Siyamukamulonga might have received an evil spirit (*muzimu mubi*) from her. If that were the case, any other woman whom he would marry and sleep with might die, being affected by it. His former wife's kin would be responsible for her death and it would be their duty to have him cleansed of the evil spirit and to pay for the treatment. To find out whether Siyamukamulonga had received an evil spirit from Cikuni, her kin arranged for her paternal half-sister, Mukajene, to sleep with him for two nights during the *mayobo* with an option to marry him afterwards. As she did not die after having slept with him, it was established that he was free of the evil spirit. If he marries in the future and should his wife die, her death will not have been caused by the evil spirit and Cikuni's kin will not be responsible for it.

There is concern with the purification of the widow when it is suspected that she might have been given *lunyoka* – a medicine aimed at preventing her

152

from committing adultery. On the request of the man, *lunyoka* can be administered to his wife by a witchdoctor, very often without her knowing. Sometimes it is administered to both the man and his wife. *Lunyoka* works in such a way that every man except her own husband dies after intercourse with her. A woman who has been given *lunyoka* cannot remarry without endangering her new husband unless she has been cleared of it. If a husband of such a woman dies, she will approach his kin, usually through her own grandmother, with a request to take her to a witchdoctor who will free her from *lunyoka*. If they fail to do this, the husband's kin will be fully responsible for providing her with shelter, food and clothing.

When Thomas died, his wife, Eni, told her parents that she had been given *lunyoka* by him. They approached Thomas's kin and asked them to take her to a witchdoctor, as it was their duty to free her from it. Thomas's kin refused, insisting that he never administered any medicine to her. Eni's parents sensed trouble and before the *mayobo* was to take place, they went to see the chief, asking him to attend it. The chief sent one of his assessors to the *mayobo*. Thomas's eldest son was chosen as a successor. Eni's kin insisted that a kinsman of Thomas should sleep with her for three nights to free her from *lunyoka*. Thomas's kin again refused to admit that Eni had *lunyoka* and it nearly came to a fight between them and Eni's kin. It was eventually agreed that one of Thomas's kin would sleep with the widow. At first Thomas's sister was asked to let her son sleep with her but she refused the request, pointing out that he would certainly die. Eventually, Thomas's elder brother volunteered to sleep with the widow for three nights.

When generalising about the composition of meetings for choosing successors, the Toka never mention that the deceased's affines take part, although eleven affines were present at seven meetings which I observed: nine of them were men and two were women. Out of these eleven, eight were spouses of the *basimukowa* of the deceased (Diagram 17); they were all present for a specific reason and they were all without exception from villages other than those in which the mourning ceremonies were held. Such people are the guests of the village members, and in particular of the deceased's kinsmen who provide them with board and lodging. As guests they are treated with the same respect as the deceased's *basimukowa* who come to attend the ceremony from other villages, and during the night they sit in one group with them. It is some of the members of this group who later in the night move away from other people to hold the private meeting in which the successor is chosen. The respect which is due to all the guests and with which the deceased's affines from other villages are treated, extends so far that they are not turned away when they decide, as some of them sometimes do, to attend the meeting. Everybody knows that the meeting is the affair of the *basimukowa* and that the affines should not really attend it, but as long as they do not try to influence the deliberations, their presence is tolerated. The deceased's affines from the same village as himself do not have to be treated with the same respect as those from other, particularly distant, villages. They are neighbours, not guests; should they try to attend the

The role of the mukowa in succession

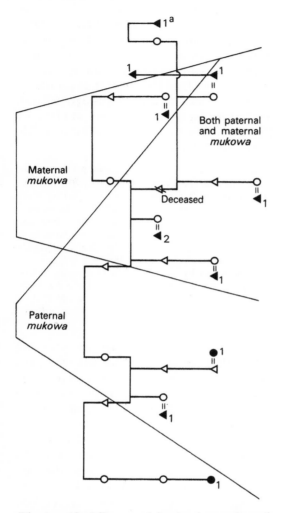

Diagram 17. Affines participating in meetings choosing successors to the deceased

Affines present at the meetings are indicated in black and the numbers behind the symbols indicate the number of individuals of each kinship type actually present.

[a] The brother of the deceased's wife did not attend the meeting as a representative of his sister; the latter had been dead when the man to whom she had been married died.

meeting, they would be reminded that they are not *basimukowa* and would be turned away; particularly if they are young they might be reminded of their status in a way which is far from polite by Toka standards.

The meetings in which successors are chosen vary considerably in size as Table 8 indicates. The biggest meeting (11), in which twenty-three people took

Table 8. *The number of participants in the meetings for choosing the successor*

Meeting	*Basimukowa*	Affines	Wife's representatives	Unrelated	Total
1	9			2	11
2	6	3			9
3	7	1			8
4	6	2			8
5	8				8
6	3		3		6
7	6				6
8	5				5
9	3	1			4
10	2	1			3
11	19	2		2	23
12	5	1	2		8
13	2		2	2	6
Total	81	11	7	6	105

Mean number of participants: 7.9; median: 8.

Table 9. Mukowa *affiliation of the participants in the meetings for choosing the successor*

	Men	Women	Total
Members of the paternal *mukowa* of the deceased	18	11	29
Members of both the paternal and maternal *mikowa* of the deceased	8	18	26
Members of the maternal *mukowa* of the deceased	14	12	26
Total	40	41	81

part, was a meeting for choosing the successor of a village headman. Another meeting in which a headman's successor was chosen (4) was of average size.

Affines, wife's representatives and men unrelated to the deceased participate in only some of the meetings; *basimukowa* participate in all of them. Of the 105 participants in the thirteen meetings I witnessed, 81 (i.e. 77.1%) were *basimukowa* of the deceased (Diagram 18). These are the people I am now going to consider in more detail.

The numbers of male and female *basimukowa* are virtually equal: forty of them were men, forty-one women. There is also no considerable difference in the numbers of paternal and maternal *basimukowa* of the deceased; their *mukowa* affiliation is indicated in Table 9.

The role of the mukowa in succession

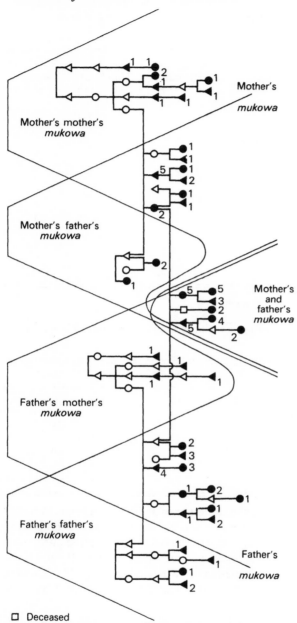

□ Deceased

Diagram 18. *Basimukowa* participating in meetings choosing successors to the deceased (summary of thirteen meetings)

Basimukowa present at the meetings are indicated in black and the numbers behind the symbols indicate the number of individuals of each kinship type.

The role of the mukowa in succession

Table 10. *Participation of the paternal and maternal* basimukowa *in the meetings for choosing the successor*

	Men	Women	Total
Members of the deceased's paternal *mukowa*	26	29	55
Members of the deceased's maternal *mukowa*	22	30	52
Total	48	59	107

Table 11. *Affiliation of the meeting participants with the four* mikowa *of the deceased*

	Men	Women	Total
Members of the deceased's father's father's *mukowa*	22	29	51
Members of the deceased's father's mother's *mukowa*	22	28	50
Members of the deceased's mother's father's *mukowa*	17	26	43
Members of the deceased's mother's mother's *mukowa*	22	27	49
Total	83	110	193

Twenty-six *basimukowa* taking part in the meetings were the siblings of the deceased and their descendants; they were members of the deceased's paternal as well as maternal *mukowa*. In Table 10 they are counted as members of both categories and hence the total figure is higher than in Table 9: the figure 81 in Table 9 indicates the actual number of people taking part in the meetings, the figure 107 in Table 10 indicates the number of their social identity relationships to the deceased in terms of their *mukowa* membership. Twenty-six individuals have dual social identity relationships with the deceased, being both his paternal and maternal *basimukowa* (81 + 26 = 107). The table indicates that the maternal *basimukowa* participate about as frequently in the meetings as do the paternal *basimukowa*.

The deceased's paternal *basimukowa* are members either of his father's father's or of his father's mother's *mukowa*. Some of them, again, are members of both. Equally, his maternal *basimukowa* are members either of his mother's father's or of his mother's mother's *mukowa*, with some of them being members of both. Table 11 shows the participants' membership of the four *mikowa* with which the deceased can affiliate himself; it is again based on the number of their social identity relationships with him, defined in terms of their membership in the four *mikowa* considered. The table indicates that the paternal *basimukowa* of the deceased who take part in the meeting are

157

as likely to be members of the deceased's father's father's *mukowa* as of his father's mother's *mukowa*. On his mother's side, the members of his mother's mother's *mukowa* prevail slightly over the members of his mother's father's *mukowa*. The figures concerning the members of the mother's mother's and mother's father's *mikowa* in Table 11 are skewed as a result of one particular case (1), in which six members of the deceased's mother's mother's *mukowa* participated in the meeting. It took place in Mangulwani village; the maternal *basimukowa* of the deceased are Bancindu who live in Mangulwani and its three neighbouring villages (Diagram 15). For the deceased, the Bancindu are his mother's mother's *mukowa*. If this particular case is disregarded, there would be forty-one members of the deceased's mother's father's *mukowa* and forty-three members of his mother's mother's *mukowa*. These latter figures would indicate that maternal *basimukowa* taking part in the meeting are about as likely to be members of the deceased's mother's father's as of his mother's mother's *mukowa*. Different conclusions, seemingly of a predictive nature, can thus be reached depending on whether or not one particular case is included in the statistical description of the pattern of regularity. This situation is methodologically significant.

It indicates, first of all, that any prediction based on the statistically derived pattern of the distribution of relationships can concern only a future pattern of their distribution arrived at through the same computing procedures which were employed in formulating the pattern in the first place. This means that all we can say is that, in any sufficiently large sample of randomly selected meetings, the number of paternal *basimukowa* of the deceased will be roughly equal to the number of his maternal *basimukowa*, and that the paternal *basimukowa* will be equally recruited from among the members of the deceased's father's father's and father's mother's *mikowa*, while the maternal *basimukowa* will be equally recruited from among the members of his mother's father's and his mother's mother's *mikowa*. What we are not, however, able to predict, is the participation of the members of these four descent categories in any individual case. The reason, naturally, is that the factors on which the prediction is based are not social, but statistical.

The statistically derived pattern of the distribution of relationships not only has a limited predictive value, but what is more important, it has no explanatory value (Keesing 1967). It is 'the cumulative result of a number of separate choices and decisions made by people acting *vis-à-vis* one another' (Barth 1966: 2). Unless these choices and decisions are described, the pattern which is generated through the process of exercising them cannot be explained. As Barth put it: 'Explanation is not achieved by a description of the patterns of regularity ... but by exhibiting what *makes* the pattern, i.e. certain processes' (ibid.).

The statistical pattern of distribution of the participants' relationships in terms of their *mukowa* membership, is a composite account of thirteen actual meetings. As such it is normal rather than normative in Leach's sense (Leach 1961: 300), although it displays a remarkable degree of consistency with the norm to which the Toka subscribe. When they generalise about *basimukowa* participating in meetings for choosing successors, they say that it is both the paternal and maternal *basimukowa* of the deceased who attend. This statement is not a generalisation of what, in their experience, normally happens. It is a statement of the norm, for when questioned further on the subject they explain that this is what should, but does not always, happen in actual meetings. Although the number of members of the deceased's paternal *mukowa* is virtually equal to the number of members of his maternal *mukowa* (fifty-five as against fifty-two), this can hardly be taken as a manifestation of the Toka behavioural adherence to the norm which they explicitly recognise. For us to be able to take it as this, the congruence with the norm would have to be apparent, not only in the composite account of all the meetings, but also in each individual one; if only the former is the case, the possibility that the congruence is the result of the statistical manipulation of data, rather than a statement of the relation between actors' behaviour and their notions about that behaviour, cannot be eliminated. To be able, firstly, to elucidate the processes that generate the pattern of the distribution of the *basimukowa* who take part in the meetings, and secondly to consider how far that distribution is a reflection of the norm that both the paternal and maternal *basimukowa* of the deceased should decide on his successor, the thirteen meetings must be considered individually. To avoid lengthy description, I present them in a diagrammatic form (Diagram 19).

In only five of the thirteen meetings (1, 3, 5, 11 and 12) did both the paternal and maternal *basimukowa* take part and the norm that members of both categories should participate was thus observed. In none of these meetings was the number of the paternal *basimukowa* equal to that of the maternal ones. In three of the meetings (3, 5 and 12) their respective numbers were not grossly disproportionate; in the remaining two cases (1 and 11) *basimukowa* on one side predominated numerically over those on the other. The reasons why this was so are the same as the reasons behind the fact that in most meetings only representatives of one of the *mikowa* with which the deceased was affiliated, are present. I have already mentioned Meeting 1, in which six of the participants were members of the deceased's mother's mother's *mukowa*, the Bancindu (see also Diagram 21). Most of the Bancindu live in Mangulwani, the village in which the final mourning ceremony was held, and in three neighbouring villages. All the six Bancindu who took part were either from Mangulwani itself or from these neighbouring villages; either they were the immediate neighbours of the deceased, Siyamukwiza (V4), or Mangulwani was within easy walking distance of their own village. As it was easily accessible to them, they turned up in great numbers at the final mourning ceremony, and as quite a number of them were considered

The role of the mukowa in succession

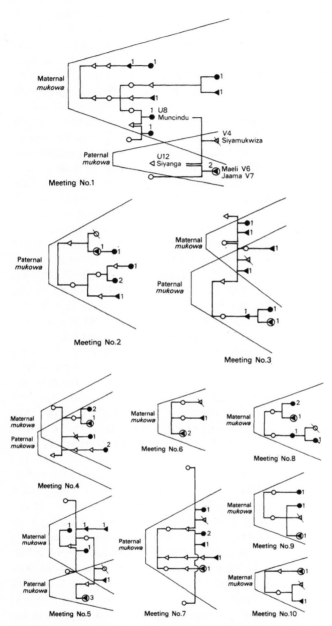

Diagram 19. *Basimukowa* participating in meetings choosing successors to the deceased *Basimukowa* present at the meetings are indicated in black and the numbers at the symbols indicate the number of individuals of each kinship type present. (Diagram continues on p. 161.)

160

The role of the mukowa in succession

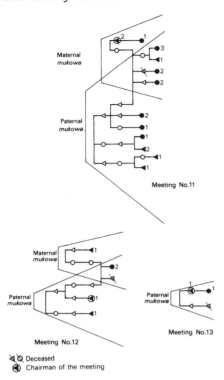

Maternal
mukowa

Paternal
mukowa

Meeting No.11

Maternal
mukowa

Paternal
mukowa

Meeting No.12

Paternal
mukowa

Meeting No.13

Deceased
Chairman of the meeting

Diagram 19 (cont.)

to be sufficiently senior to attend the meeting, they were either invited to do so or simply joined it on their own initiative. Siyanga (U12), Siyamukwiza's father, who was himself dead at the time of his son's death, had been from Bucwani village, which is about 80 km from Mangulwani. He married in Bucwani and his two sons from his first marriage, Jaama (V7) and Maeli (V6), live there. After he had divorced his first wife, he married Muncindu (U8), a divorcee from Mangulwani, and had been living in her village. With him to Mangulwani came his elder brother, Siyamakanda (U13), with his wife and their son, Mwilima (V5). Siyamakanda (U13) and his wife both died in Mangulwani; their son, Mwilima (V5), still lives there. He is the only member of Siyamukwiza's paternal *mukowa* living in that village and he attended the mourning ceremony. Because of his young age, he did not take part in the meeting for choosing Siyamukwiza's successor, as attendance at these meetings is generally considered to be the prerogative of older people, and young people do not attend them unless they are specifically invited.

161

The role of the mukowa in succession

Because Bucwani, where most of the members of Siyamukwiza's paternal *mukowa* live, is so far away from Mangulwani, only two of Siyamukwiza's paternal *basimukowa* came from there to attend the mourning ceremony. They were Jaama (V7) and Maeli (V6) and they took part in the meeting as the representatives of Siyamukwiza's paternal *basimukowa*. They were the only paternal *basimukowa* who participated in the meeting. The other six participants, whom I have already mentioned, were Bancindu – members of Siyamukwiza's mother's mother's *mukowa*. The ninth and last participant was Cinyama (U11), paternal half-sister of Siyamukwiza's mother, who lives in a nearby village. She counts as one of Siyamukwiza's *basimukowa* but is not a member of the Bancindu *mukowa*; she is a member of Siyamukwiza's mother's father's *mukowa*. Although it was the Bancindu who acted as Siyamukwiza's maternal *basimukowa* in the meeting, Cinyama (U11) was allowed to take part in it for the same reason as that for which affines are often allowed to participate. As a guest from another village and an old woman, she had been treated with respect, and it would not have been polite to turn her away when she followed Siyamukwiza's mother (U8), her own half-sister, to the meeting. The meeting for choosing Siyamukwiza's successor was the only one in which the maternal *basimukowa* of the deceased were members of two separate *mikowa*. In all other meetings, the maternal *basimukowa* were all members of either the deceased mother's father's or his mother's mother's *mukowa*, and for that matter, the paternal *basimukowa* of the deceased were all members of either his father's father's or his father's mother's *mukowa*.

Whereas in Meeting 1 it was the maternal *basimukowa* of the deceased who outnumbered the paternal ones, in Meeting 11 many more paternal than maternal *basimukowa* attended, while some of those who took part in it were members of both these categories. The paternal *basimukowa* of the deceased were members of the *mukowa wa* Linda, a numerous *mukowa* whose apical ancestor was one of the past headmen of Linda village, of which the deceased (Simayumbola) was himself a headman. Most of the inhabitants of Linda and some of the neighbouring villages are members of Linda's *mukowa*. They turned up in big numbers at the final mourning ceremony and many of them attended the meeting for choosing Simayumbola's successor. Simayumbola's mother is from another area than Linda and most of her own *basimukowa* live in that area. Owing to its distance from Linda only a few turned up at the final mourning ceremony and consequently only a few attended the meeting.

At each meeting, one man acts as its informal chairman and eventually declares who will succeed to the deceased's name. He does not necessarily have the main say in suggesting the successor, nor indeed does the candidate whom he himself has backed, necessarily succeed. The role of the chairman is to direct the discussion, to reconcile the opposing views of the participants and eventually to sense their feelings before finally proposing a candidate for the formal approval of all present.

The chairman of Meeting 1 was Jaama (V7), one of the members of the paternal *mukowa* of the deceased. Meeting 11 was chaired by one of the mother's brothers of the deceased, a member of the deceased's maternal *mukowa*. In both these cases, the chairmen were members of the *mukowa* whose representatives were in the minority at the meeting. There is no rule stipulating that the man convening the meeting of the *basimukowa* should himself be a member of a specific *mukowa*, nor has he to be a member of the *mukowa* numerically predominant at the meeting. The fact that he usually belongs to the *mukowa* whose members are in the minority is a consequence of quite different considerations. I have mentioned before that *basimukowa* of the deceased who come to attend the final mourning ceremony from other villages than his own are treated with respect and deference by the deceased's *basimukowa* who themselves live in his village, and in fact by all its members. In a way they are guests of honour of the *basimukowa* who live in the deceased's village. This is particularly so if they come from an area which is considerably distant from the village in which the mourning ceremony is held. If this is the case, it is very likely that at least some of the deceased's *basimukowa* living in his village do not even know them personally, or know them only superficially from some previous encounter. The fact that they are strangers adds to the respect and deference with which they are treated, for all strangers among the Toka are treated in this way. The fact that the local organiser of the mourning ceremony asks the man who has been acting as the spokesman of the visiting *basimukowa* to convene the meeting is an integral part of the deferential treatment which the visiting *basimukowa* enjoy. As their number is as a rule smaller than the number of *basimukowa* from the deceased's village and from the villages immediately neighbouring it, it is quite common that a man who plays a prominent role at the meeting is a member of the *mukowa* whose members are in the minority.

Seven of the thirteen meetings I witnessed were attended by members of only one of the deceased's *mikowa* (Meetings 2, 6, 7, 8, 9, 10 and 13). At four of them (6, 8, 9, 10), only members of the maternal *mukowa* of the deceased were present, and at three of them (2, 7 and 13), only members of the paternal *mukowa* were. The reasons why members of one of the deceased's *mikowa* are absent are the same as those behind the fact that the numbers of participants from the two *mikowa* are usually disproportionate in cases when representatives of both of the deceased's *mikowa* attend. Two meetings held in Mujalanyana village (Diagram 11) illustrate these reasons well. Mweene (N6), whose successor was chosen at Meeting 6, had originally lived in Katapazi, a village about 80 km from Mujalanayana. After a dispute with his brothers, he left Katapazi and settled in Mujalanyana, his wife's village, where he died and where the final mourning ceremony was held. Although members of Mweene's paternal *mukowa* in Katapazi were informed about his death, none of them came to attend either his funeral or the final mourning ceremony, about which they were also informed by Mweene's younger brother. Unlike the members of Mweene's paternal *mukowa*, some of the members of his maternal *mukowa* live in villages which are not too distant from Mujalanyana. Five of them came to attend the final mourning ceremony and three of them assembled at night to choose his successor. Only three of Mweene's neighbours belong to the same *mukowa* as himself: his own daughter, his sister's daughter and his sister's son. Although the latter was in charge of the preparations for the ceremony, he did not attend the meeting of the *basimukowa* as he himself was a potential successor; neither of the two women was considered to be senior enough to be invited to attend.

Meeting 7, which also took place in Mujalanyana village and at which the successor of Bulawayo (N8) was chosen, was attended only by Bulawayo's paternal *basimukowa* (Bwoono). Bulawayo's father was Cabakani (M2), the former headman of Mujala village. His mother, Simwembe (M1), was from an area about 100 km away and she had lived virilocally in Mujala, where Bulawayo (N8) was born. Although he had met some of his mother's kin when they had occasionally been to visit her in Mujala, he had never himself been to the area from which his mother had come. Simwembe (M1) died in Mujala and since Bulawayo had moved to Mujalanyana, together with other people from Mujala village, he had not seen any of his maternal *basimukowa*. When he died, neither his wife nor anybody else in Mujalanyana knew who his maternal *basimukowa* were. Consequently, only the Bwoono, his paternal *basimukowa*, attended the final mourning ceremony. The most important man among the Bwoono in Mujalanyana was Ilumbela (N14), the village headman; the most important man among the Bwoono who came from outside Mujalanyana was the headman of Kanema. Ilumbela (N14) asked him to convene the meeting of the *basimukowa*; six people, all members of Bulawayo's paternal *mukowa*, took part in it.

Obviously, when only members of one of the deceased's *mikowa* attend the meeting, the question of the *mukowa* membership of its chairman does not arise. The rule that he should be chosen from among the visiting *basimukowa* is, however, observed. Not only was Meeting 7 chaired by a member of the deceased's *mukowa* from a village different from that of the deceased, but so were all other meetings in which the members of only one *mukowa* participated.

The last of the thirteen meetings (4) was attended by six people; one of them was the deceased's own daughter, the others were all descendants of his siblings. All of them shared with him the membership of the same paternal and maternal *mikowa*. When generalising about the composition of the meeting for choosing the successor, the Toka state that younger *basimukowa* of the deceased do not take part in it because the successor of the deceased is chosen from among them. As the Toka explain it, it is the *basimukowa* older than the deceased himself who decide on his successor, as they themselves do not come into consideration for succession. It might, of course, happen, as it did in Meeting 4, that the deceased is an old man who has no surviving *basimukowa* older than himself. In such a case the onus of deciding on his successor falls of necessity on the younger *basimukowa*. However, the rule that those who might be eligible to succeed him do not attend is still observed; as it is considered desirable for men to succeed men and women to succeed women, the onus of choosing a successor to a man who had no *basimukowa* older than himself, falls of necessity on the female members of his *mukowa*. The near kinsmen of the deceased are those from among whom the successor will be chosen; being potential candidates for succession, they try to avoid attending the meeting. It is these considerations which account for the fact that of the six *basimukowa* attending Meeting 4, five were women. The sixth member of the meeting was the sister's son from a village different from that of the deceased; he was asked to convene the meeting and acted as its chairman. He accepted this role as he knew that he would not succeed the deceased. He himself had already inherited two *mizimu* and the Toka try to avoid choosing anybody in that position to succeed to yet another name. In this particular case it was unlikely that the sister's son would have to be chosen, as the deceased had sons who were an obvious choice; one of them was appointed to succeed his father. Knowing perfectly well what the chances were, it was both safe and sensible for the sister's son to take part in the meeting when he was asked to do so. In fact, he was asked to do so in the first place as everybody else concerned knew perfectly well what the chances were.

The Toka's generalisation that those who are eligible for succession do not attend the meetings is an accurate description of what actually occurs. Expressing this generalisation in terms of age relative to that of the deceased is, however, not accurate for all cases. Six out of the thirteen meetings were attended by a number of the *basimukowa* who were actually younger than the deceased. All of them, however, knew that they were themselves not eligible. I have dealt already with Meeting 4; the others were Meetings 1, 2, 3, 7 and 11. One category of *basimukowa* younger than the deceased who attended all these meetings were the deceased's distant collateral kinsmen. The successor is always chosen from among the deceased's close *basimukowa*: his children, younger siblings and siblings' descendants. More distant kin do not qualify as successors and they can thus safely attend the meeting even when they are actually younger than the deceased. Meetings 2, 3 and 11 were, however, attended by those of the deceased's *basimukowa* who fall within the range of those eligible for succession. In this respect, they were similar to Meeting 4 and the reasons for the participation of the younger *basimukowa* were similar to those which accounted for their participation in that meeting. Two of the deceased's own daughters and five of his nieces took part in Meeting 11. As females they were not eligible to succeed a deceased man, particularly as he was a village headman and not only succession to his name but also to the headmanship was involved. The deceased's sister's son who participated in this meeting did so again because he already had two inherited *mizimu* and it was practically certain that he would not be chosen to inherit a third one. Meeting 3 was also attended by the sister's son of the deceased man. He did not have any inherited *mizimu* and he was theoretically eligible for succession. But, practically, there was hardly any chance that this would happen. The deceased had three sons of whom one had been ploughing with him for several years. It was clear to everyone present that he would succeed his father and this indeed was the case. Similarly the niece of the deceased woman whose successor was chosen at Meeting 2, participated in the meeting knowing that the deceased had daughters and that one of them was likely to succeed her. The possibility that succession could go to a niece instead of a daughter could be safely eliminated.

The point is that although the deliberations of every meeting for choosing the successor are conducted in the utmost secrecy, their outcome is easily predictable. On the basis of their knowledge of relevant cultural rules, almost all adult Toka are able to say beforehand who the deceased's successor will be. Consequently, every member of the deceased's *mukowa* who is eligible to attend the meeting due to his seniority, knows whether he should exercise his right or whether he should act instead as somebody who is eligible and abstain from the meeting.

The successor has to be a member of the same *mukowa* as the deceased. As I have already mentioned, not all the younger members of the deceased's *mukowa* are, however, eligible. The successor is always chosen from among his children, his younger siblings and his siblings' children.

I collected information on successors of twenty-six men and nineteen women whose deaths occurred during my fieldwork. The relation of the successors to the deceased men is indicated in Table 12.

Disregarding younger brothers, who are eligible under both systems, cases of agnatic succession outnumber cases of uterine succession by almost six to one (17:3). Considering that the succession is ideally monosexual, it is only the succession of men that is indicative of any change in the pattern of succession. The succession of daughters to their mothers' names as opposed to the succession of sisters' daughters to their mothers' sisters' names[1] does not have the same significance in this respect as has the succession of sons to their fathers' names as opposed to the succession of sisters' sons to their mothers' brothers' names: the succession of daughters to their mothers' names is compatible both with the succession of sisters' sons to their mothers' brothers' names (conceptualised as members of the same

The role of the mukowa in succession

Table 12. *Successors of deceased men*

Relation of the successor to the deceased	Number of cases	Total
Agnatic		
Son	15 ⎫	
Brother's son	1 ⎬	17
Daughter[a]	1 ⎭	
Adelphic		
Younger brother	6	6
Uterine		
Sister's son	2 ⎫	
Sister's daughter's son	1 ⎭	3
Total	26[b]	26[b]

[a] It is unusual for a woman to succeed a deceased man and the case of the daughter succeeding her father was the only case of cross-sexual transmission (Goody 1962: 315) I came across. The deceased had lived uxorilocally in his wife's village. He was himself from an area over 100 km distant from his wife's village and most of the members of both his paternal and maternal *mikowa* live in that area. None of them came to attend the final mourning ceremony. Only three members of his paternal *mukowa*, who live in the village of his wife and in another village near it, attended. Two of them were women, the third one was the headman of the village in which the deceased lived. Having himself already inherited two *mizimu*, he declined the succession. As the deceased had no sons, his daughter or one of his two female *basimukowa* present were the only choices.

[b] The figure does not include successors of three headmen whose death occurred during my fieldwork. Included in the figure are sixteen of the seventeen cases which I have already considered in Chapter 3. The seventeenth case considered in Chapter 3 concerns a headman.

matrilineal descent category) and the succession of sons to their fathers' names (conceptualised as members of the same cognatic descent category). As matrilineal descent has not changed into patrilineal, the succession of females was not affected in the same way as was the succession of males. A woman's daughter is her nearest kinswoman within the same descent category, irrespective of whether it is conceptualised as a matrilineal or a cognatic one.

Table 12 clearly indicates that cases of agnatic succession at present considerably outnumber those of uterine succession. In order to find out whether any trend towards the change in succession could be detected over time, I paid particular attention to the succession to village headmanship. Successors of headmen are remembered by more people than are successors to non-headmen. In the case of a succession to headmanship, the statements of numerous informants can be compared with one another and the danger of their interpretation of what happened in the past being coloured by present-day norms can thus be more easily eliminated than it can be if the informants are limited to the direct descendants of the man in question, as is always the case when he is not a village headman. By questioning independently not less than five informants in each village, I obtained what I consider to be reliable histories of fifteen villages in Ngwezi. When collecting these, I recorded twenty-eight cases of succession to headmanship, which were spread over at least the last eight decades. Their distribution in time is shown in Table 13, which clearly indicates a trend of change from uterine to agnatic succession. Instances of succession which occurred in the first two decades of the twentieth century were of the uterine type; since the 1940s not a single uterine succession has been recorded and headmanship has been consistently transmitted through agnatic succession. The 1920s and 1930s seem to be the main period in which both modes of succession coexisted. Although the cases available are numerically too small to be fully conclusive, it seems that in the 1920s uterine succession still predominated over agnatic succession, whereas in the 1930s the instances of agnatic succession already equalled those of uterine succession.

The succession of daughters' sons to headmanship, which was recorded three times, is interesting and merits a comment. All its instances occurred prior to the 1940s, that is, at the time when uterine succession was still normative. As in Guta and Cifokoboyo, a village headman in Ngwezi should also be ideally succeeded by an inhabitant of the village. As can still be the case nowadays in Guta and Cifokoboyo, the ideal of keeping the headmanship in a given descent category through uterine succession probably quite often conflicted with the ideal of choosing the headman from among the inhabitants of the village. The succession of one of the daughters' sons could be seen, like the succession of sons in Guta and Cifokoboyo where uterine succession is still firmly held as an ideal, as a result of the effort to reconcile the reality of village composition with the headmanship, in the sense of enabling the numerically strongest descent category in the village to hold the office.

When discussing the strategy of a hamlet head in Guta and Cifokoboyo, I mentioned that, apart from his own uterine kinsmen, he also tries to attract his sons and daughters to his hamlet. The success of this strategy depends directly on his success in retaining his own wife. If he manages to retain her, the children who live with him in his settlement and who, together with their own descendants, may constitute the majority of its inhabitants, are not members of his own, but of his wife's, descent category. They may outnumber the members of his own descent category in the village and after his death they might try to assume the headmanship. Provided his daughters and their descendants form the majority of the inhabitants of the village, the

168

Table 13. *Succession to village headmanship in Ngwezi*

	1900s and earlier	1910s	1920s	1930s	1940s	1950s	1960s	1970s
Uterine	ZS	ZS	ZS	ZS				
	ZS		ZS	ZS				
			ZS					
Adelphic					B		B	B
							B	
Agnatic			S	S	S	S	S	S
				S	S	S	S	
					S	S		
						BS		
Other types	DS		DS	DS				

The table indicates the relationship of the successor to the deceased headman.

headmanship will pass to the numerically strongest descent category in the village if one of the daughters' sons succeeds his grandfather as headman.

There is some evidence that this type of succession might have been the outcome of the tendency to have the headmanship transferred to the numerically strongest category within the village. One of the recorded cases of a daughter's son succeeding to headmanship occurred in Cileya (Diagram 15), when, during the 1920s, Simufunde (R4), the founder of this village, was succeeded by Malumo (T10), the father of the present headman (U9). It is impossible to say precisely what the composition of Cileya was in the 1920s, but the genealogy in Diagram 15 gives us some clues. The villages of Mangulwani, Siyakalaluka and Siyacinga split off from Cileya during Malumo's time. The oldest living members of these four villages and those of their ancestors who are buried in them, lived in Cileya village at the time of Simufunde's death and Malumo's succession. Simufunde's brothers were apparently the only members of his matrilineal descent category living in his village. On the other hand, the children of Simufunde's daughter, Mwaandu (S7), were numerically the strongest matrilineal descent group within the village, with Malumo (T10) being its senior member.

Although under the mode of uterine succession a younger brother can succeed his elder one, as has sometimes happened in Guta and Cifokoboyo, the fact that all the cases of a brother succeeding as a headman in Ngwezi have occurred in the last four decades when the norm of agnatic succession has been fully established, merits special consideration. I shall return to the question of adelphic succession in Ngwezi in Chapter 10.

The successor inherits the *muzimu* (spirit, shade) and kinship duties and responsibilities of the deceased. If the deceased himself had an inherited *muzimu*, usually two successors are chosen: the main one inherits the deceased's own *muzimu*, the other one the *muzimu* which the deceased had himself inherited.

The deliberations of the meeting which chooses a successor are kept secret until the successor is formally installed. There is a fear that he would run away if he knew that he had been chosen, especially if the person whom he is to succeed died as a result of witchcraft. He might feel that by inheriting the deceased's *muzimu* he will likewise become a target for witchcraft. The people who have chosen the successor ask two men, if the successor himself is a man, or two women, if the successor is a woman, to capture the successor early in the morning. The fact that he has succeeded the deceased is supposed to come as a surprise to him. It is usually two of those who have attended the meeting at night who capture the successor in the morning; but he can just as well be captured by people from his village who are not his kin.

Immediately after the successor has been captured, a white scarf is tied round his neck. Then he is brought to the house of the deceased; he sits down in front of it on a mat or on a thatch removed from its roof together with one of his kin, usually his mother, his sister, his mother's mother, or the brother or brother's son of the deceased.

Close kin of the successor (his sister or his mother's or father's sister or brother) put strings of white beads round his neck and one of them (usually his mother's or father's brother or sister, or sometimes his elder sister) smears his arms, legs and hair with vaseline. Usually the brother of the successor's father or mother takes a handful of millet gruel from a pot and puts it on a stone from which the successor eats it, spitting out the first mouthful and swallowing the second one. The same kinsman strikes him with the stone on his chest and back to give him strength. Instead of gruel, the successor is more frequently given beer. He again spits out the first mouthful and swallows the second. He then takes the beer and gives it, to drink, to the kinsman who first offered it to him. A small plate is put on the mat beside the seated successor, on which the people who come to 'greet' him usually put 5n or 10n. Each one receives a drink of beer from him and everybody again spits out the first mouthful and swallows the second. Close kin of the successor come to greet him first, being followed by other people from the village, and the guests who have come from other villages to attend the mourning ceremony. Sometime during the morning a black or dark hen is killed and the successor eats its heart to ensure that the *muzimu* of the deceased will enter into him.

The successor remains seated on the mat until the mid-afternoon. He is not supposed to leave the mat and when he has to go to relieve himself, he is accompanied by one of his close kinsmen, who will escort him back to it.

170

In the late afternoon, the successor, escorted by one of his close kinsmen, walks through the village from one house to another at the head of a procession formed by his kin and other guests who have come to attend the mourning ceremony. One woman carries a basket into which a woman from each household puts a plate of grain, a few maize cobs, or a plate of peanuts as her household's contribution towards the hospitality provided by the organiser of the *mayobo*.

The guests from other villages return home in the evening and only kin of the deceased, headmen, and possibly other important men from neighbouring villages stay overnight to participate in the division of the inheritance, which takes place the next morning. They again sleep in the open in front of the house of the deceased.

A *mayobo* is always held for all married people, but a *mayobo* for a woman is very frequently a much simpler affair than a *mayobo* for a man. It is quite often attended only by a few female kin of the deceased and older women from her village, who spend the night sitting and sleeping in front of the deceased's house. There is no beer and no dancing. The successor is formally installed in the morning but the entertainment of participants is limited to a simple meal of millet gruel.

As a rule, there is no *mayobo* held for children, as children up to the age of five years or so do not yet have a *muzimu*. It depends on their kin whether a *mayobo* will be held for adult men and women who die before they are married. If they are buried without a *mayobo* and their *muzimu* is not inherited, it may start causing disease to their kin, particularly small children. When the cause of the disease is investigated by a diviner, he will point out that the *muzimu* of the deceased is looking for somebody to inherit it. A *mayobo* is then eventually arranged to appease the *muzimu* and to relieve the kin of the deceased of their troubles.

8

The role of the *mukowa* in inheritance

The division of the deceased's estate among his *basimukowa* is the last stage of the mourning ceremony. If the ceremony starts on a Saturday night, the division of the estate takes place on the Monday morning, when all the movable property of the deceased is assembled in front of his house. Until then the spouse or the son of the deceased acts as the guardian of the property. The guardian always has to be present at the division of the deceased's estate for he or she knows which cattle in the kraal belong to the deceased, to whom he has loaned cattle, and where he has claims on other people's property. Before the estate of a deceased man is divided, whichever of the deceased's *basimukowa* chaired the meeting for choosing the successor, and later played the prominent role in his installation, asks the widow, her children and possibly some of her near kin, about the debts of the deceased, his cattle, cash which was in the house when he died, and about the bridewealth received for his married daughters and the way in which it was disposed of. Inquiries are made as to whether all the things left behind by the deceased have been declared by the guardian of his property, whether the things assembled in front of his house represent all his personal and household effects, and whether any of them do not in fact belong to someone else. When the deceased is a woman, similar questions are put to the widower or his nearest kin. The inquiry preceding the division of the estate is also concerned with whether the bridewealth was transferred when the deceased married because, in many instances, the fact of whether or not he was legally married determines whether or not the cattle in his kraal are part of the estate. The man who has not paid bridewealth for his wife is not entitled to bridewealth for his daughters if he is their genitor. If cows were received in bridewealth for them or purchased with the bridewealth money, their offspring belong solely to his wife and are not part of his estate, although his kinsmen might try to treat them as such. In the case of his wife's death, they are part of her estate and the widower is pressured into declaring them as such. When a man has paid bridewealth for his wife, all the offspring of the cows received for his daughters are his and his wife's joint property. In the case of the death of one of them, only half of their joint herd is part of the estate; the other half is the personal property of the surviving spouse.

The role of the mukowa *in inheritance*

The nearest kinsmen of the deceased are all informed about his or her property, and as long as the guardian's answers tally with their own knowledge, his questioning is a formal matter and usually does not take longer than a few minutes. It gains in importance when it is open to dispute whether all the cattle in the deceased's kraal were actually his or, alternatively, when his kinsmen claim that the cattle in the care of other people constitute a part of the estate. The inquiry also gains in importance when the kinsmen of the deceased are suspicious that the guardian has not declared all the property, is unable to account for part of it, or has misappropriated some of it. As the deceased did not necessarily have to keep all his cattle in one kraal, it is usually the cattle which might be difficult to trace and which the guardian is called upon to account for.

Inquiries preceding the division of every estate are thus typically concerned with three issues: the legality of the deceased's marriage, establishing what the estate properly consists of, and ensuring that the guardian has accounted for it in full and has not misappropriated any of it. Cattle, fields[1] and other property apart from the deceased's personal effects and 'the things in the house' (furniture, household utensils, agricultural implements, etc.), are allocated to individual inheritors during the inquiry. This part of the estate can sometimes be quite substantial, particularly when the deceased was a man who had a well-paid job in town. Every Toka is domiciled in a particular village even when he has been living in a town for several decades. Even when he has been buried in the town in which he was employed, the final mourning ceremony is held in his village and his estate is divided there.

For example, Siyamukwiza (V4) was domiciled in Mangulwani, where his mother and his maternal half-siblings live. He had been working as a police officer on the Copperbelt and after being killed in a car accident, he was buried there. The final mourning ceremony for him was held in Mangulwani, to which all his personal belongings were brought to be divided among his *basimukowa* (Case 1, Diagrams 20 and 21). Part of his estate was a car valued at K600 and insurance of K5360 which had been paid by the insurance company to his wife, who was his beneficiary under the terms of the policy. Both the car and the insurance were, however, treated as part of the estate and allocated to individual inheritors during the inquiry. The car was given to Siyamukwiza's maternal half-brother (V2), who has employment in town and holds a driving licence. The insurance was divided so that Siyamukwiza's four half-siblings received K480 each, his four children K600 each, his mother K540 and his wife K500.

After the questioning of the guardian and the inquiry into the deceased's property have been completed, one of the deceased's kinsmen straightens the blades of the spears and knives belonging to the deceased, which were all deliberately bent when he died. Afterwards, all the spears, axes, knives and hoes belonging to the deceased are purified with chicken's blood before they are divided as a part of the estate.

The role of the mukowa in inheritance

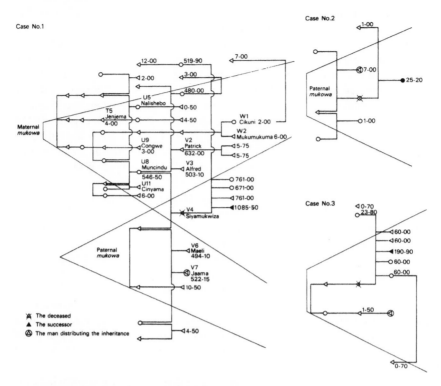

Diagram 20. Division of the deceased's estate

Following this ritual, the personal belongings of the deceased which have been assembled in front of his house are divided among his *basimukowa*, his spouse, usually a few other affines, and sometimes even unrelated people who are present during the division. As a rule, the division is carried out by the chairman of the meeting for choosing the deceased's successor. Only when he has left the village because of some other urgent business, before the division of the estate, does another of the deceased's kinsmen take care of it. He picks up one thing after another and hands them over to individual inheritors. Only those who are present during the division of the estate receive a share; the *basimukowa* of the deceased who do not attend the final mourning ceremony are excluded from inheritance. The exceptions to this rule are his children, who receive a share even if they do not attend. It is very often the labour migrants who are unable to attend. As far as their right to a share of the estate of their deceased parent is concerned, they do not suffer any disadvantage against their siblings who stay in the village and are able to attend the mourning ceremony.

174

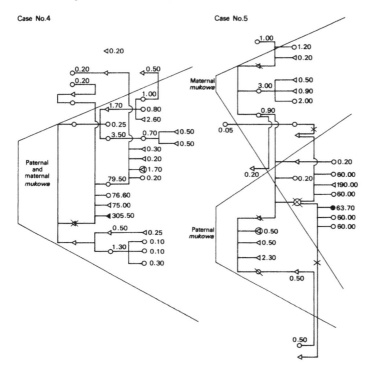

Diagram 20 (*cont.*)

I observed the division of the estates of ten people who died during my fieldwork (Diagram 20). Three of them were women (Cases 2, 5 and 8) and seven men (Cases 1, 2, 4, 6, 7, 9 and 10). The ten cases which I discuss here correspond to the first ten cases of choosing the successor discussed in the preceding chapter. For one reason or another, during the final mourning ceremonies 11, 12 and 13, which were considered in the preceding chapter, the estate was divided later and I had no opportunity to observe it.

The monetary value of the ten estates[2] ranged from K23.30 (Case 8) to K7052.75 (Case 1), the mean value being K1065.00. The value of women's estates tends to be much smaller than that of men's estates (K188.60 compared with K1440.45 in the case of men), though some of the women's estates (Case 5) are much larger than some men's estates (Cases 3, 6, 7 and 10).

The number of inheritors ranged from four (Case 2) to thirty-six (Case 7), the mean number being 17.9 and the median 23. There is no direct relationship between the size of the estate and the number of inheritors. The

175

The role of the mukowa in inheritance

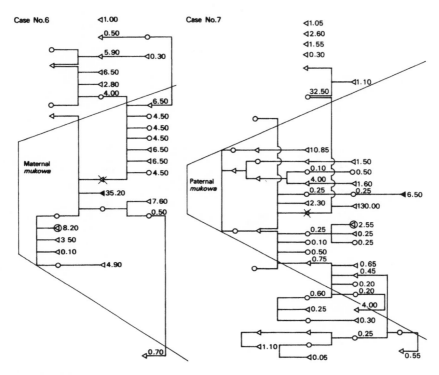

Diagram 20 (cont.)

smallest estate (Case 8) was divided among twelve inheritors, which was not the smallest number by a long way: three others (2, 3 and 9), all larger than Estate 8, were divided among fewer people. In fact, the second largest estate (9) was divided among only seven people, the second smallest number of inheritors recorded. The biggest estate (1) was divided among twenty-six inheritors, again not the largest number; two other estates (4 and 7), substantially smaller than Estate 1, were divided among a larger number of inheritors. In fact, the estate that was divided among thirty-six people, the biggest number of inheritors recorded, was considerably below average size. Rather than depending on the size of the estate, the number of inheritors depends on the number of *basimukowa* who come to attend the final mourning ceremony, which in itself is dependent on various factors, of which the distance between the deceased's village and the village in which his *basimukowa* live, is the most important.

The number of inheritors of women's estates tends to be smaller than the number of inheritors of men's estates. It varies from four to twenty-three

176

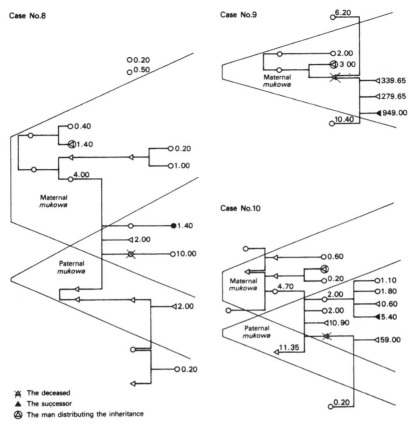

Diagram 20 (*cont.*)

with the mean number being thirteen, while the number of inheritors of men's estates varies from seven to thirty-six with the mean number being 19.9. But again, the number of inheritors of some of the women's estates (5) is larger than the number of inheritors of most of the men's estates (3, 6, 9 and 10).

The value of the ten estates and the number of people among whom they were divided are indicated in Table 14. Of the 179 inheritors among whom the ten estates were divided, 133 were the deceased's *basimukowa*. The remaining 46 were their spouses, their other affines, and people unrelated to them by kinship or affinity. I shall first analyse the inheritance by the *basimukowa* and then consider the affines and people not related to the deceased.

The ideally recognised rule that both the paternal and the maternal *basimukowa* inherit, is, in its practical application, modified by another rule

177

Table 14. *The value of the estate and the number of inheritors*

Estate	Sex of the deceased	Monetary value of the estate	Number of inheritors
1	M	K7052.75	26
2	F	K34.20	4
3	M	K457.60	9
4	M	K554.20	27
5	F	K508.35	23
6	M	K119.20	22
7	M	K209.65	36
8	F	K23.30	12
9	M	K1589.90	7
10	M	K99.85	13

stipulating that only those present during the division of the estate, with the exception of the children of the deceased, are entitled to a share. In practice, the inheritance is divided among the members of the deceased's paternal and maternal *mikowa* only when members of both attend the division. Such was the situation in Cases 1, 5, 8 and 10.

The range of *basimukowa* who inherit (apart from the deceased's own children, who always inherit), depends as much on how many of them are present as on the size of the estate. There is a marked tendency to allocate the shares to the members of a *mukowa* of a wide generational span only if the estate is sizeable, as Table 15 indicates. If the estate consists of a limited number of goods, only the nearest kinsmen of the deceased can obtain a share.

In the preceding chapter, I mentioned that the number of paternal and maternal *basimukowa* attending the final mourning ceremony is often disproportionate and that often only the members of one of the deceased's *mikowa* attend. In Cases 2 and 7, only the deceased's paternal *basimukowa* were present and consequently only they inherited. There were two members of the maternal *mukowa* of the deceased (his maternal half-brother and sister) present during the ceremony in Case 3 and they both attended the meeting for choosing his successor. Both were from a different village from his and they left for home before the division of his estate. Consequently, as in Cases 2 and 7, only the paternal *basimukowa* inherited.

In Cases 6 and 9, only the members of the maternal *mukowa* inherited as no paternal *basimukowa* of the deceased attended the final mourning ceremony.

In Case 4, all inheritors were direct descendants of the deceased or descendants of his siblings. Thus they all shared membership of the same paternal and maternal *mikowa* with him. As I explained in the preceding

Table 15. *The size of the estate and the range of the* basimukowa *inheriting*

Estate	Value of the estate	Total number of basimukowa inheriting (Children of the deceased excluded)	Number of the members of the *mukowa* of a				
			2-generational span	3-generational span	4-generational span	5-generational span	6-generational span
8	K23.30	8	2	1	5		
2	K34.20	2	2				
10	K99.85	11	5	6			
6	K119.20	7	1	6			
7	K209.65	21	6	8	4	3	
3	K457.60	1		1			
5	K508.35	13	2	11			
4	K554.20	19		9	8	2	
9	K1589.90	2	1	1			
1	K7052.75	16	6	4	2	2	2
Total		100	25	47	19	7	2

chapter, this was because the deceased was an old man who had no surviving *basimukowa* older than himself.

Although the ten estates differ considerably in size and value, their division is mutually comparable for the differences affect only the shares allocated to the deceased's children, siblings and parents but not the shares of his other *basimukowa*. When the estates differ in size, the value of the children's, siblings' and parents' shares varies considerably (see e.g. the shares of the deceased's children in Cases 6 and 9). The shares of all the other *basimukowa* do not differ greatly whether the estate is large or small – cf. e.g. the shares of the distant kinsmen in Case 8 (FBSS, MMZS, MBSD, MMZD) with those of the distant kinsmen in Case 4 (BSS, ZSS, BDD, ZDD, ZSD). For this reason, Cases 2–10 are treated together in the analysis of inheritance by the *basimukowa*. Although the division of Estate 1 displays, to a large extent, the same pattern as the other cases, it is treated separately from them for the following reasons:

(1) Due to the exceptionally high value of the estate, the shares of the deceased's siblings are much higher than in any other case. Moreover, the deceased in Case 1 had no full siblings and the shares were allocated only to his paternal and maternal half-siblings. If this case were to be considered with the others, the mean value of the shares allocated to members of the deceased's paternal and maternal *mikowa* of a two-generational span (the *mikowa* containing his paternal and maternal half-siblings) would considerably surpass the mean value of shares allocated to the deceased's full siblings, who share with him membership of the same paternal and maternal *mikowa* of a two-generational span, thus distorting the actual relations between the shares of the three categories of members of the deceased's *mukowa* of a two-generational span (members of his paternal *mukowa*, members of his maternal *mukowa*, and those who share membership of both his paternal and maternal *mikowa*).

(2) There were many more members of the deceased's maternal *mukowa* than of his paternal *mukowa* attending the final mourning ceremony in Case 1. Consequently, thirteen members of the maternal *mukowa* and only three members of the paternal *mukowa* inherited (four inheritors – the deceased's own children – were members of both his paternal and maternal *mikowa*). Due again to the exceptionally large size and value of the estate, the mean value of the shares received by them surpasses the mean value received by their counterparts in all other cases. Should Case 1 be considered together with the others, the mean value of the shares of members of the maternal *mukowa* would be inflated and that of the shares of members of the paternal *mukowa* deflated, thus considerably distorting the actual relations between the mean value of the shares of members of these two *mikowa*.

(3) Due to the large amount of goods of which the estate consisted, distant kin of the deceased (e.g. members of his *mikowa* of a five- or six-generational

Table 16. *Inheritance of Estate 1*

	Deceased's children		Members of the *mukowa* of a 2-generational span		Members of the *mukowa* of a 3-generational span		Members of the *mukowa* of a 4-generational span		Members of the *mukowa* of a 5-generational span		Members of the *mukowa* of a 6-generational span		Total		Men and women
	Men	Women	Men	Women	Men	Women	Men	Women	Men	Women	Men	Women	Men	Women	
Paternal *mukowa*			1016.25 / 2 / 508.10		10.50 / 1 / 10.50								1026.75 / 3 / 342.25		1026.75 / 3 / 342.25
Both paternal and maternal *mukowa*	1846.50 / 2 / 923.25	1432.00 / 2 / 716.00											1846.50 / 2 / 923.25	1432.00 / 2 / 716.00	3278.50 / 4 / 819.60
Maternal *mukowa*			1135.10 / 2 / 567.55	1026.50 / 2 / 513.25	12.00 / 3 / 4.00		9.00 / 2 / 4.50		6.00 / 1 / 6.00	2.00 / 1 / 2.00	8.50 / 2 / 4.25		1170.60 / 10 / 117.05	1028.50 / 3 / 342.85	2199.10 / 13 / 169.15
Total	1846.50 / 2 / 923.25	1432.00 / 2 / 716.00	2151.35 / 4 / 537.85	1026.50 / 2 / 513.25	22.50 / 4 / 5.60		9.00 / 2 / 4.50		6.00 / 1 / 6.00	2.00 / 1 / 2.00	8.50 / 2 / 4.25		4043.85 / 15 / 269.60	2460.50 / 5 / 492.10	6504.35 / 20 / 325.20
Total (men and women)	3278.50 / 4 / 819.60		3177.85 / 6 / 529.65		22.50 / 4 / 5.60		9.00 / 2 / 4.50		8.00 / 2 / 4.00		8.50 / 2 / 4.25				

In each line, the first figure indicates the total value of the shares inherited by members of the given category, the second figure indicates the number of inheritors of the given category, and the third figure indicates the mean value of the share per inheritor.

span) received shares whose value considerably surpassed the value of the shares of their counterparts in other cases (in Case 1 the value of the shares of MMZSSD was K2.00, and the mean value of the shares of MMMFBSSDS and MMMFBSS was K4.25). Should Case 1 be considered with the others, the mean value of the shares of the members of the *mukowa* of a wider generational span would be inflated and that of the shares of the members of the *mukowa* of a narrower generational span deflated, thus considerably distorting the actual relations between the mean value of the shares of members of the *mikowa* of the wider and of the narrower generational span.

The division of Estates 2–10 among the deceased's *basimukowa* is summarised in Table 17. The sex of the inheritors, their membership of the deceased's paternal or maternal *mukowa* and the generational span of the *mukowa* whose members inherit, are the variables considered in the analysis. It is based on the mean value of the shares allocated to individual inheritors falling into the three analytical categories considered. The actual value of the share allocated to a particular kinsman in the division of a particular estate can differ considerably from the mean value of the share of one member of the analytical category into which that particular kinsman falls. For example, the mean value of a son's share is K189.85. The three sons who inherited in Case 9 received shares worth K949.00, K339.65 and K279.65, whereas the three sons who inherited in Case 6 each received a portion of the estate worth K6.50. The reason is, of course, that the actual value of the share allocated to a particular kinsman in any concrete instance depends on many contingent factors (of which the size of the estate and the number of the *basimukowa* present are the most important, although not the only ones), which are disregarded in an analysis carried out in terms of analytical categories and based on the consideration of a composite account of all nine cases. The mean value, although subsuming contingencies of observed cases, cannot be used as the basis of a prediction about the division of the estate among the deceased's *basimukowa* in any actual case, for here the actors' decisions will be based on numerous specific contingencies which cannot be predicted beforehand. The mean values on which the analysis is based thus have no predictive value in themselves; the analysis, nevertheless, reveals certain regularities in the distribution of the estate which display a fairly consistent pattern from one case to another.

The first regularity that clearly emerges from the analysis of Cases 2–10 (Table 17) is that the biggest part of the deceased's estate is allocated to his children and only a very small part is widely distributed among his other *basimukowa*. The aggregate value of the shares of the deceased's children (K3291.20) was 94.5% of the aggregate value of the nine estates (K3482.15); the aggregate value of the shares allocated to all the other *basimukowa* (K190.95) was only 5.5%. In all the nine cases taken together, the mean value of the shares of the deceased's sons (K189.85) was about 4.5 times bigger

Table 17. *Inheritance of Estates 2–10*

	Deceased's children — Men	Deceased's children — Women	2-generational span — Men	2-generational span — Women	3-generational span — Men	3-generational span — Women	4-generational span — Men	4-generational span — Women	5-generational span — Men	5-generational span — Women	Total — Men	Total — Women	Men and women
Paternal *mukowa*			12.10 / 2 / 6.05	1.85 / 4 / 0.45	9.20 / 9 / 1.00	0.65 / 3 / 0.20	16.85 / 3 / 5.60	0.10 / 1 / 0.10	3.60 / 3 / 1.20		41.75 / 17 / 2.45	2.60 / 8 / 0.30	44.35 / 25 / 1.75
Both paternal and maternal *mukowa*	2658.20 / 14 / 189.85	633.00 / 15 / 42.20	60.40 / 6 / 10.05	4.45 / 4 / 1.10	18.00 / 8 / 2.25	10.50 / 10 / 1.05	9.35 / 3 / 3.10	3.00 / 6 / 0.50	1.00 / 2 / 0.50		2746.95 / 33 / 83.25	650.95 / 35 / 18.60	3397.90 / 68 / 49.95
Maternal *mukowa*				9.60 / 3 / 3.20	18.30 / 7 / 2.60	9.00 / 6 / 1.50	1.40 / 1 / 1.40	1.60 / 3 / 0.55			19.70 / 8 / 2.45	20.20 / 12 / 1.70	39.90 / 20 / 2.00
Total	2658.20 / 14 / 189.85	633.00 / 15 / 42.20	72.50 / 8 / 9.05	15.90 / 11 / 1.45	45.50 / 24 / 1.90	20.15 / 19 / 1.05	27.60 / 7 / 3.95	4.70 / 10 / 0.45	4.60 / 5 / 0.90		2808.40 / 58 / 48.40	673.75 / 55 / 12.25	
Total (men and women)	3291.20 / 29 / 113.50		88.40 / 19 / 4.65		65.65 / 43 / 1.55		32.30 / 17 / 1.90		4.60 / 5 / 0.90		3482.15 / 113 / 30.80		

Table 18. *Mean value of the shares of sons and daughters*

Estate	The deceased	Mean value of sons' shares	Mean value of daughters' shares
3	Father	K103.65	K60.00
4	Father	K190.25	K78.05
5	Mother	K190.00	K60.75
6	Father	K6.50	K4.50

than the mean value of the daughters' shares (K42.20). These differences can, however, be much smaller in individual cases (Table 18). That the sons' shares are bigger than daughters' shares holds true irrespective of whether the deceased was the children's father or mother, as Table 18 indicates. I am not considering in this table the remaining six cases when the deceased had children of only one sex.

The same pattern as in Cases 2–10 is also observable in Case 1 (Table 16), although in the latter the difference between the value of the children's shares and the value of the shares of the other *basimukowa*, compared with the difference between the value of the sons' and daughters' shares, is not so pronounced.

The next highest shares to those of the deceased's children are allocated to his siblings or parents (members of his *mukowa* of a two-generational span). The shares of all other *basimukowa* are much smaller and they decrease in size with the increase of the inheritor's genealogical distance from the deceased. All ten cases clearly indicate this tendency. In fact, the mean value of shares allocated to the genealogically distant *basimukowa* is not bigger than the mean value of shares of the deceased's affines, and only slightly bigger than the mean value of shares allocated to those who are not related through kinship or affinity, as Table 19 indicates. The mean value of the shares allocated to widows is actually bigger than the mean value of the shares of the deceased's *basimukowa* (with the exception of the shares of the children).

The successor of the deceased is the main heir. If he is his son (Cases 1, 3, 4 and 9), he always receives the biggest share of the estate.[3] When a daughter succeeds her mother (Cases 2 and 5), her share does not necessarily have to be bigger than that of her brothers, who may often inherit all their mother's cattle and fields; it is, however, bigger that the shares of her sisters. In Case 5, the share of the successor was worth K63.70 while her brother's share was worth K190.00.[4]

When the successor is not a child of the deceased (Cases 6, 7, 8 and 10), his share is not necessarily bigger than that of the deceased's children, siblings

The role of the mukowa in inheritance

Table 19. *Inheritance by the spouses, affines and unrelated people*

	Spouse		Affines		Unrelated people	
	Husband	Wife	Men	Women	Men	Women
Estate 1						
VI		K519.90	K28.50			
No.		1	5			
MVPI		K519.90	K5.70			
Estates 2–10						
VI	K1.00	K77.10	K25.65	K2.75	K7.40	K0.70
No.	1	6	17	7	7	2
MVPI	K1.00	K12.85	K1.50	K0.40	K1.05	K0.35

VI = Total value of the shares inherited by members of the given category.
No. = The number of inheritors of the given category.
MVPI = The mean value of the share per inheritor.

or parents,[5] but it is always bigger than it would have been had he not been the successor. For example, in Case 10 the biggest share of the estate (worth K59.00) was allocated to the son of the deceased. The deceased's father inherited goods worth K11.35, and his brother goods worth K10.90. The sister's son who succeeded the deceased received a share worth only K5.40. His share was, however, considerably larger than that of another sister's son who received goods worth only K0.60.

Another regularity which clearly emerges from the analysis of Cases 2–10 is that both men and women inherit, irrespective of the sex of the deceased. The practice is to allocate things associated with the performance of male roles to the men and things associated with female roles to the women. The men inherit fields, ploughs, bicycles, axes, spears, tools, men's clothes, etc., whereas women inherit hoes, pestles and mortars, cooking-pots, cutlery, crockery, glasses, women's clothes, etc. Both men and women inherit cattle and cash. Obviously things associated with the performance of women's roles form a larger part of women's estates than they do of men's, and thus it is not surprising that women predominate among inheritors of women's estates. Three such estates in my sample (Cases 2, 5 and 8) were divided among twelve male and twenty female *basimukowa*. Conversely, men predominate among inheritors of men's estates. The six estates of the deceased men (Cases 3, 4, 6, 7, 9 and 10) were divided among forty-six male and thirty-six female *basimukowa*. But women sometimes predominate even among the inheritors of men's estates. For example, in Case 4 twelve women and eleven men inherited and in Case 10 there were seven female and five male inheritors.

Case 1 displays the same pattern of distribution of male and female inheritors as the remaining nine cases, although in this particular case the number of male inheritors was much bigger than the number of female inheritors. The fact that male inheritors predominate in all ten cases taken together (there were altogether seventy-three male and sixty female inheritors) is mainly due to the fact that there were seven deceased men and only three deceased women in my sample.

Although both men and women inherit, the mean value of shares allocated to men and women is not equal. Just as the mean value of the daughters' shares is smaller than that of the sons' shares, so the mean values of the shares allocated to other female *basimukowa* are consistently smaller in Cases 2–10 than the shares of the male *basimukowa*, again irrespective of whether the deceased was a man or a woman: in all nine cases considered together, the mean value of the shares allocated to male inheritors was K48.40, whereas that of the shares of females was K12.25. These figures include the shares of sons and daughters. When these are excluded, the mean value of men's shares was K3.40 and that of women's shares K1.00. Similarly, the mean value of shares allocated to female affines is smaller than that of the shares of male affines and the shares of women not related by kinship or affinity to the deceased are smaller than those of unrelated men.

As I mentioned before, only five female *basimukowa* were allocated shares in Case 1. Two of them were the deceased's daughters, another two his maternal half-sister and his mother, who both received large shares (totalling K1026.50), and the last was a distant matrilateral relative (MMZSSD), who received a share worth K2.00. Although the mean value of the shares of the female members of the maternal *mukowa* of a two-generational span (the category including the deceased's mother and his maternal half-sister) is smaller than that of the male members of this category (K513.25 as against K567.55), the mean value of the shares of all female members of the maternal *mukowa* is much bigger than the mean value of all its male members (K342.85 as against K117.05). This is due to the fact that there were many more distant male members of the maternal *mukowa* among the inheritors than distant female members (eight against one). The male members received only small ̇ares and, as these were included in the calculation of the aggregate value ˅ne shares of all the male members of the maternal *mukowa*, their low value affected the aggregate mean value.

When both the paternal and the maternal *basimukowa* of the deceased attend the mourning ceremony, they hardly ever equal one another in numbers. In all four cases when both were present (1, 5, 8 and 10), the maternal *basimukowa* outnumbered the paternal ones, and they outnumber them by 33:28 even when all the ten cases are considered together. As already mentioned, however, this cannot be taken as an indication of greater importance being ascribed to the maternal *mukowa*.

The analysis of the division of the ten estates in terms of shares allocated to the members of the two *mikowa* might, nevertheless, be taken as indicative of a preference for the maternal *basimukowa* as inheritors. Although the mean value of the shares of the male members of the paternal and maternal *mikowa*[6] in Cases 2–10 is precisely the same (K2.45), the mean value of the shares of the female members of the maternal *mukowa* is much higher than that of the female members of the paternal *mukowa* (K1.70 as against K0.30) and the aggregate mean value of the shares of all the maternal *basimukowa* is higher than that of the paternal *basimukowa* (K2.00 as against K1.75). But this difference again cannot be interpreted as an indication of preference for the maternal *basimukowa*. The inheritors' membership of either of the two *mikowa* is not a primary consideration governing the allocation of particular shares. When more paternal than maternal *basimukowa* attend the mourning ceremony, a greater part of the estate is allocated to the paternal *basimukowa*; when more maternal *basimukowa* attend, the situation is reversed. That the shares of the female maternal *basimukowa* in my sample are higher than those of the female paternal *basimukowa*, is due simply to the fact that more female than male members of the maternal *mukowa* attended the division of the estates and, in the absence of male inheritors, received rather higher shares than they would have if more male members had attended.

The division of Estate 1 bears out this conclusion. Ten male and only three female maternal *basimukowa* attended it. The fact that the aggregate mean value of the shares of the female members of the maternal *mukowa* is higher than that of the shares of its male members is clearly due to the high shares of the deceased's mother and maternal half-sister, which were not offset, in the calculation of the aggregate value, by lower shares of more distant kinswomen, as it was in the case of the aggregate value of the shares of the male members of the maternal *mukowa*.

The choosing of the successor and the division of the estate among the deceased's *basimukowa* are situations widely open to manipulation. Although ideally a particular person's membership of either the deceased's paternal or his maternal *mukowa* is not taken into consideration when shares are allocated, members of both *mikowa* often try to manipulate the situation to their advantage. The choosing of the successor and the division of the estate in Case 1 provide an illustration (Diagram 21).

The deceased was Siyamukwiza (V4), who had been working as a police officer on the Copperbelt. He was the youngest son of Muncindu (U8), from Mangulwani village, begotten by her second husband, Siyanga. After Siyamukwiza's death, his wife, Monde, moved with her four children from the Copperbelt to Mangulwani.

Some time after the death, Alfred (V3), Muncindu's son from her previous marriage, and Monde, disappeared from the village. Alfred's explanation was that they had gone to buy a bicycle for his mother. In fact, together with Alfred's full-brother, Patrick (V2), who had been working in Livingstone,

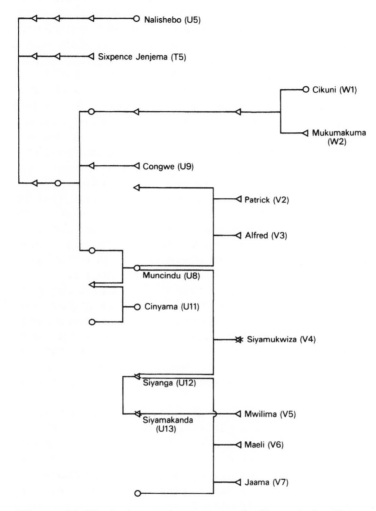

Diagram 21. The final mourning ceremony for Siyamukwiza (Case 1)

they had gone to see a diviner to enquire about the cause of Siyamukwiza's death. They returned to the village after five days and did not give any account of their journey. It was generally assumed that the diviner had indicated that the maternal *basimukowa* of the deceased, to whom Alfred (V3) and Patrick (V2) belong, had been responsible for the death. If it had been otherwise, people reasoned, Alfred and Patrick would have mentioned the result of the divination.

The general feeling before the final mourning ceremony was that either

Jaama (V7) or Alfred (V3), Siyamukwiza's paternal and maternal half-brothers respectively, were likely to succeed, as Siyamukwiza had only two small sons. The question of the successor was a rather important issue as a major estate was at stake and, as usual, a substantial portion of it would go to the successor. In spite of the suspicion of witchcraft, Alfred (V3) was backed by the inhabitants of Mangulwani, who are all maternal *basimukowa* of the deceased. Being a potential candidate, he avoided attending the meeting at which the successor was chosen.

Jaama (V7), from Bucwani village, knew that Alfred (V3) was supported by all the inhabitants of Mangulwani, where the final mourning ceremony took place. He realised that the maternal *basimukowa* of the deceased would be in the majority at the meeting, and that his own candidacy did not stand a chance against this body. Being a member of Siyamukwiza's *mukowa* and a guest in Mangulwani, he was asked to convene the meeting of the *basimukowa* to decide on the successor. Unlike Alfred (V3), he decided to take part in it and to influence its deliberations to his own and Siyamukwiza's paternal *basimukowa*'s advantage.

The following people took part in the meeting: Muncindu (U8), Cinyama (U11), Cikuni (W1), Jenjema (T5), and Nalishebo (U5), all Siyamukwiza's maternal *basimukowa*, and Jaama (V7) and Maeli (V6), his paternal *basimukowa*. Because an argument between the members of the two *mikowa* was expected, Muncindu (U8) asked the headman of a neighbouring village and another old man from a neighbouring village, who were not Siyamukwiza's kinsmen but who came to attend the final mourning ceremony, to attend the meeting.

At the meeting, Muncindu (U8) proposed her son Alfred (V3) as Siyamukwiza's successor. Jaama (V7) strongly opposed this. He pointed out that, should Alfred (V3) succeed, all the estate would go to the maternal *basimukowa*, and the paternal *basimukowa* would be left with nothing. He said that Muncindu (U8) was like a grain-bin in that she was only keeping Siyamukwiza's property, but its owner had a right to come and take it. This argument, which fairly summarised the reasons behind the struggle for succession, left the maternal *basimukowa* unimpressed. Jaama's second argument was more convincing. He said that Siyamukwiza (V4) most probably died because he was bewitched (not indicating who was responsible for his death); should an old successor be installed, he might also be bewitched as the deceased was. A little boy cannot speak for himself (i.e. cannot claim any property for himself) and therefore does not face the danger of being bewitched. At the end of his speech Jaama (V7) proposed Siyamukwiza's four-year-old son as the successor. This compromise solution was acceptable to the maternal *basimukowa*; the struggle between the paternal and maternal *basimukowa* was postponed until the division of the estate.

Shares of the estate were allocated by Jaama (V7). Although this obviously displeased all the maternal *basimukowa*, the most prominent of whom were Muncindu (U8), Alfred (V3) and Patrick (V2), there was no way they could stop it. Jaama (V7) was a senior member of Siyamukwiza's *mukowa* and was a visitor in Mangulwani. As such he had to be asked to convene the meeting for choosing the successor and, as a result of this, it was his prerogative to allocate the shares of the estate to the assembled inheritors. Very slowly, he picked up one thing after another and handed them over to individual people. Although the maternal *basimukowa* could not stop him allocating the shares, they expressed their dissatisfaction with the way in which he was handling the situation by loud groaning and, ostensibly to speed the division of the estate, Patrick (V2) stepped in and started helping Jaama (V7).

The conflict between the paternal and maternal *basimukowa* came into the open when the sewing-machine was to be allocated. Jaama (V7) claimed it for himself. By doing that, he actually behaved as a successor, for a sewing-machine, like a gun, a plough, a bicycle, or a grinding-machine, is normally inherited either by the successor or by the children of the deceased. Muncindu (U8) strongly objected and suggested that it should be given to Alfred (V3), who was the best tailor around. Just as Jaama (V7) was assuming the role of successor for himself by claiming the sewing-machine, Muncindu (U8) was now in fact assuming this role for her son, Alfred (V3), whom she had already pushed forward as a successor at the meeting. The conflicting claims of the paternal and maternal *basimukowa* at the meeting had been resolved by recourse to an alternative solution: that of appointing the deceased's son, although a minor, as his father's successor. This solution, by virtue of being a normative one and not harming one party at the expense of the other, was acceptable to both. Similarly, the conflicting claims to the sewing-machine were resolved after a heated discussion by recourse to a normative solution: it was allocated to the deceased's children, for whom it would be kept in custody by their mother. Neither of the rival parties gained or lost and both could thus accept this solution.

Similar conflicts about the allocation of shares to the paternal and maternal *basimukowa* regularly accompany the division of inheritance when a substantial estate is at stake both in Guta and Cifokoboyo, where the *mukowa* is conceptualised as a category of matrilineal kin, and in Ngwezi, where it is seen as a cognatic descent category. The changing notion of descent reckoning and the accompanying changes in the norms of succession and inheritance in Ngwezi lead to a new type of conflict which did not exist previously: a conflict triggered off by the possibility of invoking in any particular situation either the traditional matrilineal or the new cognatic ideology. I shall return to such conflicts in the final chapter.

9

Mukowa: representational and operational models

Among the Ngwezi Toka, the term *mukowa* refers to a collectivity of people who are all cognatic descendants of one common ancestor supposed to have lived some five or six generations before his present youngest living descendants were born. The Toka are able to define various situations as those into which people are recruited because of their *mukowa* membership. When talking about these, they present them as *mukowa* affairs.

So they say that the *basimukowa* have to give consent for the marriages of *mukowa* members, that the *basimukowa* of the deceased decide during the final mourning ceremony on the successor to his name, that they inherit his estate and that the *mukowa* performs rain-making rituals. Unlike in Guta and Cifokoboyo, the Ngwezi Toka claim that those who belong to the *mukowa* whose member or apical ancestor founded a village, are its owners.

In these statements they speak of the *mikowa* as social groups which clearly crystallise in various interactional contexts, and ascribe to them a distinct corporateness. It would be easy to see them in the way in which they obviously talk about them, i.e. as descent groups, and then to describe and analyse them as such. Although anthropologists use other data apart from the verbal statements of their informants, it seems that it is probably the actors' own verbalisations which are responsible for the anthropological model of corporate descent groups, whose essential elements have been presented in the classic studies of African lineage systems. Such a model treats groups whose members are recruited on the basis of descent criteria as the main elements of the social structure.

Scheffler criticises this model in his stricture that a communality of descent does not itself 'make' a group (Scheffler 1966: 544), and I take it that Keesing had this model in mind when he observed that 'perhaps more theorists of kinship over the years have come to grief or caused confusion by losing track of the difference between social groups and cultural categories than by any other conceptual flaw' (Keesing 1975: 9), and that 'the anthropological literature is full of confusions about "clans" and "lineages" and "kindreds" where the distinction between groups and categories, corporations and action groups, have been blurred or overlooked' (ibid.; see also Keesing 1971).

191

If 'group' is merely an analytical concept, as La Fontaine explicitly suggests (1973: 38), and when the object of the analysis is not an explanation of the actual social processes but of the actors' cultural notions or the cognitive structure of a given society, the group can be ideologically defined, as Scheffler expresses it (1966: 547), i.e. defined in terms of the ideology of group membership. A distinction between categories and groups is then not an issue, or at least not the major one.

The situation becomes quite different when the object of the analysis is an explanation of the actual social processes as opposed to merely a study of the actors' notions or their ideological representations, or when its object is an explanation of the relations between the events and transactions in which the actors engage and the cultural notions or representations which they hold. When, as Keesing expresses it, 'we pay closer attention to who does what with whom' instead of trying 'to explain the behaviour of individuals as a product of (or deviation from) the system' (1975: 126, 122), the distinction between groups and categories becomes of crucial importance.

Scheffler has demonstrated the analytical importance of this distinction in his study of Choiseul Island social structure, which aims at an explanation of the relationship between the social processual order and the notional order of the Choiseul Islanders. In his analysis of the *sinangge*, a kin unit consisting of all descendants, through both males and females, of an apical ancestor known to have founded the unit, he distinguishes cognatic descent categories (Scheffler 1965: 53–62) and descent groups which form the 'primary residential proprietary segments' of Choiseul society (ibid.: 92ff). This analytical distinction follows closely Choiseulese conceptualisations, according to which 'the descent group is sometimes viewed as those of the *sinangge* who have, literally translated "stayed put" as opposed to those who have "gone out"' (ibid.: 57).

The distinction between groups and categories is central also to Keesing's analysis of Kwaio social structure, which I closely follow here. Keesing distinguishes clearly the level of actual social processes from the level of Kwaio notions. He points out that Kwaio social structure could be described as a set of primary segments (consisting of descent group members domiciled in their estate, plus their spouses) 'forming discrete corporations and independent political units; but interlocked into a wider system by cross-cutting webs of cognatic kinship, by secondary interest of complementary filiation, and by affinal alliance' (Keesing 1971: 125). But such a model is deficient in that it confuses the realm of the actors' conceptual world with the realm of processual order (ibid.: 126). Keesing argues that Kwaio individuals who live in the same settlement or territory cannot usefully be viewed as a 'descent group'. Rather they 'fall into a complex pattern of partially overlapping categories. Cultural principles governing interactions, rights and transactions are structured in terms of these categories; and it is from these categories that different social groups are crystallised in defined contexts' (ibid.).

In a way similar to that in which Kwaio social structure could be described, Toka social structure could be seen as a set of *mukowa* segments localised in particular villages and interlocked into a wider system by ritual ties that bind the segment members within a *mukowa* of a wider span, and both the *mikowa* and their segments could be seen as social groups that convene and have a certain form and degree of continuity, discreteness and organisation. Such a notion could easily be derived from the Toka's own verbalisations. It is, however, important to realise that when the Toka speak of the *mikowa* convening for the performance of certain activities, they are providing us merely with an insight into their representations, or with an insight into notions about the form of their society, and not with a description of what actually happens on the ground. A Toka who says that it is the *basimukowa* who chose a successor to the name of one of their number would certainly be astonished if he saw, during the final mourning ceremony, all those whom he considers to be the deceased's *basimukowa* trying to attend the meeting at which the successor is to be chosen. Similarly, a Toka who says that it is the deceased's *basimukowa* who inherit his estate would hardly comprehend a situation in which all those whom he distinguished as the deceased's *basimukowa* demanded, and were given, a share.

The terms *mukowa* and *basimukowa*, which the Toka use in their general descriptions of the structure of their society, are highly indexical. When they speak of the *basimukowa* as convening for the performance of certain activities, the term *basimukowa* is not incorrect; it is simply too general and unqualified, for all the qualifications which would be needed for a description of the actual processes and rules that govern them are left unspoken. I would suggest that the main deficiency of the anthropological model of corporate descent groups is the analytical failure to realise the indexicality of the actors' descent group idiom, and the treatment of the descent group in terms of an absolute, unqualified meaning. The result is then an unwarranted presentation of the actors' representations as isomorphic with the actual social processes which they guide and determine.

When it comes to the way the actors practically respond or act, they are not guided by their representations. They invoke their operational model, whose elements are the concepts, categories and cultural rules for making decisions about affiliation and appropriate action in particular situations which every individual actively manipulates in the course of his behaviour. It is these rules that enable the actors to make decisions, behave appropriately and anticipate one another's actions. Keesing points out that these 'cultural "rules", like linguistic "rules", are largely unconscious' (1971: 125) in the sense that the actors are seldom able to verbalise them. They belong to the vast amount of intersubjectively shared background expectancies; because the actors take these expectancies for granted, they hardly ever make them explicit. When an actor behaves in a specific way, he is 'responsive to this background, while at the same time he is at a loss to tell us specifically of what the expectancies consist. When we ask him about them, he has little or nothing to say' (Garfinkel 1967: 36–7). It does not follow, however, that if the actors themselves hardly ever make verbally explicit the rules which they actively operate in the course of their behaviour, that these rules have to remain unavailable for sociological analysis.

To describe the rules which the Toka operate in making decisions about affiliation and appropriate action in the situations about which they themselves talk as *mukowa* affairs, it is useful to view '*mukowa* member' as a social identity (Goodenough 1965) which individuals assume in certain situations. Central to Goodenough's analysis of 'roles' is his perception that in real-life situations actors seldom occupy only one social identity at a time. Appropriate action is defined by combining the role entailments of the component social identities.

The social identity of a '*mukowa* member' gives its bearer the right to attend a meeting for choosing the deceased's successor only if it is combined with some other social identity. Apart from being a '*mukowa* member', he has at the same time to be either a member of a more senior generation than the deceased himself, or to be older in age than the deceased. 'Senior to the deceased' is a social identity relationship which may be assumed on the basis of age (if membership of the deceased's own generation is concerned). Only if no senior *basimukowa* of the deceased are alive or present, will those *basimukowa* with the social identity of 'junior to the deceased' attend the meeting. Apart from being a '*mukowa* member', an individual will be entitled to attend the meeting only if he is genealogically closely related to the deceased. 'Close kinsman' is a social identity relationship which is not defined on the basis of descent but on the basis of kinship. Again, apart from being merely a '*mukowa* member', an individual will be entitled to attend the meeting if he combines this social identity with that of a 'distinguished guest' in the deceased's village. Basically, all *basimukowa* of the deceased who come to attend the final mourning ceremony from other villages, assume an identity of distinguished guests. This identity itself is graded. The more distant the individual's own village is from that of the deceased and the older he or she is, the more distinguished a guest the individual is and the stronger is his or her entitlement to participate in the meeting.

Descent criteria are intertwined with criteria of cognatic kinship (as well as criteria of seniority or residence), not only in the assumption of the identity of a participant at the meeting for choosing the successor to the name of the deceased, but also in the assumption of the identity of an inheritor of the deceased's estate. Again, primarily those in the identity relationship of *basimukowa* to the deceased are entitled to inherit. The size of the inheritance allocated to them depends, however, on the closeness of their cognatic kinship to the deceased. The shares next highest to those of the deceased's children are allocated to his siblings or parents. The shares of all other *basimukowa* are much smaller and they decrease in size with the increase of the inheritor's genealogical distance from the deceased. In fact, the mean value of shares allocated to the genealogically distant *basimukowa* is not bigger than the mean value of shares allocated to the deceased's affines, and only slightly bigger than the mean value of shares allocated to those who are not related to the deceased through kinship or affinity. We can see here that the concept of cognatic kinship is operationally used alongside the descent concept to define the boundary of the *mukowa*. This boundary, conceptualised in kinship terms, is not sharp and clear-cut. As the notion of kinship fades with increasing genealogical distance until it gradually turns into non-kinship, so in a sense can the *mukowa* be visualised as a field of gradually decreasing intensity of relationship. At one end of this continuum are the people who are clearly *basimukowa* in all contexts, at the other end are those who are not *basimukowa*. There is an area in the continuum where the social identity of a '*mukowa* member' may be assumed in some situations but not in others.

A situation in which even those people who stand at the very edge of *mukowa* membership in certain situations (like that of inheritance) will interact on the basis of their social identity as '*mukowa* member', is the rain-making ritual. Again, it is only people with the social identity of a '*mukowa* member' who become its participants. But again, as in other situations, it is not this social identity alone which recruits participants. They get recruited only as long as they are, at the same time, residents in the neighbourhood in which the rain-making ritual is performed.

The closeness of cognatic kinship qualifies the status of a '*mukowa* member' not only when the successor is chosen and the estate of the deceased divided among his inheritors, but also when the approval of the *basimukowa* for the marriage of one of their number is sought. The parents of the boy or girl to be married usually inform one of their close kinsmen living in the same village as they are, about the marriage. The social identity relationship of '*mukowa* member' *vis-à-vis* the person to be married is assumed here by an individual who stands, at the same time, in the social identity relationship of close kinsman and village co-resident.

In Ngwezi, the only social identity based directly on that of '*mukowa* member' and unqualified by any other identity, is that of a village owner. It is simply one's membership of the *mukowa* which defines one's ownership of a village. Not even one's actual residence qualifies one in any way as an owner of a village. One can be an owner of a certain village, and one is entitled to exercise one's ownership rights in it, even when one resides in a different village.

195

Mukowa: *representational and operational models*

The Toka representational model which conceives of the situations which I have briefly surveyed here as *mukowa* affairs is not incorrect in the sense that only people with the social identity of a '*mukowa* member' are entitled to participate in them. Where the Toka's representational and operational models differ, is that the operational model takes into account various other identities that have to accompany the social identity of a '*mukowa* member' to entitle him actually to participate. What follows is that the entity which the Toka call *mukowa* in their verbal statements is not one and the same thing in all the situations to which their verbal statements refer. The meanings of the terms *mukowa* and *basimukowa* vary contextually on two scales. One scale is that of the size of the *mukowa*, which varies from one single individual who approves somebody's marriage, the approval being taken as that of the *mukowa*, to the inhabitants of several villages of the same neighbourhood who participate in the same rain-making ritual, which is conceived of as a *mukowa* affair in the same way as the approval of a marriage is. The other scale on which the meaning of the term *mukowa* contextually varies is that of the rigidity with which the criterion of descent is applied in the definition of the social identity of a *mukowa* member in a given context. Here we have, at one end of the scale, an owner of a village (whose social identity is assumed solely on the basis of the descent criterion), and at the other end a participant in a meeting for choosing a successor to the name of the deceased. The social identity of the participant is assumed on the basis of the criteria of descent, cognatic kinship, seniority, and residence. At the level of Toka verbal statements, village ownership, like the selection of a successor, is again a *mukowa* affair. There are thus shifts in the ranks of one's *basimukowa* from context to context, although there may be some individuals who act as one's *basimukowa* in all of them.

If, following Scheffler (1965, 1966) and Keesing (1971, 1975), we define a social group on the basis of interaction and not on the basis of some formal criteria of membership, a *mukowa* is not a social group, even less a corporate social group, although the Toka representational model may present it as such. It is simply a cultural category – a class of individuals who share a common attribute, which in this case is their descent from a common ancestor. Aggregates of people which can be seen as groups are the co-residents of a village, the participants in a meeting for choosing a successor, those who have assembled to divide the estate of a deceased or to participate in a rain-making ritual. As far as all these groups are concerned, it is the membership of the *mukowa* category which defines entitlement to membership of them. But membership of the *mukowa* does not assign members to these groups or define their boundaries. Actual membership decisions involve many cultural principles unrelated to descent, the most important of these being kinship, residence and seniority.

We might think of these groups as descent groups in the sense that they consist 'of a cluster of persons acting in social identity relationships defined on the basis of descent ... or assumed partly on grounds of descent entitlement or obligation' (Keesing 1971: 129). These social identities may in turn be elements within complex social personae, other elements of which are not based on the criterion of descent (for example kinsman, old man, distinguished visitor, village resident). Descent groups, so conceived, exist only insofar as they periodically crystallise in particular interactional situations. Outside these situations, they have no temporal continuity. It is only the descent categories that have such temporal continuity.

Most of the above-mentioned groups crystallising in different interactional situations are what most sociologists or anthropologists would call action or task groups. Many sociologists and anthropologists would consider as a group, not only a unit that convenes for the performance of a specific task, but also a unit that has a certain form and degree of continuity, corporateness, discreteness and organisation, though these characteristics may be variously defined (see for example Firth 1963: 36; Fortes 1953: 36; Freeman 1961: 202–3; Goffman 1961: 9–14; Sprott 1958: 9–22). A 'descent group' so conceived among the Toka has a continuing existence in any one of its various manifestations only in the sense that the same cluster of actual persons recurrently assume the social identity of *mukowa* members.

To return to the model of corporate descent groups which it would be possible to construct as an explanatory model of Toka social structure if we took the Toka's own representational model and failed to distinguish it clearly from their operational model, we can see that by talking of descent groups instead of merely descent categories, we would ascribe continuity and discreteness to something which has no such continuity or discreteness either on the Toka's notional or on their transactional level. In other words, we would reify something which simply is not there among the Toka.

10

Norms as a strategic resource

The discussion in the preceding chapters has concentrated on the description of the new way of conceptualising the *mukowa* and on the new norms of succession and inheritance which have emerged in Ngwezi during the past few decades. The traditional notions about descent, village ownership, succession and inheritance, described in Chapter 1, have, however, not disappeared from consciousness. They coexist alongside the newly emerged notions and are part of the cultural knowledge not only of those who advocate their continuing validity, but also of those who dispute or challenge it. In this respect, the culture of the Ngwezi Toka is less homogeneous than that of Guta and Cifokoboyo in that it encompasses two different ideologies and two different normative systems. In this chapter, I consider how these ideologies and their accompanying norms are being manipulated in the course of people's strategic behaviour.

In the discussion of the change in the inheritance system among the Ngwezi Toka, I pointed out that the norm stipulating the relationship of the successor and main heir to the deceased has been adapted to include the son, who was traditionally excluded from succeeding his father and becoming his main heir. The sister's son, however, has not been barred from his traditional prerogative of becoming the successor and main heir. If we take the norm stating that a man's son should succeed him and become his main heir as a norm of agnatic succession, and a norm stipulating that the sister's son should be his successor and main heir as a norm of uterine succession, the system of inheritance and succession in Ngwezi can be seen as one in which both these norms are recognised as valid and exist side by side. It has changed from the previous system in which only the norm of uterine succession and inheritance was recognised as valid, but it has not changed in the sense that this norm has become obsolete and been replaced by the norm of agnatic succession and inheritance.

Similarly, the norm of tracing descent for the purpose of *mukowa* membership has been adapted in the sense that the traditional matrilineal descent has not become obsolete, but the cognatic descent has also been recognised as a valid qualification for *mukowa* membership alongside it.

Norms as a strategic resource

It has already been pointed out in Chapter 2 that norms do not bring about behaviour by themselves but only by being invoked in action by specific individuals. Any such invocation is successful only when the appropriateness of the norm is accepted by all others concerned. Among the Ngwezi Toka, both the norm of uterine succession and that of agnatic succession can be invoked and both are recognised by others as valid. Invocation of these two norms is differently legitimised. The norm of agnatic succession is legitimised by an appeal to what might be considered a principle of natural justice: another norm, which stipulates that those who have helped to produce a man's wealth are entitled to inherit it, is invoked in support of the norm of agnatic succession. The norm of uterine succession is invariably legitimised by the invocation of the Toka tradition: 'This is what we have always done' or 'This is what our ancestors have always done. Surely, what was the way of our ancestors, is the right way for us' is the usual way of expressing it. As the legitimisation of the norm of uterine succession is always expressed on this abstract level, its effective invocation depends on its collective support. The legitimisation of the norm of agnatic succession is much more specific. In this case, it is not a question of invoking in general terms what the ancestors have always done, but a question of specifically invoking the fact that the prospective successor had ploughed with his father and thus helped to build up the wealth whose greater portion ought to go to him and will go to him if he succeeds.

Two ideologies with their associated norms and values thus exist side by side in Ngwezi: the matrilineal ideology with its accompanying notion of uterine succession validated by tradition and the correctness of the way of the ancestors, and the new cognatic ideology with its accompanying notion of agnatic succession and the concomitant value of natural justice.

The norms of uterine and agnatic succession can be invoked in the same situation. Their invocation and legitimisation has, however, different weight in cases of succession to the names of non-headmen than in cases of succession to the names of village headmen.

Choosing a successor of a non-headman is a situation that directly involves only a limited number of people. It is for this reason that the norm of uterine succession, which needs a collective recognition or support, is easily disregarded when it conflicts with the principle of natural justice that legitimises the norm of agnatic succession. This is due to the fact that, in a situation in which only a limited number of people are involved, the specific opposition to tradition is more telling than the non-specific traditional opposition to natural justice. Because this is so, the legitimisation of the norm of agnatic succession by an appeal to the principle of natural justice usually clinches the argument. Only when the traditional way cannot be repudiated by the invocation of this principle does the legitimisation of the norm of uterine succession, by an appeal to the ancestors' way, clinch the argument.

Norms as a strategic resource

It is significant that in the three recorded cases of uterine succession to the names of non-headmen (see Table 12 and also Chapter 3, p. 82), what is considered to be the traditional Toka way was adhered to because it did not conflict with the recognised principles of natural justice.

The interplay of the norms of agnatic and uterine succession, or the interplay of what the Toka recognise as their traditional ways and what they recognise as principles of natural justice, is more complex in cases of succession to village headmanship. Not only do these two notions, which can be mutually conflicting, enter here, but very often the traditional and modern conceptualisation of the *mukowa* as well. The reasons for this complexity derive from the fact that, in a case of succession to the name of a non-headman, only the succession to the deceased's personal position is concerned. This is not so when the deceased was a village headman because, apart from the succession to his personal position, succession to the village headmanship itself is automatically involved. The social position of the deceased as a village headman overrides in importance his personal position, as many more people are affected by the succession to the former than by the succession to the latter. Obviously, the fact that many more are concerned brings in a wider range of personal interests in whose pursuit the different existing norms and ideologies may be invoked by different people, thus making the situation more open to manipulation than when the deceased was not a village headman. On the other hand, the fact that the position of the deceased as a headman overrides in importance his personal position, automatically adds more weight to the traditional matrilineal ideology.

Whereas this ideology can be repelled by a resort to the principle of natural justice when the deceased was not a headman, it can hardly be repelled in the same way when succession to village headmanship is the issue. Should the son not succeed and become the main heir of his father, who was a village headman and with whom he cooperated in ploughing, the recognised principle of natural justice would be violated. But it would only be the deceased's son himself, or possibly a few of his nearest kin, who would be adversely affected. On the other hand, should the son succeed because the principle of natural justice is observed, the majority of the village inhabitants might suffer. In this respect, the situation of succession to the position of a village headman is in a way a reversal of that of succession to the position of a non-headman: in the former situation it is the norm of agnatic succession and its supporting principle of natural justice which are easily disregarded when opposition to them is clearly expressed. Although they are known to everybody and shared by all, they are directly relevant only to a few whose succession to the headmanship would be upheld by them. They are not relevant to the rest of the community; the norm of agnatic succession would not qualify the rest of the community for the office, and they therefore have no vested interest in positively invoking it. By remaining ideologically neutral

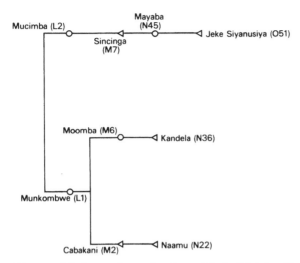

Diagram 22. Succession to headmanship in Mujala village

in this way, the rest of the community automatically tends to support the traditional norm and its accompanying ideology. It is for this reason that the traditional matrilineal ideology is almost invariably accepted by all concerned when someone opposes the succession of a son and invokes the matrilineal ideology in support of some other candidate.

The efficacy of the invocation of the traditional matrilineal ideology is well illustrated by the case of succession to the village headmanship in Mujala village (Diagram 22). Cabakani (M2), the headman of Mujala, died in the mid-1930s, but the way in which his successor was chosen is still well remembered by people both in Mujala itself and in Mujalanyana, which split off from it soon afterwards. There were no discrepancies in the ways in which my several informants recounted the events. They all agreed that there were three main contestants for headmanship: Cabakani's eldest son, Naamu (N22), and his 'grandson', Jeke (O51), who both lived in Mujala, and his sister's son, Kandela (N36), who had been born and was living in Cabalanda, his father's village, into which his mother had moved after her marriage. It was generally expected that Naamu (N22) would succeed. While his father was still alive, he had run errands for him and he was much better acquainted than anybody else with the duties and responsibilities of headmanship. He was from Mujala village and everybody there knew him well, which was another factor that was strongly in his favour. Jeke (O51) was aware of Naamu's popularity and support and tried very hard to gain the backing of his fellow-villagers. When there were visitors in the village, he took care of them, thus performing a duty which is normally that of the village headman. Most of the time he was sitting under the shelter in the middle of the village ready to be seen by everybody, and whenever beer was brewed in the village he would buy it for all the villagers. Kandela (N36) was generally considered the least likely candidate. Not only was he much younger than Jeke (O51) and Naamu (N22), but he did not even live in Mujala and some of the people there hardly knew him at all.

At the meeting where Cabakani's successor was to be chosen, both Naamu (N22) and Jeke (O51) were proposed. But Kandela's mother, Moomba (M6), rejected them both on the same grounds and suggested her own son as the successor. She pointed out that Cabakani's mother, Munkombwe (L1), had herself been born in Mujala and that she was an owner of the village into which Cabakani's father had married. Like his mother, Cabakani (M2) was an owner of the village and was its headman by right. According to her, Naamu (N22) was in a different situation, for his mother was not an owner of the village. She had merely been brought into it by Cabakani (M2) and, according to Moomba (M6), she was just like a slave there. Although Sincinga (M7), like Cabakani, was an owner of Mujala and could also have been a headman there, his daughter, Mayaba (N45), was not an owner of Mujala. Sincinga's wife was from Citengu village and her daughter, Mayaba (N45), like her mother, was an owner of Citengu; so was her son, Jeke (O51). Although he was Cabakani's 'grandson', unlike Cabakani (M2), he was not an owner of Mujala; he could become headman of Citengu but not of Mujala. It would be wrong to support either Naamu (N22) or Jeke (O51) as a successor to Cabakani (M2) as neither of them was an owner of the village and the people of Mujala would suffer should either one of them succeed to the headmanship. Moomba (M6) pointed out that, although she had been married to Cabalanda, she was an owner of Mujala village as her mother had been born there and was one of its owners. Her son, Kandela (N36), like she herself, was an owner of Mujala. He was the only one who could succeed to Cabakani's name and to the headmanship of the village as he was the only candidate who was an owner of the village. Her argument, which was based on the straightforward invocation of the traditional matrilineal ideology, won and Kandela (N36) was chosen as Cabakani's successor. The fact that Moomba (M6) was the oldest person present at the meeting contributed to her argument being so readily accepted.

As I mentioned before, Naamu (N22) and his followers moved out of Mujala soon after Kandela had succeeded to the headmanship and founded their own village, which became known as Mujalanyana (Diagrams 10 and 11). When Naamu (N22), its first headman, died in 1965, a similar argument to that of Moomba (M6) was put forward by his own sister, Cuma (N9). There were three main contestants for the headmanship of Mujalanyana after Naamu's death: his eldest son, Daniel (O32), his sister's son, Siyabola (O13), and his brother, Ilumbela (N14). Each of them tried to manipulate the situation to his own advantage by invoking different situationally relevant norms and values. The three most important people at the meeting for choosing Naamu's successor were Kandela (N36), the headman of Mujala Mupati and head of Cabakani's *mukowa*, Chief Musokotwane, and Naamu's and Ilumbela's sister, Cuma (N9). Kandela's candidate was Daniel (O32) and Kandela (N36) advocated his appointment by pointing out Daniel's cooperation with his father. Cuma's candidate was her son, Siyabola (O13), and she advocated his appointment by quoting the traditional matrilineal ideology and by stressing that the way of the ancestors is the only right way. Ilumbela (N14) himself had effectively solicited Musokotwane's support and was Musokotwane's candidate.

All my informants agreed that the final mourning ceremony for Naamu (N22) was a situation of great tension. They told me that while the meeting was still in progress somebody had informed Daniel (O32) and his brother, Johnsen (O31), that Ilumbela (N14) would most probably succeed and they almost had a fight with Ilumbela after they heard the news. The meeting for choosing the successor was unusually long and difficult. One of my informants described the situation graphically by saying that the sun was already high above the horizon and the successor had not yet been chosen and installed. There was no agreement about the events which preceded and followed Naamu's death. Before Naamu (N22) died, Daniel (O32) and his brother, Johnsen (O31), had been away from Mujalanyana as labour migrants. Ilumbela (N14) and his children and brothers maintained that Daniel (O32) and Johnsen (O31) had sent a letter to their father telling him to eat his wealth as the rains would bury him (i.e. that he would die in the rainy season). Naamu (N22) gave the letter to Ilumbela (N14) and, when he indeed died in the rainy season, Ilumbela (N14) sent the letter to Musokotwane. The letter was proof that Naamu's sons had killed him by sorcery to inherit his wealth. Ilumbela (N14) also told Chief Musokotwane that because sorcery was involved, he expected trouble during the final mourning ceremony and had asked him to attend it to make sure that an upright and honest man would be selected as Naamu's successor, and not a sorcerer, because then all the people in the village would suffer.

Daniel (O32) and Johnsen (O31) denied that they had ever sent a letter to their father; according to them Ilumbela (N14) had fabricated the whole story. He wanted to be a headman and he knew that he had no chance as all the people in the village would support Daniel (O32). So he had to disqualify Daniel by accusing him of having killed his own father through sorcery. Daniel (O32) and Johnsen (O31) maintained that not they themselves but Siyabola (O13) had killed Naamu by sorcery, and they claimed to have been proved right by the fact that Siyabola (O13) died soon after he had eaten the meat of Naamu's cow killed for the mourning ceremony. According to them, Ilumbela (N14) was appointed Naamu's successor because people at the meeting had always suspected Siyabola (O13) of sorcery, although Ilumbela (N14) claimed that it was Daniel (O32) and Johnsen (O31) who had killed Naamu (N22).

Whatever actually happened, the fact is that Ilumbela (N14) won the day by soliciting for himself the support of the chief. For the chief, he was an ideal candidate for headmanship for, by unmasking the sorcerers who had killed the previous headman and by asking him to intervene for the sake of justice being carried through, he had shown that the welfare of the villagers was his prime concern. To involve the chief was Ilumbela's best bet. For many years he had worked as a court messenger and the chief knew him very well personally. Ilumbela (N14) could be sure that he would support him and that his authority would eventually win. After having heard the accusation of Daniel's sorcery, Kandela (N36) stopped insisting on his being chosen as a successor. Cuma (N9) fought against Daniel (O32) by invoking the traditional matrilineal ideology. She could not invoke it against Ilumbela (N14), who, as Naamu's uterine brother, was, according to the norm of uterine succession, just as eligible to succeed as was her own son. The matter was eventually decided on the basis of Ilumbela's and Siyabola's personal qualities and Ilumbela succeeded to village headmanship.

Although I have no information on the circumstances of the other three cases in which a brother succeeded to village headmanship (Table 13) to prove my point, it seems nevertheless, that the appointment of a brother might very often be a compromise solution between uterine and agnatic succession, chosen in a situation in which both norms of succession and their accompanying legitimisation are invoked in support of rival candidates. The emergence, since the 1940s, of adelphic succession to village headmanship in Ngwezi, alongside succession by sons, would also seem to support this interpretation. When a brother of the former incumbent is appointed to succeed in a situation when both the son and the sister's son contest the headmanship, the decision about whether the succession should follow one normative system or the other is, as it were, postponed. At least, it was the feeling in Mujalanyana village that this is precisely what had happened when Ilumbela (N14) succeeded Naamu. At the time of my fieldwork, Ilumbela (N14) was well into his seventies and the question of who would succeed him as the village headman was openly discussed on many occasions. It was generally felt that, should Ilumbela (N14) die before Cuma (N9), Cuma would push through her other son, Joseph (O9), in exactly the same way in which Moomba (M6) had pushed Kandela (N36) to headmanship in Mujala. Should Cuma (N9) be dead at the time of Ilumbela's death, Joseph (O9) would be left with no support and the main contestants would be Ilumbela's son (O15) and Ilumbela's full-brother, Siyalwindi (N4). It was also expected that Daniel (O32) would make another bid for the headmanship, which he had failed to gain after his father's death, although the general feeling was that such a bid would be unsuccessful.

The feelings of the people in Mujalanyana clearly indicate that the Toka are fully aware that it is the interests of particular people which determine whether one or another normative system will be brought to bear on the action. It is both men and women who favour their own sons as candidates for succession against other people, but it is always a man's mother who pushes him through against her brother's son by invoking the traditional matrilineal ideology. His father is not a member of the deceased's *mukowa* (however that *mukowa* is conceptualised) and unlike his wife, he has no right to attend the meeting for choosing the successor. If he manages to attend it, he is, like his wife, likely to invoke the norm of uterine succession backed by the ideology of matrilineal descent. The deceased headman's wife has herself less opportunity to push through her own son for she again is excluded from attending the meeting. Her son is, however, backed up by her own *basimukowa*, both male and female, who attend the meeting as her representatives; to push forward their candidate, they invariably invoke the norm of agnatic succession backed by values of natural justice. The members of the deceased's *mukowa*, other than his own sister, are more or less impartial about the two candidates. They are both members of their *mukowa*: one a child of their 'son' and 'brother', the other a child of their 'daughter' and 'sister'. They are more likely than anyone else to take into account their personal qualities and, depending on their choice, will invoke either one or the other ideology. In this situation, it is typically the deceased's own sister who pushes through her own son as the candidate for succession. A sister's son's chances of succession thus differ considerably depending on whether his mother is still alive or dead, a fact of which the people in Mujalanyana showed themselves to be quite clearly aware.

The cognatic ideology and the matrilineal ideology are not only invoked by various people in the pursuit of their own interests when a successor to the deceased is to be chosen, but in many other situations of everyday life as well. One such situation was a dispute between Johnsen (O31) and Diksi (O24) in Mujalanyana village (Diagram 23). Diksi (O24) called a case against Johnsen (O31) in front of the village headman:

Diksi (O24) (addressing the headman): I am coming to report to you that on Sunday, when there was a beer party, people left the party and went to sleep. Johnsen [O31], instead of going to sleep, went to our place and wanted to enter the hut where Jeni [P11] and Mbeeda [O25] were sleeping. I was standing outside and he did not see me. When he opened the door, I asked him: 'What are you doing here?' He asked me for a cigarette. I pushed him and he fell down. When he got up, he started to insult me: 'You, Diksi [O24], this is not your village. It is my father's village [Johnsen's father (N22) was the founder and first headman of Mujalanyana]. If you want, you [O24] and Abraham [O22], and Malambo [N17] and Mukampande [N18], you all can go to Mukuni, from where you came.

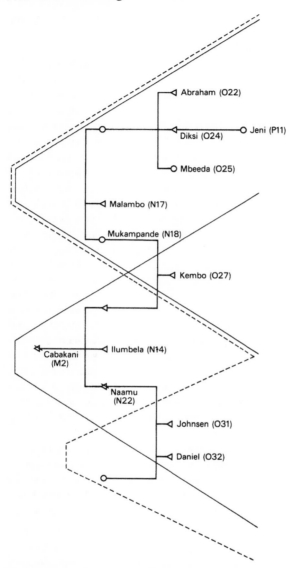

Diagram 23. Conflict between members of two *mikowa* in Mujalanyana village

Solid lines indicate Johnsen's (O31) conceptualisation of the boundaries of the two *mikowa*, conceived of as categories of cognatic descendants of a common ancestor. Dotted lines indicate Mukampande's (N18) conceptualisation of the two *mikowa*, conceived of as categories of matrilineal descendants of a common ancestor.

Why do you want to stop us from inspecting our village at night? It is our village; they are our children and we are supposed to look after them at night.' Then Gidion came and told Johnsen: 'If Diksi [O24] spears you because you came to him at night, what shall you do?' Johnsen [O31] did not answer. Then Johnsen said: 'If they want, they can prevent me from visiting this village at night, but they must not curse me.' Then he left. Thank you.

George (a 'stranger' in the village living about 4 km west of the headman's hamlet): Johnsen [O31], are these words which we heard from Diksi [O24] true? Tell us whether they are only backbiting you or whether you really said that.

Johnsen (O31): They are not backbiting me; all that Diksi [O24] said is true. I made this mistake because I was drunk.

Dahlias (another 'stranger' in the village living some 200 m south of the headman's hamlet): Diksi [O24], what do you think about this matter now you have heard that Johnsen [O31] agrees? What is your suggestion?

Diksi (O24): I cannot suggest anything now. Johnsen [O31] has his father here [reference to Ilumbela (N14), Johnsen's father's brother]; then his father should tell us what he is thinking, whether Johnsen [O31] is right and we should leave the village and go back to Mukuni.

Ilumbela (the headman): Johnsen [O31], do you persist in what you said to Diksi [O24], Abraham [O22], Malambo [N17], Mukampande [N18] and the family of Diksi and Malambo? Do you think that they should leave this village and go to Mukuni?

Johnsen (O31): I agree I said so. I was drunk and people heard all that I said.

Ilumbela (N14): You were wrong to say that this is not Diksi's village because Diksi [O24] was born here and he is staying here because he has kinsmen here. If he had no kinsmen here, he would not be here. Nobody is the owner of a village, not even me, the headman; all who live in a village are its owners; without people there would be no village. Now I am going to finish this case. Johnsen [O31], from now on, do not drink beer and avoid insulting people and chasing them out of the village. If you do it once more, I will send you to the court.

Mukampande (N18): I still say that you should advise Johnsen [O31] because he is always insulting us [reference to Mukampande's and Malambo's *mukowa*]. He does not know that even I myself am his mother. It is wrong when he says that the village is his. Every time when he is drunk he wants to open the door of the house where Mbeeda [O25] sleeps and the daughter of Diksi [P11] sleeps because he does not know that they are his sisters. I was married to the young brother of his father and brought by him to this village. Johnsen's mother was married to Mujalanyana [Naamu – N22] and brought to this village from Siyamuntu. Even he and his mother should go back to Siyamuntu because even for them this is not their village. Siyamuntu is their village. I was not chased from Mukuni myself. I was just married and brought here. So was his mother. She was not chased away from Siyamuntu but married and brought here. I have a son called Kembo [O27]. If Johnsen [O31] is chasing us away saying that we should go back to Mukuni, to where we came from, what is he going to call him? Johnsen [O31] thinks that we are not of his *mukowa* because we come from Mukuni. He is also not of Cabakani's *mukowa* because he comes from Siyamuntu. He should stop saying these words when he is drinking beer. How come that he is cursing us while his elder brother [Daniel – O32] listens to our advice because he knows that we are his parents.

Johnsen (O31) tried to justify the way he had behaved to Diksi (O24) when he had been caught by the latter trying to enter Jeni's (P11) and Mbeeda's

(O25) hut, by invoking the notion of cognatic descent, according to which he was a member of Cabakani's *mukowa* while Diksi was not. According to the cognatic ideology, Johnsen (O31) was an 'owner' of Mujalanyana village and Diksi (O24) was a stranger there. But even as an 'owner' of the village he had no right to behave in the way he did, and during the hearing of his case, he explained that he was drunk. The Toka recognise that drunks are not responsible for their actions. When the headman advised Johnsen (O31) to stop drinking and thus to keep out of trouble, he was doing his best under the circumstances. But the case was concerned with more than a particular incident of Johnsen's drunken behaviour. As Mukampande (N18) pointed out, Johnsen (O31) had perpetually pointed out to her, Malambo (N17), Diksi (O24) and Abraham (O22) that they were strangers in Mujalanyana. When asked specifically by Ilumbela (N14) whether he still thought that they should leave the village, Johnsen (O31) did not retract his opinion. Ilumbela (N14) tried to solve the conflict by pointing out that nobody, not even he himself, owns the village and that everybody who lives in the village owns it equally. It is in his interest to attract as many people to his village as he possibly can because through being a headman of a big village he builds up his name. Were he to admit that some people are 'owners' of a village and others are not, he might lose those who are not. In spite of the headman's words, everybody knew that only some people are 'owners' of the village in which they live. The headman did not specify who they were. For this reason it was Mukampande (N18) herself and not the headman who concluded the case; it was her status in Mujalanyana and the status of other members of her *mukowa* living there which was threatened by Johnsen (O31). Had she accepted Johnsen's interpretation of village ownership, she would have had to accept that Johnsen (O31) was an 'owner' of Mujalanyana, being cognatically descended from Cabakani (M2), while she and other members of her *mukowa* in Mujalanyana were not its owners. She would have had to admit that Johnsen's rights and the rights that she and the members of her *mukowa* in Mujalanyana had, were different. She also knew that, however the concept of village 'ownership' might be interpreted, she and the members of her *mukowa* could never pass as 'owners' of Mujalanyana. To achieve equal status with Johnsen (O31) within the village, she had to demonstrate that even Johnsen (O31) himself was not an 'owner' of Mujalanyana. This she did by invoking the ideology according to which village 'ownership' is perpetuated in the matrilineal line. By reference to herself and to Johnsen's mother, she made it clear that, according to Toka tradition, their status in Mujalanyana was equal, and that consequently the status of Johnsen (O31) and Diksi (O24) in Mujalanyana was also equal. Strictly speaking they were both 'strangers' in this village and neither of them was an 'owner' of it.

To strengthen her argument that Johnsen (O31) and Diksi (O24) were of equal status and that it was thus wrong for Johnsen to behave towards Diksi as if he were of lower status within the village than Johnsen, she made recourse to kinship terminological usage. Johnsen (O31) addresses Mukampande (N18), the wife of his father's brother, and Mukampande's sister by the same term as his own mother (*bama*). Kembo (O27), a member of his own paternal *mukowa* (conceptualised as a cognatic descent category) is his *muzialwama*. As he addresses not only Mukampande (N18) but also her sister as *bama*, Diksi (O24), like Kembo (O27), is also his *muzialwama*. He addresses him by the same term as that by which he addresses his own elder brother (*mukalenangu*), and Diksi (O24) addresses him by the same term as that by which he addresses his own younger brother (*mwencangu*). Mbeeda (O25) is also Johnsen's *muzialwama*, and he addresses her by the same term by which he addresses his sister (*mucizangu*). Mukampande's effort to stress Johnsen's (O31) and Diksi's (O24) equal status by allusion to herself (N18) and her siblings as both Johnsen's and Diksi's parents and to Kembo (O27), Diksi (O27) and Mbeeda (O25) as Johnsen's siblings was based on this terminological usage.

In various situations, people pursue their interests and legitimise or justify their actions by invoking different norms and ideologies. They are able effectively to manipulate the norms and their accompanying ideologies in pursuit of their immediate interests and goals only because all the norms invoked in a specific interactional situation, and their accompanying ideologies, are mutually intelligible and understandable to all parties concerned. This means that all the Toka are able to understand and actively to operate both the cognatic and the matrilineal ideology. Empirically, the same individual can invoke one ideology and normative system on one occasion and another ideology and normative system on another occasion. For example, Kandela (N36), who succeeded to the headmanship in Mujala village because the norm of uterine succession was invoked and adhered to, later supported the son of the headman of Mujalanyana village as a successor to the headmanship. Although in each situation the two available ideologies and normative systems are mutually conflicting, they do not have to be conflicting at the level of individual cognition. Although the Toka operate both ideologies and normative systems, they do not hold conflicting views. A view invoked in one situation does not necessarily have to be invoked in a different situation if it is contrary to the individual's momentary interests. By the differing ideologies and normative systems being adhered to by the same individual in spatially and temporarily separate situations, any conflict on the individual's cognitive level is effectively eliminated.

In spite of the fact that most Toka manipulate both ideologies and their concomitant normative systems and accompanying values in the pursuit of their immediate interests, there were people among them who were 'traditionalists' in the sense that they subscribed more consistently than others to the traditional matrilineal ideology, and others who were 'progress-ives' in the sense that they subscribed more than others to the cognatic ideology brought about by modern technological development. When applying these labels, I would be hesitant to see the 'traditionalists' as those who are morally more strongly committed to the matrilineal ideology and the 'progressives' as those who are morally more strongly committed to the cognatic ideology. In my view, the 'traditionalists' are rather those who, in the course of their lives, have more consistently invoked matrilineal ideology to achieve various goals, while the 'progressives' are those who, due to their own circumstances, have more consistently invoked the cognatic ideology for the same reasons. While some Toka are 'traditionalists' and others are 'progressives' in this sense, most of them are definitely 'pragmatists'.

Anthropologists who have rejected the thesis of universal male dominance have often turned to matrilineal societies for examples of women's high status and their active role in political and economic decisions. The traditional Toka society confirms the emerging view of the relative importance of women in matrilineal societies; women certainly played in it as important a role in decisions about succession and inheritance as men did. Their important decision-making role did not change after the concept of cognatic descent evolved and the principles of agnatic succession and inheritance became part of the normative system. Women still actively participate in meetings for choosing the successor to the deceased's name and often it is their word which carries the weight. Although it is typically a man's mother who invokes the traditional matrilineal ideology to push forward the succession of her son to the name and position of her deceased brother, it would be incorrect to conclude that women are more deeply committed than men to the matrilineal ideology, with its accompanying notion of uterine succession. They invoke it more often than men do because it more often suits their own particular interests. They are, however, as ready to invoke the norm of agnatic succession, with its concomitant value of natural justice, when the cognatic ideology better serves their immediate interests.

Appendix 1: Village fission in Guta

The emergence of the other two villages in Guta illustrates further the principles of village fission discussed in Chapter 1.

Kataba (Diagram 3)

Kataba's mother's brother, Kamela (G2), was dead in 1935 when Kamenyani (H15) moved his village from Guta to Nyawa. Kataba (H5) was thus the senior male member of Mukasilumbe's (F1) *mukowa*. Like Kamenyani (H15) and Matongo (H12), Kataba (H5) is a son of Lunga's sister's daughter. When Kamenyani (H15) succeeded to Lunga's headmanship, Kataba (H5) exercised his right to become a village headman by forming a village of his own; if he had stayed in the village of which Matongo (H12) became a headman, this would have amounted to recognising Kamenyani's and Matongo's right to headmanship and forfeiting his own. Unlike Matongo (H12), however, Kataba (H5) did not command the wide support of his *basimukowa* and their children nor the support of his own children. Of the members of his own *mukowa*, he attracted only his uterine sister, Bene (H3), to his own village. Nowadays Bene's son, Siyamonga (I4), and the latter's son, Alec (J2), live with their families in Kataba's village.

Most of the village inhabitants are members of the Muntanga clan. They are kinsmen of Kataba's first wife, Muntemba (I5), who is herself a member of this clan, and they were attracted to the village because of their relationship to her. They are Muntemba's mother's sister, Mukacoobwe (H7), and her children (I7 and I8), Muntemba's brother, Malumani (I6), and the father and father's brother of Malumani's wife, who are also members of the Muntanga clan.

After Kamela (G2) died, his wife, Mukwazi (G1), did not move back to her own village but, together with her son, Nason Muyoba (H2), stayed in Guta. When Guta split, she followed Kataba (H5) into his village as she was more closely related to him than to either Matongo (H12) or Siconda (G7). She was a member of the Mudenda clan, of which Kataba (H5) is a child. Musiko (H1) had lived virilocally in her husband's village; after his death she came to Kataba to live with her mother, and with her came, with their families, her two children, Anderson Limwanya (I1) and Nasimoono (I2), whose son, David Liyambai (J1), now has his own household in Kataba.

Anderson Limwanya (I1) now lives in his own hamlet apart from the other members of the village, who all live in Kataba's hamlet. Anderson Limwanya's hamlet consists of two households only: the other one besides his own is that of his mother-in-law, who moved in to join her daughter, Limwayna's wife. Anderson Limwanya (I1) hopes, however, to attract his own sister, Nasimoono (I2), and her son, David Liyambai (J1), to his hamlet and to start a settlement of Musiko's *mukowa* of the Mudenda clan. When he moved out of Kataba's hamlet, he hoped that his maternal uncle, Nason Muyoba (H2), would follow him and that the members of Mukwazi's *mukowa* of the Mudenda clan would eventually establish themselves in their own hamlet and, when their numbers grew bigger in the future, hopefully in their own independent village. This idea appealed to Nason Muyoba (H2), but there was a snag. Had he moved to Limwanya's hamlet, he would have accepted the leadership of a man who was not only younger than he is but also his potential successor, and this he was not prepared to do. He argued with Limwanya (I1) that there were not enough members of Mukwazi's *mukowa* successfully to start their own village; he dismissed as wishful thinking Limwanya's argument that, once the members of Mukwazi's *mukowa* had started a settlement of their own, other *basimukowa* who have been scattered in different villages would come and join them and a big independent village would result. The fact that Nason Muyoba (H2) did not join the new hamlet seriously affected Limwanya's plans. He was not able to attract his sister, Nasimoono (I2), and her son, David Liyambai (J1), only because he was not able to attract Nason Muyoba (H2): Nasimoono (I2) prefers to stay with her maternal uncle (H2) in the main hamlet of the village, where there are many people, instead of joining Limwanya's 'lonely place in the bush', as she put it. Anderson Limwanya (I1) is now virtually waiting for Nason Muyoba (H2) to die. He hopes that after his death, as his sister's son, he will succeed to his name and that Nasimoono (I2) and Liyambai (J1) will join him in his hamlet; possibly other members of Mukwazi's *mukowa* who live scattered in different villages will join their own village, of which Anderson Limwanya (I1) will be the headman.

In Kataba, as in Matongo, there are very few members of a *mukowa* four generations deep who occupy the same hamlet. Mukwazi's *mukowa* is the only one in Kataba which has a depth of four generations and only the heads of three households in Kataba's hamlet belong to it: Nason Muyoba (H2), Nasimoono (I2) and David Liyambai (J1).

Kataba's village consists of members of three different clans: the Mucimba, the Muntanga and the Mudenda. Kataba's own clan, the Mucimba, is numerically the smallest and it is generally expected that after Kataba's death the village will split. The expectation is that Kataba's sister's son, Siyamonga (I4), will succeed him as headman, but that he will not be able to keep in his village the members of the Muntanga or the Mudenda clans who will secede and establish their own villages or hamlets. The desperate efforts of Anderson Limwanya (I1) to establish his own hamlet are generally seen as a step in this direction.

A split along clan boundaries, which is expected to happen in Kataba after the present headman's death, is common in village fission. As the spouses are not of the same clan, each matricentric family attached locally to the husband and father through ties of virilocal residence, represents potentially a nucleus not only of a distinct *mukowa* segment, but also of a foreign matriclan. Not every virilocal marriage results in the creation of such a nucleus within what might otherwise be a homogeneous village in *mukowa* terms. This is due to the fact that, after her husband's death or after she has been divorced, the wife will leave her husband's village and, together with her children, will return to her own. If, for whatever reasons she fails to do so and continues to live as a widow or divorcee in her husband's village, her sons and her single, widowed or divorced daughters will reside there as well. The unity of the matricentric family will in this case result in the formation of the nucleus of a foreign clan within the village. The growth of the Mudenda clan within Kataba's village is an illustration of this process. If such a foreign clan becomes numerically strong within the village, its fission will occur along the clan boundaries; the emergence of Siconda's village is a case in point.

Siconda (Diagram 3)

Siconda (G7) was the son of Lunga (F3) and his junior wife, Namayapi (F4). When the village split after his father died and was succeeded by Kamenyani (H15), Siconda (G7) founded his own village. He was joined there by his son, Nelson (H8), and his wife and by two of Namayapi's other children, Simangwede (G11) and Kalemba (G10). Siconda's three full-siblings – Malumani (G14), Thom (G8) and Mukambala (G9) – were dead at that time and Siconda (G7) did not succeed in attracting their descendants to his village. I have no information about the whereabouts of Thom's children, who, after his death, followed their mother and migrated from Guta. The residence of Matongo (H12) (Malumani's son) and Jangulu (H9) (Mukambala's son) is an illustration of some further implications of the process whereby the unity of the daughter's matricentric family disrupts the unity of the mother's matricentric family, or, more precisely, the unity of the group of uterine siblings which is a remnant of the matricentric family. As long as her husband is alive and follows his wife and her children in residence, the unity of his wife's matricentric family also disrupts the unity of his own group of siblings and consequently the spatial unity of his own *mukowa*. Malumani (G14) was the husband of Caangu (G15), Matongo's mother. When Matongo (H12) founded his own village, Malumani (G14), together with Caangu (G15), joined him there. Malumani (G14) thus took up residence in a different village than that in which his siblings resided. In his case the unity of his wife's matricentric family disrupted the spatial unity of his own sibling group. Jangulu (H9) is married to Moono (H10), who lives with her sons, Jakalas (I11) and Kepi (I12), in their own hamlet in Matongo's village. Jangulu (H9) resides there with them away from his own *basimukowa* (Muzamba), who live in Siconda. In his case, as in Malumani's (G14), the unity of his wife's matricentric family disrupts the unity of his own sibling group and consequently the spatial unity of his own *mukowa*.

When Siconda (G7) died in 1943, he was succeeded as headman by his maternal half-brother, Simangwede (G11). Soon after, the village split into two. Siconda's children moved out and founded their own hamlet, which now consists of three houses: that of Nelson (H8), Siconda's son, that of Sainet (I10), Nelson's own son, and that of Lameck (I9), Nelson's sister's son. The emergence of Nelson's hamlet is a result of the same process as the emergence of Siconda's village. Both came into existence as a result of the split of the original village along the clan boundaries. Siconda's wife, Moonga (G5), was a member of the Mutanga clan and Nelson's ambition is to start a settlement of the members of Moonga's *mukowa* of the Muntanga clan. Like Anderson Limwanya's plans mentioned above, Nelson's plans have so far been frustrated. His own mother, Moonga (G5), was dead when he started his own settlement and he did not succeed in maintaining the local unity of his own sibling group against the centrifugal tendencies of his sisters' matricentric families. He did not succeed in attracting his own sister, Mukacoobwe (H7), who went on living in Kataba's village together with her two children. Neither did he succeed in attracting Malumani (I6), a son of his other sister, Muncindu (H6), who also lives in Kataba's village. Malumani (I6) stayed in Kataba, where his own sister, Muntemba (I5), is married to the headman (H5). Nelson (H8) is one of those who predict the disintegration of Kataba's village after his death and he pins his hopes on it. He expects that Muntemba (I5), who has no children of her own, will join him in his hamlet and that her brother, Malumani (I6), will follow, bringing with him his parents-in-law and the brother of his father-in-law. Nelson (H8) also hopes that his sister, Mukacoobwe (H7), and her children (I7 and I8), instead of staying alone among foreigners in Kataba, will then join their other *basimukowa* in his own village.

The second hamlet in Siconda is the headman's own. Apart from Simangwede (G11) and his married daughters, it consists of members of the matricentric family of Simangwede's sister, Kalemba (G10). To the latter cluster of houses is attached the house of Kalemba's daughter's mother-in-law.

The hopes of eventual success in founding one's own village, which Nelson

(H8) entertains, can remain unfulfilled for ever. Jimson Siyamundele (G13), the head of Kantumbi hamlet in Siconda's village, is a case in point. He is Lunga's sister's son and was thus also qualified to succeed Lunga (F3) as a chief and headman. In his own opinion, supported by some other people in his hamlet, he should by right have succeeded Lunga (F3) instead of Kamenyani (H15) as he was more closely related to Lunga (F3) than the latter. When Matongo (H12) and Kataba (H5) founded their own villages as an expression of their genealogically given right to headmanship, Jimson Siyamundele (G13) decided to do the same. He was equally, if not more, qualified than Matongo (H12) and Kataba (H5) to become the headman of Lunga's village. Although he had very few followers at the time of Lunga's death, he did not join either Matongo's or Kataba's village as this would in fact have amounted to a recognition of the leadership of men who are his juniors. On the other hand, he could not have started his own village as he did not command the support of at least nine other tax-payers, as demanded by the Native Authority. The only alternative left to him was to settle down in his own hamlet, formally recognising Siconda's village headmanship. He had no married children at that time and he succeeded in attracting only three other households to his hamlet. One was that of Simusinga (G12), his mother's sister's daughter, another was that of Kabayo (F7), the widowed wife of his mother's brother, and the third was that of Kabayo's son. Later, Kabayo's son's daughter settled in Kantumbi together with her husband, who himself is a member of the Mucimba clan. Jimson Siyamundele (G13) was not discouraged at first by the small number of his followers as he expected that his own children would settle, after their marriages, in Kantumbi. He married another wife to bear him more children. But his plan misfired. Only two of his daughters are living with their husbands in Kantumbi. He was not able to attract his two other daughters, who settled virilocally, one in Kataba (Alec's (J2) wife) and the other in Simangwede's hamlet (the wife of Kalemba's (G10) son). Forty years after it was founded, Jimson Siyamundele's hamlet consists only of eight households. Jimson Siyamundele (G13) is an old man now and he is philosophically resolved to the capricious fortune of political ambitions.

Appendix 2: Aspects of individual mobility in Ngwezi

Change of residence upon marriage

Out of 134 women in Ngwezi, 117 (87.3%) changed their residence on marriage and moved to the villages of their husbands; 14 of them did so twice during their lives. The remaining 17 (12.7%) were either joined by their husbands in their own villages or married men from their own villages. The women in my Ngwezi sample accomplished altogether 220 changes of residence, of which 121 (55.0%) occurred upon their marriage.

Only 25 men out of 119 (21.0%) changed their residence upon marriage and left their own villages for those of their wives. As in Guta and Cifokoboyo, most of them had to reside uxorilocally because they had not completed the transfer of bridewealth. For many of them, uxorilocal residence was only a temporary arrangement and later they moved, with their wives, either to their own or to some other village. Because of the otherwise low inter-village mobility of men, uxorilocal residence is a more significant reason for a man's move from one village to another in Ngwezi than in Guta and Cifokoboyo. The Ngwezi men in my sample accomplished altogether 94 moves from one village to another, of which the 25 changes of residence upon marriage represent 26.6% (as against 10.5% in Cifokoboyo).

Change of residence upon the death of the spouse

Thirty-five women in my Ngwezi sample had experienced widowhood, six of them twice. Three had also experienced divorce. Twenty-one of these women did not change residence after their husbands had died; four experienced widowhood twice and did not change their residence in either case. One other woman who had experienced widowhood twice changed residence following the death of one of her husbands but not after the death of the other. My sample thus yielded altogether twenty-six cases in which a woman did not change residence after her husband had died. In twelve out of these twenty-six cases she did not change residence because she had been living in her own village (in seven of the twelve cases the residence of the couple was uxorilocal at the time of the husband's death, the remaining five cases were intra-village marriages). Compared with Cifokoboyo, where only one woman did not change residence after her husband's death although she was living in his village, and where six widows out of seven who changed residence did so because their residence was virilocal (after the husband's death they moved back to their own villages), there were fourteen widows in Ngwezi who did not leave their husbands' villages but continued to live there with their married sons, or more rarely, their daughters. It is the reluctance of men to leave their fathers' villages which directly affects the mobility of women in these cases. In Guta and Cifokoboyo, if a woman has lived in her husband's village, she usually moves back to her own after his death; her sons usually follow her there, and widowhood and divorce eventually bring her daughters there as well. As men in Ngwezi are unwilling to leave their natal villages even after their fathers' deaths, their widowed mothers usually stay with them. Cases in which widows live with their married son or sons in villages into which they were brought by their marriages are a normal occurrence in Ngwezi, where mothers and children reside together in the same settlement as often as they do in Guta and Cifokoboyo. Unlike in the latter areas, however, the matricentric family does not reconstitute itself as a spatial unit in the mother's village but rather stays together in the father's locality.

The effect of the stability of men's residence on the pattern of mobility of women is manifest, not only in the cases in which women did not change residence following their widowhood, but also in cases in which they did. There were altogether fourteen women in my Ngwezi sample who changed residence following their widowhood; one of them experienced widowhood twice and changed her residence in both cases; another also experienced widowhood twice but changed her residence in only one case. There were thus fifteen cases in which the woman changed residence after her husband's death. In thirteen of them the couple's residence had been virilocal at the time of the husband's death. In four of these thirteen cases the widow soon remarried and moved to the village of her new husband. The changes of residence which the widows accomplished in the remaining nine out of these thirteen cases, clearly indicate that it is the decreased mobility of men in Ngwezi which again affects the pattern of the mobility of women. In five of these nine cases the widows moved back to the village from which they originally married; they were all either childless or had only small children. In three cases out of the nine the widows moved to the village in which their daughters were married; none of them had any married children residing in the village in which she had lived with her husband. In the remaining case, the widow moved to the village of her brother; again, she had no married children residing in the village into which she had herself married. In two cases in which a woman changed residence following her widowhood, the residence of the couple was uxorilocal at the time of the husband's death. In one case, the couple was residing in the wife's mother's natal village into which the wife had moved before her marriage, together with her mother, following her father's death. When she married, her husband moved to live with her in that village. When he died, her mother was already dead. She had only small children and none of her siblings were residing in the village so she moved to the village of her brother. In the other case, the couple resided in the wife's natal village. During her married life, the wife's parents moved with their other children to another village. After her husband's death, their daughter followed them there. She had only one small child at the time her husband died.

Due to the prevalence of virilocal residence, men's residential arrangements are less affected by widowhood than women's arrangements are. There were eight men in my Ngwezi sample who experienced widowhood, one of them twice. All these men were residing virilocally at the time of their wives' deaths (seven of them in their natal villages) and none of them changed residence because of his widowhood.

Change of residence upon divorce

The reluctance of men to change their residence affects the residential arrangements of divorced women in the same way as it affects the residence of widows. Thirty-four women in my Ngwezi sample experienced divorce and eleven of them did not change their residence upon it. One woman of these eleven had been divorced twice and did not change her residence in either case; another had also been divorced twice but did not change residence following only one of her divorces; yet another of the eleven had been divorced three times and did not change her residence after any of her divorces. The census thus yielded fourteen cases in which a divorcee did not change her residence. In five of these fourteen cases the couple's residence was uxorilocal at the time of their divorce and the woman continued to live in her own village; the same situation obtained in three other cases in which the husband and wife were from the same village. In the remaining six cases in which the woman did not change her residence, this was in spite of the fact that the couple were residing virilocally at the time of their divorce. All six couples had adult children who were themselves married and had their own households in their parents' village. They were ploughing with their fathers and would have been unwilling to follow their divorced mothers to their own villages where they would have been faced with the problem of acquiring suitable land for growing maize and establishing cooperative relations. Muzamba (N15), in Mujalanyana village, did not change residence after her divorce for this reason.

Twenty-four women in my Ngwezi census changed their residence after they had been divorced (including one woman who was divorced twice and changed her residence after one of her divorces, and two women who were divorced twice and changed their residence following both their divorces). The sample thus yielded twenty-six cases of change of residence following divorce. In only one of them was the couple's residence uxorilocal at the time of the divorce. The woman changed her residence because both her parents were dead, she had no brothers and all her sisters were married and living in the villages of their husbands. She moved with her small children into a village in which one of her sisters was living. In the remaining twenty-five cases in which a divorced woman changed her residence, the couple were residing virilocally. In five of these twenty-five cases the woman remarried immediately after her divorce and followed her new husband to his village. In one case the divorcee, whose parents were dead, moved with her small children into a village in which one of her married sisters was living. In another case the divorced woman, whose mother was, herself, divorced and living with her new husband in his village, returned to her father's village, where one of her sisters was living, after her own second divorce, with her small children by her second husband. Her children by her first husband were all already married at the time of her first divorce and had stayed with their father. In only two of the twenty-five cases did a divorced woman whose father was dead, move to her mother's village together with her married children. In the remaining sixteen cases she moved back to her parents' village, which in most cases was also her natal village. It is significant that all the sixteen women who returned to the village in which they had lived prior to their marriage had either small children or no children at all. None of their sons was yet old enough for his economic contribution to his father's household to be a factor which had to be taken into consideration when a change of residence was contemplated.

It is again due to the prevalence of virilocal marriage that divorce affects the pattern of the mobility of men in Ngwezi less than it affects the pattern of women's mobility. There were nineteen men in my sample who had experienced divorce, three of them twice, making a total of twenty-two cases. In only five did the men change residence following their divorce, and it is significant that all five who did so had been living uxorilocally when their marriages collapsed. The parents of two of them were dead at the time of their divorce. One of these two moved to a village in which his married sister was living, the other moved to the village of his late father (which was not his own natal village), in which his brothers lived. Both had only small children, who remained with their divorced mothers. The remaining three returned to their parents' villages. Two of them had children at the time of their divorce, one had small children, who stayed with their mother. Of the seventeen cases in which men did not change residence after their divorce, fifteen involved men residing virilocally (eleven of them in their natal villages), and two involved men who had been married to women from their own villages.

Notes

Introduction

1 The validity of postulating these contradictions has itself recently been questioned. It has been argued that they are a function of the primacy given to jural authority and power in defining the essential form of society, and of the jural model of society as the system of rules governing the exercise of authority that is effectively equated with power and control (James 1978: 144ff.), or, simply the function of the unwarranted assumption of universal male dominance (Poewe 1981).

1. Descent categories and local ties in traditional Toka society

1 A new village headman has to be recognised by the chief and by the administration. The chief's recognition is usually not a limiting factor, but the administration requires that each man who wants to found his own village must be joined by at least another nine adult males who will accept him as their headman. The administration may refuse recognition if the secession diminishes the original village to under the limit of ten adult males.
2 The rain-making ritual is described more fully in Chapter 6.
3 These include the succession to the Nyawa chieftainship in the 1930s. The succession to the same chieftainship in 1964 is not included; the chosen successor has not been approved by the administration and there are now two men who claim the title of Chief Nyawa. This case of succession is discussed later.
4 The name of the village is used as an honorific title of its headman; he is addressed and referred to not by his own name but by that of his village.

2. Technological development and the restructuring of the relations of production

1 1K (Zambian *kwacha*), divided into 100n (*ngwee*), was worth approximately £0.60 during the time of my fieldwork (1968–72).
2 The largest sum which I recorded, raised by a household through the sale of maize to the National Agricultural Marketing Board, was K180. This sum is quite exceptional; the household in question was that of a man who regularly grows maize for sale on very fertile soil. The next highest sums recorded were K150 and K90. Most households which depend on cash income for the sale of maize raise considerably less.
3 The figures naturally fluctuate from year to year due to the changes in both the human and cattle populations. In 1968–9, there was an average of 0.78 plough animals per household in Mujalanyana, a figure closely approaching that for Siyabalengu. The lower figures for Mujalanyana are mainly due to the fact that

here a higher percentage of households than in Siyabalengu are those of widows who do not own oxen.

3. Changing norms of inheritance

1 Proven or strongly suspected sorcery on the part of a kinsman disqualifies him from becoming the successor.

4. The structure of local groups

1 The percentage of men who have never left their natal village is probably underestimated for the whole of the Ngwezi area as my census is biased in favour of men who have taken up residence elsewhere. Two of the villages in which I carried out the census were founded during the lifetime of all the men I interviewed there, another was founded during the lifetime of all but the youngest men in my sample. On top of the fifty-two men who had never left their natal villages, there were another twenty-one for whom one of the three newly founded villages was their second place of residence; most of them had moved into it from their natal village, from which the newly founded village had split off. Most of these men would probably still have been living in their natal villages had not some of their members emigrated to found new settlements. If we count these men as still living in their natal villages, we get 69.0% instead of 43.7% of men residing in their natal villages. It is my impression that the percentage of men in the whole of the Ngwezi area who have never left their natal villages falls somewhere in between these two figures.
2 The census is based on 216 male residents in Ngwezi, but the hamlet heads themselves are not included among the 191 men. Sixty-five men were living with their wives' kin in uxorilocal residence, fourteen were residing with affines (i.e. with husbands of their kinswomen), twelve had no kinship link with others in the village in which they resided, and seven resided in the village in which both their parents lived. As the parents of the last seven men had either affinal links with others in the village or were strangers there, it was impossible to classify the residence of the seven men as being with either agnatic or uterine kin.
3 Although most hamlets are founded by men aspiring to headmanship, not all of them are. Sometimes people live in a small hamlet of their own built some distance from the main body of the village, to which they moved after some quarrel or dispute with their neighbours, usually following a witchcraft accusation. Other small hamlets have come into existence for various other reasons. Mafuta's hamlet in Mujalanyana, built half-way between Mubalu and Kacenje, is an example. Mafuta (N29) married a kinswoman of Cabakani and at first resided uxorilocally in Mujala Mupati. When his wife (N28) died in 1951, he moved with his son, Maxwell (O41), to Mujalanyana, where they both lived in the headman's hamlet. Mafuta remarried and his mother-in-law (M4) followed her daughter (N30) to Mujalanyana. In 1960, Mafuta built his house on its present site as he was keeping pigs, which were a nuisance to the other inhabitants of the village, and he wanted to keep them away from other people's fields. His son (O41) and his mother-in-law (M4) moved with him to his new hamlet. Mafuta considers his small hamlet to be an integral part of Mujalanyana village and his contact with the people in the headman's hamlet is much more intensive than his contacts with the inhabitants of Kacenje, Kakala and Kawayo's hamlet.

Notes

5. The changing concept of the *basimukowa*

1 These conditions seem to prevail among Luapula businessmen and -women, who find their obligations arising from the notion of shared matrilineal descent an obstacle to economic growth. They sever their relations with their close kin in an attempt to temper their demands; they justify their behaviour by substituting the religious ideology of the Seventh-Day Adventists for the traditional matrilineal ideology (Poewe 1981: 80–1).

2 The existing notion of descent can be sustained even under the conditions of a changed spatial distribution of the members of the descent category if the couple's membership of the same category is held to be a bar to their marriage (Fox 1967: 110). Among the Toka, marriage is allowed with bilateral cross-cousins. Traditionally, one of the spouses could have thus been the child of the *mukowa* of the other one. When people count as members of either the paternal or the maternal *mukowa*, it can happen that cross-cousins share the same *mukowa* membership. This is not considered to be a bar to their marriage and rather than emphasising the spouses' *mukowa* membership, the Ngwezi Toka take into account their kinship relationship when judging the suitability of their marriage.

6. *Mukowa* and ritual

1 Following the Toka usage, I use the term 'ancestor' to refer to all the deceased members of the *mukowa*.

2 Such a place is called *itwido* from *kutwa* – to pound; *itwido* was a women's version of men's houses (*inkuta* or *cikuta*) which also do not exist any longer in Toka villages.

3 UNIP (United National Independence Party) was the ruling party in Zambia during the time of my fieldwork and it became the only political party in the country when Zambia was declared a one-party state in 1971.

4 Ancestral spirits.

5 Congwe is here referring to his position as the head of the *mukowa*, responsible for its members in the same way as the ancestors were during their lifetime.

6 A loin cloth worn before it was replaced by European clothing. It is still sometimes worn when ploughing after heavy rains, when the soil is muddy, to prevent the regular clothes from getting dirty, or when ploughing in the rain, to prevent the clothes from getting soaked.

7 *Siyakabela nakabila kazondi* – one of God's names.

8 The importance of matrilineally traced descent in Ngwezi is discussed in Chapter 10.

7. The role of the *mukowa* in succession

1 Of the nineteen women who died during my fieldwork, thirteen were succeeded by their daughters, five by their younger sisters and one by her sister's daughter.

8. The role of the *mukowa* in inheritance

1 The fields are usually inherited by the successor or by the sons of the deceased. The daughters inherit fields only rarely as it is expected that they will be provided with land by their husbands. When fields are allocated to individual inheritors, their existing land holdings and their future needs are taken into consideration and kinsmen who have sufficient land are excluded, or they themselves waive any claim.

222

Notes

As a rule, fields are inherited only by the deceased's kinsmen who live in his village and can thus work his land. If a widow goes on to live in the village of her late husband, all his fields are often left to her and her children.

2 Based on the current value of the things comprising the estate. The value of cattle is included but not the value of the fields as land is never sold.

3 In Case 1, the successor received a share worth K1085.50, another son and daughter of the deceased each received a share worth K761.00 and another daughter a share worth K671.00. The shares of all other *basimukowa* were smaller than these. In Case 3, the value of the successor's share was K190.90, whereas all the other children received a share worth K60.00 each. In Case 4, the successor's share was worth K305.50, while the mean value of shares of the remaining children was K77.05. In Case 9, the successor's share was K949.00, while the mean value of the shares of the other two sons of the deceased was K309.65.

4 In Case 2, the daughter who succeeded her mother was the only child. She received the biggest share of all inheritors.

5 Case 6 was an exception. The brother succeeded the deceased and received the biggest share of his estate, worth K35.20. The shares of the deceased's sons were worth only K6.50 each.

6 When comparing the inheritance by the paternal and maternal *basimukowa*, I am disregarding all kinsmen who share with the deceased membership of both his *mikowa*.

References

Aberle, D. F. 1961. Matrilineal descent in cross-cultural perspective. In Schneider, D. M. and K. Gough (eds.), *Matrilineal Kinship*. Berkeley and Los Angeles, University of California Press

Barth, F. 1966. *Models of Social Organisation*. Royal Anthropological Institute Occasional Papers 23

Bauer, P. and Yamey, O. 1957. *The Economics of Underdeveloped Countries*. Cambridge Economic Handbook, London

Blake, J. and Davis, K. 1964. Norms, values and sanctions. In Faris, R. (ed.), *Handbook of Modern Sociology*. Chicago, Rand McNally

Brelsford, W. V. 1965 (2nd edition). *The Tribes of Zambia*. Lusaka, Government Printer

Cardinal, A. W. 1931. *The Gold Coast*. Accra, Government Printer

Caws, P. 1974. Operational, representational and explanatory models. *American Anthropologist*, 76, 1–10

Colson, E. 1951. The Plateau Tonga of Northern Rhodesia. In Colson, E. and M. Gluckman (eds.), *Seven Tribes of Central Africa*. London, Oxford University Press

Colson, E. 1958. *Marriage and Family among the Plateau Tonga of Northern Rhodesia*. Manchester, Manchester University Press for the Institute for Social Research, University of Zambia

Colson, E. 1960. *Social Organisation of the Gwembe Tonga*. Manchester, Manchester University Press for the Institute for Social Research, University of Zambia

Colson, E. 1961. Plateau Tonga. In Schneider, D. M. and K. Gough (eds.), *Matrilineal Kinship*. Berkeley and Los Angeles, University of California Press

Colson, E. 1962. *The Plateau Tonga of Northern Rhodesia (Zambia)*. Manchester, Manchester University Press for the Institute for Social Research, University of Zambia

Colson, E. 1971. *The Social Consequences of Resettlement: The Impact of the Kariba Resettlement upon the Gwembe Tonga*. Manchester, Manchester University Press for the Institute for African Studies, University of Zambia

Colson, E. 1980. The resilience of matrilineality: Gwembe and Plateau Tonga adaptations. In Cordell, L. S. and S. Beckerman (eds.), *The Versatility of Kinship: Essays presented to Harry W. Basehart*. London, Academic Press

Douglas, M. 1969. Is matriliny doomed in Africa? In Douglas, M. and P. Kaberry (eds.), *Man in Africa*. London, Tavistock Publications

Firth, R. 1963. Bilateral descent groups: an operational perspective. In Schapera, I. (ed.), *Studies in Kinship and Marriage*. Royal Anthropological Institute Occasional Papers 16

References

Fortes, M. 1950. Kinship and marriage among the Ashanti. In Radcliffe-Brown, A. R. and D. Forde (eds.), *African Systems of Kinship and Marriage*. London, Oxford University Press

Fortes, M. 1953. The structure of unilineal descent groups. *American Anthropologist*, 55, 17–41

Fortes, M. 1958. Introduction to Goody, J. (ed.), *The Developmental Cycle in Domestic Groups*. Cambridge, Cambridge University Press

Fox, R. 1967. *Kinship and Marriage*. Harmondsworth, Penguin Books

Freeman, J. D. 1961. On the concept of kindred. *Journal of the Royal Anthropological Institute*, 91, 192–220

Fuller, C. J. 1976. *The Nayars Today*. Cambridge, Cambridge University Press

Garfinkel, H. 1967. *Studies in Ethnomethodology*. Englewood Cliffs, New Jersey, Prentice-Hall

Geertz, C. 1966. Religion as a cultural system. In Banton, M. (ed.), *Anthropological Approaches to the Study of Religion*. London, Tavistock Publications

Geertz, C. 1970 (originally published 1965). The impact of the concept of culture on the concept of man. In Hammel, E. A. and W. S. Simmons (eds.), *Man Makes Sense*. Boston, Little Brown

Geertz, C. 1975. *The Interpretation of Cultures*. London, Hutchinson

Gluckman, M. 1951. The Lozi of Barotseland in north-western Rhodesia. In Colson, E. and M. Gluckman (eds.), *Seven Tribes of Central Africa*. London, Oxford University Press

Goffman, E. 1961. *Encounters: Two Studies in the Sociology of Interaction*. Indianapolis, Bobbs-Merill

Goodenough, W. H. 1961. Review of Murdock, G. P. (ed.), *Social Structure in Southeast Asia*. *American Anthropologist*, 63, 1341–7

Goodenough, W. H. 1964. Introduction to Goodenough, W. H. (ed.), *Explanations in Cultural Anthropology: Essays in Honour of George Peter Murdock*. New York, McGraw-Hill

Goodenough, W. H. 1965. Rethinking 'status' and 'role'. In *The Relevance of Models for Social Anthropology*. ASA Monographs 1, 1–24. London, Tavistock Publications

Goodenough, W. H. 1970. *Description and Comparison in Cultural Anthropology*. Chicago, Aldine Publishers

Goody, J. 1958. The fission of domestic groups among the LoDagaba. In Goody, J. (ed.), *The Developmental Cycle in Domestic Groups*. Cambridge Papers in Social Anthropology. Cambridge, Cambridge University Press

Goody, J. 1962. *Death, Property and the Ancestors*. London, Tavistock Publications

Gough, K. 1961. The modern disintegration of matrilineal descent groups. In Schneider, E. and K. Gough (eds.), *Matrilineal Kinship*. Berkeley and Los Angeles, University of California Press

Hill, P. 1963. *Migrant Cocoa-Farmers of Southern Ghana*. Cambridge, Cambridge University Press

Holub, E. 1975. *Emil Holub's Travels north of the Zambezi, 1885–6*, ed. L. Holy. Manchester, Manchester University Press for the Institute for African Studies, University of Zambia

Holy, L. (ed.) 1976. *Knowledge and Behaviour*. Queen's University of Belfast Papers in Social Anthropology 1

Holy, L. 1979. Changing norms in matrilineal societies: the case of Toka inheritance. In Riches, D. (ed.), *The Conceptualisation and Explanation of Processes of Social Change*. Queen's University of Belfast Papers in Social Anthropology 3

225

References

Holy, L. and M. Stuchlik (eds.) 1981. *The Structure of Folk Models*. ASA Monographs in Social Anthropology 20. London, Academic Press

Holy, L. and Stuchlik, M. 1983. *Actions, Norms and Representations*. Cambridge, Cambridge University Press

Homans, G. 1950. *The Human Group*. New York, Harcourt, Brace and World

James, W. 1978. Matrifocus on African women. In Ardener, S. (ed.), *Defining Females: The Nature of Women in Society*. London, Croom Helm

Jenkins, R. 1981. Thinking and doing: towards a model of cognitive practice. In Holy, L. and M. Stuchlik (eds.), *The Structure of Folk Models*. ASA Monographs in Social Anthropology 20. London, Academic Press

Kato, T. 1982. *Matriliny and Migration: Evolving Minangkabau Traditions in Indonesia*. Ithaca, Cornell University Press

Kay, P. 1965. Ethnography and the theory of culture. *Bucknell Review*, 19, 106–13

Keesing, R. M. 1967. Statistical models and decision models of social structure: a Kwaio case. *Ethnology*, 6, 1–16

Keesing, R. M. 1970. Shrines, ancestors and cognatic descent: the Kwaio and Tallensi. *American Anthropologist*. 72, 755–75

Keesing, R. M. 1971. Descent, residence and cultural codes. In Hiatt, L. R. and C. Jayawardena (eds.), *Anthropology in Oceania: Essays presented to Ian Hogbin*. Sydney, Angus and Robertson

Keesing, R. M. 1975. *Kin Groups and Social Structure*. New York, Holt, Rinehart and Winston

Kopytoff, I. 1977. Matrilineality, residence and residential zones. *American Ethnologist*, 4, 539–58

Kroeber, A. L. and Parsons, T. 1958. The concepts of culture and of social system. *American Sociological Review*, 23, 582–3

La Fontaine, J. 1973. Descent in New Guinea: an Africanist view. In Goody, J. (ed.), *The Character of Kinship*. London, Cambridge University Press

Lancaster, C. S. 1981. *The Goba of the Zambezi*. Norman, University of Oklahoma Press

Leach, E. R. 1960. The Sinhalese of the dry zone of Northern Ceylon. In Murdock, G. P. (ed.), *Social Structure in Southeast Asia*. Viking Fund Publications in Social Anthropology 29

Leach, E. R. 1961. *Pul Eliya: A Village in Ceylon*. Cambridge, Cambridge University Press

Lévi-Strauss, C. 1949. *Les Structures élémentaires de la parenté*, translated (1969) as *The Elementary Structures of Kinship*. Boston, Beacon Press

Lewis, W. A. 1955. *The Theory of Economic Growth*. London, Allen and Unwin

Lowie, R. H. 1920. *Primitive Society*. New York, Horace Liveright

Meek, C. K. 1957. *Land Tenure and Land Administration in Nigeria and the Cameroons*. Colonial Research Studies 22. London, HMSO

Mitchell, J. C. 1956. *The Yao Village*. Manchester, Manchester University Press

Mitchell, J. C. and Barnes, J. A. 1950. *The Lamba Village: Report of a Social Survey*. Communications from the School of African Studies, NS 24. Cape Town, University of Cape Town

Murdock, G. P. 1949. *Social Structure*. New York, Macmillan

Nakane, C. 1967. *Garo and Khasi: A Comparative Study in Matrilineal Systems*. Paris, Mouton

Oliver, D. L. 1955. *A Solomon Island Society*. Cambridge, Harvard University Press

Poewe, K. 1981. *Matrilineal Ideology: Male–Female Dynamis in Luapula, Zambia*. London, Academic Press for the International African Institute

References

Pospisil, L. 1958. *Kapauku Papuans and their Law.* New Haven, Yale University Publications in Anthropology 14

Richards, A. I. 1950. Some types of family structure amongst the Central Bantu. In Radcliffe-Brown, A. R. and D. Forde (eds.), *African Systems of Kinship and Marriage.* London, Oxford University Press

Schapera, I. (ed.) 1963. *Livingstone's African Journal, 1853–6.* London, Chatto and Windus

Scheffler, H. W. 1964. The genesis and repression of conflict: Choiseul Island. *American Anthropologist,* 66, 789–804

Scheffler, H. W. 1965. *Choiseul Island Social Structure.* Berkeley and Los Angeles, University of California Press

Scheffler, H. W. 1966. Ancestor worship in anthropology, or: Observation on descent and descent groups. *Current Anthropology,* 1966, 541–51

Schneider, D. M. 1961. Introduction to Schneider, D. M. and K. Gough (eds.), *Matrilineal Kinship.* Berkeley and Los Angeles, University of California Press

Shibutani, T. 1955. Reference groups and perspectives. *American Journal of Sociology,* 60, 562–9

Smelser, N. J. 1963. Mechanisms of change and adjustment to change. In Hoselitz, B. F. and W. E. Moore (eds.), *Industrialisation and Society.* Unesco. Paris, Mouton

Sprott, W. J. H. 1958. *Human Group.* Harmondsworth, Penguin

Stuchlik, M. 1977a. The emergence of a group: the case of a Mapuche sports club. In Stuchlik, M. (ed.), *Goals and Behaviour.* Queen's University of Belfast Papers in Social Anthropology 2

Stuchlik, M. (ed.) 1977b. *Goals and Behaviour.* Queen's University of Belfast Papers in Social Anthropology 2

Turner, V. W. 1957. *Schism and Continuity in an African Society.* Manchester, Manchester University Press for the Rhodes–Livingstone Institute

van Velsen, J. 1964. *The Politics of Kinship.* Manchester, Manchester University Press for the Rhodes–Livingstone Institute

Watson, W. 1954. The Kaonde village. *The Rhodes–Livingstone Journal,* 15, 1–30

Index

Index

Douglas, M., 1–2, 80
ducks, 15

estate: division, 8, 21, 42–4, 53, 79, 81–3, 149, 171–8, 180–2, 187, 189–90, 195–6; value, 175–80, 223

family: elementary, *see* family, individual; individual, 1, 3, 15, 56, 59, 120, 122; matricentric, 28–30, 32–3, 35–6, 47–8, 103, 109, 213–14, 217; patricentric, 109, 111, 113–15; polygynous, 15, 56
Firth, R., 197
fishing, 15, 73, 129
Fortes, M., 79–81, 122, 124, 197
Fox, R., 123, 222
Freeman, J. D., 197
Fuller, C. J., 1–2
funeral, 21, 27, 116, 118, 164

Garfinkel, H., 194
Geertz, C., 6, 55
Gluckman, M., 97
goals, 7–8, 55, 66–9, 71, 75–7, 83–4, 107, 144, 146, 148, 209–10
goats, 15, 23
Goba, 127
Goffman, E., 197
Goodenough, W. H., 6, 22, 66, 124, 194
Goody, J., 79–80, 83, 167
Gough, K., 1, 79, 121–2
graves, 38–9, 134–40, 143–5, 147
groundnuts, 16
Guta, 18–20, 23, 26, 29, 33–5, 37–41, 43, 45, 53–6, 78, 86–7, 91–2, 96–7, 99–107, 109, 115, 118–19, 123–4, 126–7, 130, 132, 134–6, 141, 145–6, 150, 168–70, 190–1, 198, 211, 213, 216–17
Gwembe District, 11–12
Gwembe Tonga, 121

hamlet, 14, 23–4, 30, 36–7, 40, 49, 70, 97–8, 102–3, 106, 112, 137, 147, 212–15; cooperation within, 70, 98, 112, 116, 131; emergence of, 111–15, 131, 214, 221; size, 23; social composition of, 28, 35
hamlet head, 25, 28–9, 98–9, 102, 104–7, 221; strategy of, 30, 106–7, 147, 169
hamlet head's *mukowa*, 33, 130, 147
headman, 13–14, 21, 23–5, 29, 35–6, 41, 50–1, 54, 97–9, 107, 109, 112–13, 129, 140–1, 144–7, 149–51, 163–5, 167, 189, 201–5, 207–9, 211–15, 220; qualifications of, 45, 54; and ritual, 38, 129, 134, 138, 145; senior, 24, 98, 142, 144; strategy of, 47, 74, 113, 146, 208
headman's *mukowa*, 26–7, 47, 54, 147

headman's representative (*ng'ambela*), 27–8, 41
heir, 42, 78–87, 118, 184, 198, 200
Hill, P., 83
Holub, E., 12–13
Holy, L., 5–6, 9, 85
Homans, G., 87
household: composition of, 15, 56, 59; cooperation in ploughing of, 59–61, 63–5, 68, 74–5, 78, 91; developmental cycle of, 59, 74, 78; head of, 96; physical aspects of, 14–15, 23; as a productive group, 56, 58–9, 68, 84, 91; size of, 59
hunting, 15
hut owners, 96, 100, 102–6

ideology: cognatic, 190, 199, 205, 209–10; matrilineal, 1–3, 52, 55, 190, 199–205, 208–10, 222
inheritance, 42–4, 55, 76–87, 172–90; by affines, 42, 174, 177, 184–6, 195; agnatic, 83; by the *basimukowa*, 43–4, 174, 177–87, 195, 223; of cattle, 43–4, 78, 81–2, 173, 184–5; change in, 1–2, 10, 79–81, 83–5, 87, 190, 198; by children, 43, 81, 86, 174, 178, 180–4, 186, 190, 195, 223; familial, 79; of fields, 43, 173, 184–5, 222–3; matrilineal, 1–3, 10, 78–80, 83–5, 198; by non-kin, 42, 174, 177, 184–6, 195; norms of, 8, 42, 76–9, 82–3, 85–7, 119, 177–8, 190, 198; of oxen, 63, 78, 81–2, 85–6; of ploughs, 44, 79, 81–2, 185, 190; by sons, 63, 78–9, 81–3, 85–7, 182, 184–5, 222–3; by spouses, 43, 174, 177, 184–5; by the successor, 43–4, 184–5, 190, 223; uterine, *see* inheritance, matrilineal
inter-village mobility, 29–33, 49, 76, 88–96, 97, 123, 216–19

James, W., 220
Jenkins, R., 6

Kalomo, 13, 18
Kalomo District, 11–12
Kalomo river, 13
Kalomo Rural Council, 11
Kancele village, 30–1
Kanjolo village, 18, 26, 31
Kasangu river, 13
Kataba village, 18, 26–7, 46–7, 211–15
Katapazi, 12, 164
Kato, T., 2
Katwamazila village, 47–8
Kay, P., 6
Keesing, R. M., 6–7, 9, 66, 77, 124, 158, 191–3, 196–7
kin groups in the village, 99–101, 104, 106

230

Index

Oliver, D. L., 125
operational model, 6, 10, 53–5, 191, 193, 196–7
owner of the village, 25–6, 29, 38, 54, 118, 137, 191, 195–6, 198, 202, 207–8
oxen, 56–7, 59–64, 67–70, 74–5, 84; gifts of, 84; inheritance of, 63, 78, 81–2, 85–6; ownership of, 58, 72, 76, 78, 82, 84–5, 91; sale of, 58, 61; training for ploughing with, 57–8, 70, 75

Parsons, T., 6
pawpaws, 23
pigs, 15, 23, 221
Plateau Tonga, 10–13, 79
plough: introduction of, 56–7, 78; ownership of, 59
ploughing, 56–65, 67–8, 70, 72–4, 76, 78, 91–2, 222; for cash, 56, 64–5, 67–70, 76; cooperation of fathers and sons in, 72, 74–6, 78, 81–6, 91, 96, 166, 199–200, 218; cooperation of kinsmen in, 65–6, 69–73
ploughing teams, 8, 59–63, 67–8, 71–3, 75, 91, 116; composition of, 63–7, 71, 73–4
Poewe, K., 1, 3, 77, 220, 222
Pospisil, L., 7
purification of widows, 152–3

rain-making ritual, 21, 37–41, 49, 116, 132–49, 191, 195–6, 220
rain medicine (*kaunga mayoba*), 136, 140
representational model, 6, 10, 53–5, 191, 196–7
representations, 5, 192–3
residence: avunculocal, 123; decisions on, 29, 99, 102; matrilocal, 27, 96, 102–3, 106; natolocal, 88, 91–2, 219, 221; neolocal, 28, 93; patrilocal, 28, 96, 102–3, 106, 123; uxorilocal, 27–8, 33, 74–5, 88, 92–3, 96–7, 126, 129–30, 133, 167, 216–19, 221; virilocal, 26, 28, 29–30, 47, 74–5, 92–3, 96–7, 123, 126, 211, 213, 215, 217–19
Richards, A. I., 3
rights over land, 25
rules, *see* norms

Scheffler, H. W., 7, 86, 191–2, 196
Schneider, D. M., 3, 79, 120
Shibutani, T., 86
shrine (*kasanza*), 38, 134–7, 140
Sichifulo river, 18
Siciyako village, 142–3, 145–8
Siconda village, 18, 37, 213–15
Simango village, 30
Siyabalengu village, 18, 58–9, 220–1
Siyacinga village, 133–4, 138–9, 147–8, 170
Siyakalaluka village, 133–4, 136, 138–9, 170

Siyamutete Ling'amba village, 18, 26, 30–3, 40, 45
Siyantalusiya village, 30
Smelser, N. J., 120
social identity relationship, 22, 124–5, 155, 194–7
sorcery, 29, 44, 82, 91, 150, 170, 189, 203–4, 221
sorghum, 16
Sprott, W. J. H., 197
statistical model, 66
Strategy, *see* goals
structural model, 72–3
Stuchlik, M., 5–7, 9
succession, 41, 55, 76, 82, 107, 142, 149–71, 194, 198, 210, 212, 222; adelphic, 80, 169–70, 204; agnatic, 167–70, 198–200, 204–5, 210; change of, 10, 45, 87, 107, 119, 167–8, 204; to chieftainship, 49–52, 215, 220; to headmanship, 7, 25, 27, 35, 40, 44–9, 50, 54–5, 99, 107, 111–15, 118, 132–3, 138, 141–4, 150, 154, 166, 167–70, 199–204, 209, 211, 213–15; matrilineal (uterine), 42, 45–6, 54, 167–70, 198–200, 204–5, 209–10; of sons, 45–7, 49, 54–5, 81–2, 87, 107, 138, 165–8, 189–90, 198, 200–1, 204–5, 210
successor, 21, 41–4, 53, 80, 118, 149–51, 153, 164–7, 175, 184–5, 187, 189–90, 193, 195–6, 198–9, 202, 205, 212, 221–2; to the chief, 50–2, 220; to the headman, 44–9, 168–70, 199; installation of, 150–1, 170–2, 203
Suku, 123

tax, 31
Tonga, 2, 10–13, 22, 79–80, 122–3
Tonga–Leya Native Authority, 11, 13
tribute, 13, 50–1
tsetse fly, 15, 18, 24, 37, 43, 56
Turner, V. W., 97, 123

United National Independence Party, 51, 139, 222

Valley Tonga, 11, 13
van Velsen, J., 123
Victoria Falls, 12
village: affiliation with 29–30, 36, 47, 96–7, 99, 102–3, 106, 115–16; change of site of, 24, 26, 142; developmental cycle of, 47; fission of, 23, 25–6, 33–7, 40, 46–7, 49, 93, 98–9, 107–18, 131–3, 136–7, 141, 147, 211–15; history of, 33–6, 45, 97, 132, 168; location of, 14; physical aspects of, 23; population of, 14, 17; social composition of, 29, 30–2, 45, 76, 87–8, 96–107, 111,

Index

233

Cambridge Studies in
Social Anthropology

Editor: JACK GOODY

235

236

*ALSO AVAILABLE AS A PAPERBACK